WALL STREET:

MEN AND MONEY

MARTIN MAYER

WALL STREET
MEN *and* MONEY

Revised Edition

COLLIER BOOKS

To the young men and women of Wall Street
especially Bob and
Wilbur,
Fred and
Mary

Contents

Preface: 1959

As ORIGINALLY WRITTEN, and published in 1955, *Wall Street: Men and Money* was a product of recent, relatively systematic research on the American financial market. It was the work of an outsider: I had no commitments, no experience to keep me from seeing the subject plain and round—if I could.

The revisions incorporated in the present edition do not grow out of systematic research. They are essentially the result of keeping in touch with a subject over a period of time. One does not recapture virginity; for good or ill, I am no longer so completely an outsider as I was four years ago.

With these advantages or handicaps, I have attempted to bring the book up to date. I have replaced 1954 figures with 1958 figures—retaining the 1954 information for comparative purposes where the comparisons are striking.

Where people have died or firms have moved, I have noted the fact, but I have not attempted to update the "color" in the book. The descriptions I wrote five years ago were part of a context of observation. I should not care to substitute new descriptions, written in the context of another time, merely for the sake of achieving the appearance of contemporaneity.

I have asked many of the men in the book to tell me what in their opinion has changed in their work since I formally interviewed them, and where necessary I have inserted the new information. Where I have seen or smelled changes in atmosphere and attitude over the last five years, I have attempted to describe them and fit them into the pattern of the book. In the perspective of 1955, much of what has happened since would be incredible—and when the project of reissuing *Wall Street: Men and Money* was first broached to me, I was most reluctant to attempt anything that might indicate to any reader that the book was new. But as I worked on it, my reluctance diminished: I found I had been trapped by my trifle of insider's knowledge. *Plus ça change....* Seen plain and round, I think, the institutions remain much the same.

Even granting the premise, of course, this book is a hybrid —part the tight reporting of 1952-54, part the loose observing of 1955-59. For encouraging me to believe that the hybrid would have some life in it, I am most grateful to John F. Childs of the Irving Trust Company. He came upon me at the moment of my greatest involvement in the surprising success of *Madison Avenue, U. S. A.,* and by overpraising this older book gave me new confidence in something which had become merely another part of the (always unsatisfactory) past.

Most of the changes in this edition are additions or simple factual alterations made necessary by the passage of time, but I have also deleted a few expressions of opinion which on rereading struck me as worthless. Virtually all the material added is in footnotes or brackets, identified as new by the date 1959. I have made no effort to maintain stylistic continuity between the existing book and the additions; indeed, I felt that the difference in their provenance demanded a somewhat different style. Where my opinions on matters of some importance have changed over the five years (or where developments have proved me wrong) I have retained what I now regard as the errors of the first edition, and given my older self the pleasure of demonstrating the stupidity of my younger self.

I should like to express special thanks to all those who did my work for me by writing me of changes which had occurred in their business since the publication of the first edition of *Wall Street: Men and Money*.

Preface: 1955

Wall Street: Men and Money paints in bright colors on a small canvas an immense and rather somber subject. To this extent the book is distorted in its very conception, and my work has been to avoid further distortions, especially that of saying something is simple when it is not.

Hundreds of people have helped me in my attempt to understand and to express the New York financial market, and my debt to them is total. This is a reporter's book. When I first came down to Wall Street, in November, 1951, I was a theoretical economist turned magazine writer, with a spectacular ignorance of the subject I was approaching. The men whose names are in these pages gave generously of their time and their documents in the cause of education. I hope they like the book.

Among the books from which I have drawn information, the most important were Arthur Dewing's *Financial Policy of Corporations,* Benjamin Graham's *Security Analysis* and Louis Loss' *Securities Regulation.* I recommend them strongly to anyone seeking to penetrate more deeply into this subject.

My special thanks to the many on Wall Street who read this book, or sections of it, in manuscript and galley form—to James Conway, James Lyles, Edward McCormick, F. Walter Murphy, David Rea, John Sheehan, Winthrop Smith, William Veit and Thomas Waage, and to others unnamed. None of these men, of course, may be held responsible for any part of the book.

The opinions expressed outside quotation marks are my own. It will be observed, of course, that I got them somewhere; but I do not think their sources can easily or profitably be tracked. I have avoided mythical examples throughout the book, because real examples are more interesting; the prices put opposite the names of real stocks, however, do not represent any opinion of their worth or prediction of their prices in the future.

Finally, my gratitude to Fred Birmingham of *Esquire* magazine, who assigned and published the long article on which this book is, in part, based, and made sure I had time enough to do the job. To Tom Morgan, who suggested the assignment and gave me the title of both article and book. To Mrs. Elaine

Weisburg, who checked the facts with great courage and initiative while I was three thousand miles away. To Miss Muriel Knapp, who typed the book under difficult circumstances.

And to my wife, who put in countless hours of work and argument to refine and direct my long, windy first drafts.

MARTIN MAYER

WALL STREET:

MEN AND MONEY

Chapter 1

The Place

A BUNCH of the boys were whopping it up in the back room of the American Stock Exchange, which happens to be a public restaurant, and the conversation turned to remarkable men on Wall Street. Somebody mentioned the name of George Woods, Chairman of the Board of the First Boston Corporation, largest of the investment banking houses.

"It's funny you should mention him," said Weston Smith, public relations director for *Financial World* magazine. "You know, Woods and I went to Brooklyn Commercial High School together, got out in the same year. And I've often thought," Smith said, very seriously, "I made a mistake. I went on to college. Woods got a job as an office boy for Harris, Forbes."

Wall Street is like that; it's a funny place.

2

It is also a small place. The Street itself is seven blocks long, less than half a mile, and the area that contains the greatest of all financial markets is no more than half a mile square. To the north it is guarded by the enormous stone palazzo of the Federal Reserve Bank of New York, itself guarded by nearly two hundred special policemen; to the south it is bounded by the wonderfully gewgawed, bright red Produce Exchange.* The Street itself begins at Broadway, at the central spine of lower Manhattan, and runs east, gently downhill, to the East River. West of Broadway is Trinity Church, Episcopalian, with a tower twenty stories high but so graceful that it seems smaller, so encircled by office buildings that it seems smaller still. West of the graveyard about and behind Trinity Church is a brick wall dropping down, down some twenty feet to a lower level of the island and Trinity Place, which is home to a stock exchange, a very few financial houses, and the New York University Business School. West of Trinity Place are printing and shipping, loft buildings and the Hudson River.

This is old New York, a disorganized maze of streets with

---

* 1959: Now gone. In its place is a most ordinary glass-and-aluminum-fronted skyscraper with cream-colored panels. The new building, however, incorporates a trading floor for the Produce Exchange.

the names common to all the American Colonies: Pine, Cedar, Oak and Stone; Broad Street and Broadway; Liberty Street, New Street, William Street, Maiden Lane, Old Slip, Front Street, South Street. According to legend, there was a real wall here once, where Wall Street runs, guarding the Dutch from the Indians and the Indians from the Dutch. Now there is a seaplane base for airborne commuters where the wall anchored at the river, and two forty-story office buildings guard the entrance from Broadway. George Washington took his first Presidential oath of office here, at the corner of Wall and Nassau, and a statue stands commemorating the event on the steps of the Sub-treasury Building. Band concerts, which occur at frequent intervals for incomprehensible reasons, form around the statue. Across the street from the Sub-treasury Building is the squat bank building of J. P. Morgan & Co., Inc., where a parked wagon once blew up in the worst of the anarchist bomb scares. The resulting pocks in the granite wall have been left unrepaired, mementos of the revolution that never came off. Nobody notices the pocks; worse things have happened since.

These are the famous canyons of New York, the high office buildings rising without setbacks from narrow streets; the sun shines on some sections of pavement less than twenty hours out of a year. Between Pine Street and Cedar Street rises the third tallest building in the world—the Cities Services building, sixty-six stories high. From the glassed-in observation room up top opens a view of a world—the great harbor to the south, the ships arriving and leaving through the Narrows, anchored, puffing jets of steam that blow towards the woods of Staten Island or the grimy oil refineries of the Jersey shore, clean and brilliant from a distance, or the sweeping curve of the Brooklyn docks, out east to the shore road. North-east are the bridges over the East River, the Brooklyn Bridge, the Manhattan Bridge, the Williamsburg Bridge, all in close conjunction, and the slums, and the red-brick public housing projects, pink at a distance. Out beyond the bridges stretches Long Island, marching east, a flat place with smokestacks, homes and factories; uptown, north, the skyscrapers of middle New York, the rectangular streets bordered with buildings, and beyond them the long green quadrangle of Central Park. West are the Hudson, the Jersey cities and the Jersey swamps, and the first low range of the Jersey hills, forested and interspersed with the homes where much of Wall Street lives. But most amazing of all the view is the sight straight down, into the buildings of Wall Street, the famous entrance skyline of New York seen from above, the bottoms of the canyons almost hidden in the shadows, south-facing Broad Street a brilliant island of sunlight, toy graves in Trinity churchyard for men and women dead 250 years, and just below the level line of vision the ornamental tops of the Wall Street towers, carved and sculpted so elaborately, hidden by their height from the gaze of ordinary mortals.*

The tower of the Cities Service building is no longer open to the public: part of the panorama is an aerial photographer's view of the Brooklyn Navy Yard.

There are other views, odd views of pieces of buildings from windows on the lower floors, also views from the higher floors of towers that seem to move as the fog rises and blows in shreds and clouds from the harbor. There are panoramas from the ground, skyscrapers rising suddenly from nests of old, small buildings, perspective effects that appear and disappear as the visitor walks by the mouths of the canyons. Wall Street is an ornamented area; brick bas-reliefs, brass sculptures, stone statues, gargoyles, figures six and seven stories high cut into the brick walls stare out unnoticed. The lobbies of the buildings are two, three and four stories high, with ceilings carved and gilded; the brass elevator doors were once considered works of art as well as entrances; the floors are mosaics. In the numerous buildings owned by Trinity Church, the richest religious establishment in America, there recurs an ecclesiastical motif: vaulted arches in the lobbies, gothic carvings on the stones that cover the steel beams. Wall Street was built in the nineteen hundreds, tens and twenties, when gold lay on the streets for a clever market operator—or a real estate boomer. Little things—the right gargoyle in the right place, the height of a ceiling, the size of a lobby—meant much in prestige. Sometimes they still do. Most of the elevators in the Cities Service building have ordinary linoleum floors, but those that service the top floors, where dwell the executives of Cities Service, have an Oriental rug for the executives to stand on. Not a very expensive Oriental rug, not a very clean Oriental rug—nevertheless, an Oriental rug.

The real luxury on Wall Street is space, space in a building, space on the street. It was not easy to crowd so many big

---

* 1959: Add to the view the plain top of the new, high, very elegant home office of the Chase-Manhattan bank, and the new splash of sunlight before the bank, where a grassy *piazza* has been planted, a great bank's contribution to its environment.

buildings on to these old alleys; they were too narrow to accommodate the huge trucks that bring steel beams and carry away dirt during the construction of a skyscraper. They were so narrow, indeed, that the lifting of beams by derricks meant a constant danger of swinging enormous crowbars against the neighboring buildings. The job was done, however, without any great loss of life. The loss has been livability.

And the traffic. There are few traffic lights east of Broadway in the financial district, no buses, and fairly little traffic (for New York). What vehicles there are, however, make life hazardous for driver and pedestrian. Streets so narrow that two cars can barely stand abreast are two-way streets—up to a point. Then, for no perceptible reason, they became one-way streets. A parked truck on William Street can hold up traffic for a quarter of an hour, and since most of the traffic is knowledgeable the result will be great clashings of gears, backings-up and turnings-around. A little of this goes a long way to make the ordinary irritable New York cabbie into a monster; and his temper worsened in 1953 when no-parking streets were turned into fully parked streets by a relaxation of the law and an installation of dime-gobbling parking meters. Wall Street is typically in a hurry, vehicular or pedestrian, and the dangers of hurry are very great. A slower, sweeter era is recalled every afternoon at four o'clock, when the black limousines materialize beside the entrances to the buildings, waiting patiently for the masters, their uniformed chauffeurs lounging on the street or in the lobbies, chatting about the stock market, smoking cigars.

3

There are two subway stops at Wall Street itself: the East Side I. R. T. stops on Broadway, and the West Side I. R. T. on William Street, which is east of Broadway.

4

The face of Wall Street is the glass, granite, and marble face of a bank. Wall Street has all sorts of banks: the Chase-Manhattan; the First National City, occupying a vast, block-square, stone building in Greek Revival style, inheritor of the Mercantile Exchange building which stood on this same Wall Street site and disappeared in the great fire of 1835*; Manu-

---

* 1959: The First National City is about to disappear from its building. A new home office on midtown Park Avenue will make it the first major financial institution to leave the haunted haunts of Wall Street.

facturers' Trust, Guaranty Trust, Bankers Trust, Chemical-Corn Exchange—six of the nation's ten largest banks, their home offices all within half a dozen blocks of one another. Besides these there are little banks, with only a billion dollars or so in total assets; French, Swiss, Canadian and other foreign banks; and a few remaining private banks, such as Brown Brothers, Harriman & Company, one flight up, but that flight private, from a separate, elaborate corner entrance on Wall Street.

Banks need first-floor space, place for depositors to come in and leave the money which the banks will then rent out to business. Beyond this basic function, the banks are beehives of service. They act as transfer agents for corporations, cancelling stock that has been sold and issuing new stock to the man who bought it. They pay the actual dividends that corporations declare on their stock, doing all the dull work of writing the checks and mailing the letters. Like banks everywhere, the Wall Street banks keep accounts, clear checks and pay out cash. Most of them have large trust departments which manage estates, pension funds and other aggregations of money; many of them underwrite municipal bonds, a few others trade actively as dealers in the government bond market.* Except on very small accounts, or certain special jobs, they make no charge for the enormous amounts of clerical work they do for their customers. Banking is a service industry, and the charge for the service is simply the use of the money deposited.

Up in the towers, well above the marble halls of the banks, dwell the underwriters, the "investment bankers," a different and more adventurous breed of men. They are the people who find the new, basic capital on which industry expands. A bank will give a shoemaker money to buy leather, and the money will come back to the bank when the shoes are sold; an underwriter will find money to pay for the building of a new shoe factory, money which will not return to its source for decades, after the sale of millions of shoes. The Wall Street underwriters not only find such long-term money for business; they take all the risks of the finding. If an underwriter believes that a company has a "good case," a profitable use for the money to be raised, he gives the company the money out of his own pocket, and then sells his risk to the public. He makes his liv-

---

* 1959: The number of banks really *active* in the government bond market has declined drastically since the collapse of the market into a state of speculative chaos in the fall of 1958.

ing the way a storekeeper makes a living: he buys wholesale from the companies and sells retail to the public. But no storekeeper in the world needs the quick skills and the brilliance that are routine matters in an underwriter's office.

Underwriting is the central business of Wall Street, and Wall Street is the center of underwriting. There are banks all over the country, and the largest—Bank of America—has its headquarters and all its branches in the West. But every underwriting house of any consequence has an office on or beside Wall Street, and for all but one or two the Wall Street office is the home office. These are the important names of finance—Morgan Stanley & Co., The First Boston Corporation, Lehman Brothers, Smith Barney & Co., Kidder Peabody & Co., Goldman, Sachs & Co., Blyth & Co., Kuhn, Loeb & Co., Dillon, Reed & Co.—a long catalogue, and every name an office behind the windows and the fancy brickwork on the towers of Wall Street.

The people who buy the stocks and bonds marketed by the underwriters can make their profits or take their losses only by selling to someone else and that someone else will himself some day wish to sell. For this reason there are trading markets, where the individuals who own corporate securities can turn their holdings into cash. This activity is the biggest and the most colorful business on Wall Street. In a good year, underwriters will sell to individuals and insurance companies and other institutional investors some six billion dollars' worth of securities; the trading markets in an ordinary year will handle nearly seventy billion. The most famous place on Wall Street is the New York Stock Exchange, a trading market on the auction principle, where prices are set by competitive bidding on the buying and selling sides. And the liveliest business is the "over-the-counter" market, where security prices are set by negotiation among hundreds of independent dealers and their customers.

There are sixteen registered stock exchanges in the United States, but the two in New York (the other is the American Stock Exchange, formerly the Curb Exchange) do more than 90 per cent of the business. Since only members, present in person, can do business on the floor of an exchange, and the floors are in New York, stockbrokerage is heavily concentrated on Wall Street; and the total take-out in brokerage commissions in 1958 was nearly half a billion dollars. The over-the-counter market, which has no trading floor and therefore no focal point, is much more spread out, and its students say that New York is the wrong place to look for it; but the five biggest dealers—Blyth & Co.; Goldman, Sachs; First Boston; Wheaton; Merrill Lynch—all have their offices, and their over-the-counter traders, on Wall Street.

Trading has all the fascination of horse racing, and all the luxury. Among the more impressive structures of finance are the large buildings that house the trading floor and the office staff of the New York Stock Exchange, occupying nearly the whole city block which fronts on Broad Street and Wall Street; among the more cheerful is the modern white stone home of the American Stock Exchange. And up in the towers, in luxuriously large offices with carpeting and heavily upholstered furniture, Old Masters on the walls, and music by Muzak piped in for the clerks, are the brokers' offices, the desks and telephones of the over-the-counter dealers.

These are the three major businesses of Wall Street—banking, underwriting and trading—and around them cluster the subsidiary trades which finance serves, and the ingenious special skills that serve finance itself. Toward the lower end of Wall Street gather the commodity exchanges and the commodity brokers—cotton, coffee, sugar, hides and metals, traded mostly by means of futures contracts, agreements to deliver or accept on such-and-such a day one to nine months away, a certain amount of a product. Because of these exchanges, farmers and mining companies and manufacturers can make big plans months in advance; because of them, too, many a reckless citizen with an urge to gamble in cotton is presently broke. The commodity exchangers had their great days directly after the war, when loopholes in the tax laws made it possible for speculators to keep what they had won and to deduct what they had lost from their tax bill. Volume has dropped since then, as it has dropped on the stock exchanges since the twenties, but the trading rooms stay busy—and very, very noisy.

Cotton brokerage houses are much like stock exchange houses, although the cotton broker's customer's man inevitably picks up somewhat more expertise in his subject, which is in turn less complicated. The coffee brokers, however, have their own district on Front Street, a block from the East River, a pleasant section of red-brick Colonial structures filled with the smell of spices, the memory of the distant Indies, an aroma of history. A smell of trouble, too, since the Federal Trade Commission decided that trading methods on the Coffee Exchange were largely responsible for the big boost in coffee prices in early 1954. Most coffee brokers are also, on the side, sugar brokers; since the fall of 1954 they have been sugar brokers first of all.*

There are other businesses which use money as the raw material of production, and which cluster round the font. Insurance companies, for example, have offices up and down the Street, to take care of other people's risks and their own investments. The commercial credit companies, which stole a long march on the banks in the rapidly expanding fields of consumer finance and equipment finance, live cosily near the banks whose business they have stolen. And some industrial corporations maintain offices on Wall Street for the convenience of keeping in touch with the financial market and the pleasures of the big city.

Then there are the offices of the special trades called into existence by the auction market itself—the stock gamblers and tipsters, big and little, the arbitrageurs, the options brokers. There are the governmental and self-regulatory groups, which keep a cold gaze on the market and investigate everything that looks peculiar. And there are the lawyers, occupying four and five floors to a firm in the office buildings, drawing the elaborate contracts of finance, keeping their clients square with the federal and state rules and the tax laws. Especially the tax laws.

Finally, there are the wonderful devices that finance uses, first of all the telephone. The financial market's telephone bill runs to several million dollars a month. Every stock trade involves at least six, and more usually a dozen, telephone calls. The underwriters form their selling groups, getting new stock to the public, by means of long-distance calls, which take substantially longer than three minutes. And "over the counter" is a misnomer for the trading market in unlisted securities; "over the telephone" would be far more accurate.

Much of this telephoning back and forth is done through leased wires, permanent connections between two firms that are always doing business with each other. Every office of any size has a dozen or so of the "PX" switchboards, square wood-panelled boxes with six little switches and twelve little lights on the front, giving the men who work before them immediate access to the trading rooms of six to a dozen other firms. Houses with out-of-town branches will have leased teletype

---

* 1959: This situation no longer holds. Indeed, considering the influence of the sugar market on the course of the Castro revolution in Cuba, the sugar brokers may now be coffee brokers first of all.

wires, providing instantaneous communication between the offices at a cost somewhat lower than telephone calls. And almost every firm of any size will have a "TWX" teletype, with a TWX code number. Whenever another TWX owner anywhere in the country types the firm's code number, the teletype starts rattling a message; the cost is slightly higher than an ordinary telegram, considerably lower than a telephone call. The profits on running this service are apparently considerable, since A.T. & T. some years ago arranged to sell Western Union the TWX wires, and has been ducking out of the deal ever since.*

All these devices are noisy; except for executive offices and a few sedate customers' rooms, Wall Street firms are noisy places.

Telegraphy and the telephone are not the only methods of communication: Wall Street is totally surrounded by print shops. On everybody's desk is a black-bound copy of the Pandick Diary, gift of Miss Pandick, who runs the Pandick Press; down the street is the Ad Press, with a bowling alley in the cellar, exclusively and gratuitously for printing customers. There are close to a hundred custom and semi-custom printers on all sides of the half-mile square, and they work for everybody who works on Wall Street.

Lawyers, for example, must print the briefs for most of the cases that go up on appeal, so that every appellate judge has a nice clean copy; and they will print their briefs on any case if the client is willing to pick up the bill. This is last-minute work, because courts set deadlines for the submission of briefs, and nobody likes to close the door on his arguments until the last minute (besides, if he waits long enough and has some luck, he may be able to meet exactly the arguments the opposition is using). So the night before a brief is due the young lawyers of the firm sit around in the printers' luxuriously appointed waiting rooms, sipping free liquor and free coffee, sometimes even napping on special hide-away beds, correcting the proofs as they arrive hot from the press. The printers can afford to give such service: charges for custom printing are high. Moreover, law firms nervously "reserve" presses from a time about twelve hours before their briefs will actually be ready; the printer then makes a double profit on his press by doing another customer's work on the lawyer's time.

* This transfer has now been accomplished.

Brokers supply their customers with printed newsletters on the state of the market or one particular industry, and every new securities issue must be sold by means of a printed "prospectus" containing all the relevant facts about the issue. This, too, is hurry-up work. Finally, the public relations bug has bit very hard at Wall Street, and many of the print shops have branched off into the fancy brochure business. Some of them have even set up their own art departments, which design covers for and lay out company magazines, reports to stockholders and such. And all this work is in addition to the printing of the many Wall Street magazines and newspapers, the many letterheads and calling cards demanded by the business. Finance makes a living for a lot of people.

5

There are two smells on Wall Street: nice days, smell of coffee, from the roasters downtown; nasty days, smell of fish, from the Fulton Fish Market a third of a mile uptown. Or so they say.

6

Creature comforts: too few.

When there is a bank on the first floor, there can be no restaurant; for the hungry citizen of Wall Street, lunch is where he finds it. Behind the New York Stock Exchange building, on narrow New Street, are a few large quick-lunch places with white tablecloths and dirty floors and bad food selling à la carte only, about $2.50* for a real lunch; they hope to get three or four shifts through the place between noon and two o'clock. Most of them have separate bars for brokers too rushed to take more than liquid refreshment. On Broad Street itself, south of the Stock Exchange, are representatives of a few of the middle-priced New York restaurant chains, open only for lunch and tea. East of the half-mile square, near the river, are fish places (especially Sweet's, in the fish market) and a few restaurants specializing in national dishes—Spanish, Italian, German. North-west, half a dozen blocks from an office in the heart of the half-mile square, is the area's most distinguished eating place: the old Chop House, still housed in an eighteenth-century building, one of the oldest in New York, proud of its traditions (Jay Gould allegedly hid there before escaping to New Jersey after the market and the police

* 1959: Inflation, now $3.00.

found out about his frauds in Erie Railroad stock), full of yellowed engravings and lithographs, serving on its bare wooden tables the best ducklings in New York.†

Full up, Ye Olde Chop House will hold about sixty to seventy people; the other 99,930 on Wall Street must eat, too. To feed them there have grown up three institutions: the employees' cafeteria, the executives' restaurant and the luncheon club. A score of Wall Street firms, mostly banks, have gone into the restaurant business, establishing private non-profit cafeterias upstairs in the office buildings; here employees can eat nourishing, wholesome, energy-providing lunches for sixty or seventy cents apiece, or in some cases—notably the Chase-Manhattan Bank, which used to rent special restaurant space outside its own building—for nothing. (Every effort is made to keep out people who don't work for the company.) Upstairs, twenty flights or so above the employees' dining room, there is usually an executives' club, with tables spaced ten or fifteen feet apart for privacy of conversation, old prints on the walls, old retainers gliding quietly over the carpet to take orders. Here the food is usually on the house. The expense to the company is considerable, but the saving on executive expense accounts is considerable, too.

For those whose companies provide no dining facilities, there are lunch clubs, ranging from the large Lawyers' Club (with annual dues as low as forty dollars) to the austere and were private India House, by the Cotton Exchange on Hanover Square, basically a club for shipping people, but open on occasion to particularly eminent men from the financial market. Most of the lunch clubs are high up in the office buildings, commanding views of the harbor, the rivers or the midtown skyline; the Bankers' Club, atop the forty-story Equitable Building, has breathtaking views of the whole city from its four dining rooms and two lounges. These are no ordinary dining rooms, either; the ceilings are nearly thirty feet up, and supported by ornamental columns, and each room is decorated in a different style. The main lounge has one of the largest Oriental rugs in America and one of the biggest collections of standing ashtrays.

At the Stock Exchange Club, which is only halfway up a medium-sized building and looks out only on shabby New Street and the monster Irving Trust building, the ashtray motif

† 1959: Ye Olde Chop House has moved, alas, and the attempt to retain the old *décor* in new surroundings cannot be called successful.

has been carried a step further: there are special cigarholders fixed to the walls, at the proper height, in the stalls in the men's room. Beyond such extravagances, each club has its own specialty: the broad stairs, old tables and open fireplaces of the Downtown Association, which occupies all of a five-story building on Pine Street; the small rooms and French Provincial *décor* of the Lunch Club (called the Boys' Club because it has a low initiation fee for young joiners), which takes up two floors of the tower at 63 Wall Street; the great vista of the lounge of the Wall Street Club, spreading on and on, an infinite stretch of chairs and tables and carpets. After the Downtown Association the most exclusive are the Recess Club and the Broad Street Club, where the waiting list is usually four years long.*

These, too, are more or less non-profit establishments, and lunch is relatively inexpensive—$1.50 to $2.25 or so, depending on the items ordered. No cash changes hands, of course; the member signs a ticket, and pays a monthly bill. Wall Street is a more serious place today than it was in the twenties, and more closely attuned to the times: the business that used to be done on golf courses is now done over the groaning board at the luncheon clubs. Unfortunately, the average member pays too much attention to business at lunchtime; the food at even the best of the clubs is often mass-prepared, overcooked and tasteless, and Wall Street suffers from ulcers.

What the food lacks is made up by the atmosphere, which is spacious and intensely masculine: women are admitted rarely if ever. The same masculine air filters down, avoiding the offices filled with secretaries, to the shops that poke out shyly between the banks all over the area: tobacconists, men's clothing stores, bookstores, two branches of Spalding's sports shop. And out to the west, in the streets that lead to the Hudson River, are monuments to the pricing sense of the Street: the first important discount houses.

Here, for example, is Cortlandt Street, a short but wide avenue flanked by large stores selling the big-ticket items— refrigerators and television sets, dishwashers and laundromats —plus phonograph records and high-fidelity phonograph equipment, sporting goods of all sorts, cameras, electric trains and other items of hobbydom, all at prices 20 to 40 per cent below list. This is where Wall Street has shopped since the

---

* 1959: I have been informed that the priorities here are wrong, and that the Recess Club is more exclusive than the Downtown Association.

early thirties, and the store windows, quite elaborate now, are monuments to the first triumph of a retailing revolution, the only revolution ever begun on Wall Street.

7

A patch of grass at Trinity Church graveyard; a little park to the south, at the Battery, tip of Manhattan Island; another small part to the north, three-quarters of a mile away, in front of New York's brown City Hall; and at Coenties Slip, once the hustling terminus of the Erie Canal, a concrete playground for nobody's children.* Otherwise, streets and sidewalks, buildings and people.

---

* 1959: A new housing project to be built around Coenties Slip will provide children for the playground, and the Chase-Manhattan Plaza has added a new square of grass.

Chapter 2

The People

PUTTING aside government employees (go *'way*, there!), everybody's income arises from a sale—a book, a fur coat, a package of soap, a ticket to a concert, a hundredweight of fertilizer. The total of sales is the national income, and each man's living fluctuates with the sales chart. No sales chart in the world bounces up and down so vigorously as the graphs that mark the sales of the pieces of paper called stocks and bonds.

Very few people on Wall Street have much idea of what they will earn next year: even the bankers are gambling.

This one band of attitude holds all the individuals together: a gambling excitement—a quickness of mind, a willingness to risk. The business of Wall Street is done mostly over the telephone, and decisions involving the fortunes of men must be made immediately, before either party hangs up. In the office of Harry I. Prankard, head of Affiliated Fund, there hangs a framed sampler: CERTAINTY GENERALLY IS ILLUSION, AND REPOSE IS NOT THE DESTINY OF MAN. It is very hard to be stuffy in such an atmosphere, and very easy for a man to love his work.

This is the true fascination of finance that draws rich lawyers to look longingly at struggling over-the-counter dealers. On Wall Street, as nowhere else, a man's decisions may be accurately judged, because he makes money or loses money on them almost immediately—and his alternatives are known. Arguments will rage for years as to whether Sears Roebuck was right to expand or Montgomery Ward to sit tight after the war ended, because the returns will not be in for a generation.* But an underwriter will know tomorrow whether he paid too much for a new stock issue, and a corporation will know whether it received too little. On Wall Street the men who make decisions are always judging tomorrow's

---

* 1959: Though it could still be argued that the returns are not yet in, Montgomery Ward, under severe stockholder pressure has abandoned its position, and was thus certainly wrong. To expand in the late 'fifties, when the job could have been done a third cheaper in the late 'forties is to admit serious error.

market, or at most next year's market, and the skills required for the judging are mysterious and compelling.

The words on the telephone which express that judgment represent a binding contract, at least as good as anything signed and sealed and notarized in the presence of lawyers. It is the shibboleth of Wall Street that in finance "a man's word is as good as his bond"; and this is quite true, because there is an unwritten bond behind the word. All the business of the Street is done on the basis of verbal contracts, and if a man cannot be trusted to keep his verbal contracts nobody will deal with him. So a man puts the entire value of his future business behind his words when he says, very casually, "Sold," or "I'll take it," or "I'll bid twenty-three." The risks he undertakes by living up to his contract are nothing next to the risks he would run by breaking it.

What counts on the Street, in the line of business ethics, is something more: a man's willingness to put his skills at the service of others, at a price which represents their true value. If a broker has an order from a customer to buy twenty thousand shares of Gulf Oil, he will take the order to Robert Stott, the Stock Exchange specialist who manages the market in Gulf Oil, and discuss it with him. The information that somebody wants to buy twenty thousand shares of Gulf Oil is worth a fortune: it places a floor under the market, and lifts the ceiling high. Stott, keeping the market orderly while the purchases are made, will earn about six hundred dollars: in Stott's terms, peanuts. The thought that he could make a fortune with this information struck Stott as "embarrassing nonsense": this would be chiseling on his job, a conception so repugnant it could never cross his mind.

There are a hundred other men on Wall Street who earn their living by exercising and selling these skills of judgment: the secret-keepers, to whom the information they receive is the material of work rather than the chance at a killing. Their judgment is so quick and so accurate that people are constantly bringing them business, and they live very handsomely off the just proceeds. They are the leaders of Wall Street, and their names are rarely heard outside the Street itself because they hate to waste good time for the shoddy glory of public relations. They are among the most remarkable and most likeable and best-paid men in America.

Though they work in New York, they come from all over the country. Allan Sproul, president of the Federal Reserve Bank of New York, was born in San Francisco; Edward

McCormick, president of the American Stock Exchange, in Arizona; Gustave Levy, Goldman Sachs' great arbitrageur, in New Orleans; Joseph Hartfield of White & Case, in Paducah, Kentucky; Charles Merrill of Merrill Lynch, in Florida; Perry Hall, managing partner of Morgan Stanley, in Springfield, New Jersey. Though they are important and wealthy men today, most of them came out of ordinary middle-class or even working-class backgrounds—an actual majority never went to college, and picked up their considerable educations on their own after they had started work.*

The leaders of Wall Street are men in their fifties and early sixties, with only a few exceptions at either end. Sixty-five is too old for this work, with its constant demands on nervous energy; and the generation now in its thirties and forties never came down here at all. Between 1930 and 1946 Wall Street was a bad word, and business was rotten, too; the financial market had no appeal for youth, and was too tired to go looking for fresh blood. All that changed after the war, and today there are training programs all over the Street, eager bright boys of twenty-eight trailing after the leaders, about to be leaders themselves. Yesterday's students in the training programs live today in nice suburban houses.

Nobody lives on Wall Street itself, or near enough to walk to work. Most Wall Streeters were born outside New York City, and during their first years in town they worked too hard to learn that love of the place which usually afflicts its naturalized citizens; for them, New York has no romantic spots. So they live in the greener and grassier and more Republican suburbs, especially in New Jersey. Wall Street is four miles south of Grand Central Station, where the commuter trains pull in from Westchester or Connecticut, and more than three miles south of Pennsylvania Station, where the Toonerville Trolley arrives from Long Island. The Hudson-Manhattan tubes, however, are only walking distance from the office, so convenient that the head of the *Wall Street Journal* can commute comfortably from Princeton, New Jersey, some sixty-five miles away. Those of Wall Street who do live in New York live mostly in Brooklyn, especially Brooklyn Heights, just across the East River from the financial district; and from their windows at home they see the morning sun gleaming

---

* 1959: Of these men, Sproul has resigned, probably because of policy disagreements within the Open Market Committee of the Federal Reserve System, and Merrill is dead. Working-class origins are by no means as common as the final sentence might suggest, but they can be found occasionally.

on their windows at the office. The Brooklyn *Eagle,* an out-of-town newspaper elsewhere in Manhattan, has pride of place on the Wall Street news-stands.*

A few executives, of course, have cars with chauffeurs and they usually live in Manhattan town houses along the East Fifties, Sixties and Seventies. Others, a little less rich, will drive themselves to work, spending $2.00 a day to park the car in one of the infrequent lots or garages on the fringes of the district. And, finally, there are those who carry Wall Street with them wherever they go. Charles Merrill, for example, had a house on the East River at Sutton Place, and another in Litchfield, Connecticut, and another in Southhampton, Long Island, and another in Palm Beach, Florida. A private wire ran down to Palm Beach from Merrill Lynch, so that Merrill could be reached immediately when business clamored to be done.

2

On Hanover Square, with a view of the Grace Bank, India House and the Cotton Exchange, there is a small, independent outdoor business: a two-chair shoeshine stand, with green chairs mounted on a wooden platform. Between the two chairs rises a short flagpole topped with a bronze plaque:

> Tony Rubino
> Hanover Square
> Business founded
> April 5, 1902

3

Not everyone who works on Wall Street is rich, or even moderately middle-class. The towers need elevator men, the Stock Exchange floor must be swept, bank guards must guard the banks. Upstairs, somebody has to ask visitors who they are, and answer the telephone, and take dictation, and type letters, and keep the files in some semblance of order, and help the machines add figures. Just as the best jobs on Wall Street are among the most fascinating in the world, the worst are among the dullest. And while the best jobs enjoy the gambling excitement of finance, the worst suffer from its resulting insecurity. The Street has terrible labor relations, because its leaders are literally incapable of understanding the

* 1959: The Brooklyn *Eagle* has disappeared.

non-financial man's desire for peace and quiet and a steady income.

They are also prejudiced against women, who are considered too guileless, too prone to talk and too weak physically to carry the burdens of financial labor. Nevertheless, the Street is full of women; early every morning and late every afternoon the narrow canyons of Wall Street become resonant sounding boxes to magnify the click-click-clack-click of the high heels emerging from the subway or the office buildings. More than half the workers in the financial district are women, and though they do not have anything resembling equal rights they can be thankful if they wish that they are on the Street at all: there were few females here before the males were drafted into the Army in 1941. Today the best-selling magazines on the newsstands that rise at every subway entrance are the women's slicks—but there is still only one dress shop to compete with the sporting goods stores for the available space. When the New York Clearing House celebrated its centenary in 1953, and invited 1,200 bank executives to a dinner, only one of the guests turned out to be a woman, and she came from a bank in Trenton, New Jersey.* Except for a few angry feminists, a few lawyers and customer's ladies for feminist customers, the women of Wall Street have no money.

Most of the people of Wall Street work on commission, or on the disguised commission represented by the annual bonus; and basic salaries are usually very low. "There are people working down here twenty-five, thirty years," says Walter Schulze, President of the United Financial Employees, A.F. of L., "and their basic pay is fifty dollars a week. They live on the overtime; maybe they'll put in twenty or twenty-five hours of overtime in what they call a good week, and that with the Christmas bonus drags them up to a living wage. Maybe, in a good year."

U.F.E. was founded in 1941, a little too late to catch the great organizing impulse of the middle thirties, and then ripped to small pieces by a disastrous strike in 1947. Schulze, who has worked on the New York Stock Exchange floor since 1927, and still works there on a full-time basis, was a charter member. He is a very blond, fair man with a youthful

---

* 1959: And she was unlucky; it was her bank which was most deeply involved in the scandal surrounding the suicide of a former governor of New Jersey, who had been embezzling public funds.

look and a bushy moustache. He was not an officer of the union during the strike.

"Mind you," he says, "it's hindsight, because I was for the strike as much as anybody." The strike started when the exchanges installed I.B.M. machines in their accounting departments, and insisted on their right to fire as they pleased the men displaced by the machines. U.F.E. demanded that the men be laid off according to their seniority, and when the exchanges refused the union struck.

The exchanges reacted vigorously, brought people down from the upstairs offices to do the more menial work on the floors and asked the brokerage firms to supply trained men to handle the more highly skilled jobs. In a remarkable display of shortsightedness, hundreds of brokerage house employees grabbed for the double-time pay offered by the Stock Exchange, and crossed the picket lines. Hundreds of others, however, were reluctant to scab on their friends; and to reassure them U.F.E. promised that its members would not go back to work until the brokerage houses guaranteed not to punish men who had refused to cross the lines. Then, five weeks later, U.F.E. went back, thoroughly licked; and some two hundred brokerage house employees were fired. Since that time it has been almost impossible for U.F.E. to organize new units; but a large loudspeaker still hangs in one corner of the union's one-room office on Stone Street, waiting for the call to arms.

In 1958, U.F.E. represented only the employees of the two stock exchanges and the Cotton Exchange, and not all of these. It is still not strong enough to assure its members certain minimum protections guaranteed in almost every other union contract: the number of holidays, for example, is unilaterally determined by the exchanges. In 1954, to the general outrage of the people who work on Wall Street, the exchanges decided to remain open on three days that had previously been holidays—Lincoln's Birthday, Columbus Day, Armistice Day.* U.F.E. was unable to get its people extra pay for their extra work; only the New York Stock Exchange could be persuaded to give as much as an extra day's vacation later in the year for every holiday worked.

On Wall Street, however, the union contract provides regularity for something that in almost every other industry is a management prerogative: the bonus. According to contract,

* 1959: The Exchanges still open on these holidays, and the U.F.E. is still powerless to prevent it.

bonuses are paid quarterly whenever the volume of trading on the floor of an exchange goes over a certain basic figure; the higher the volume, the higher the bonus, all set down in legal language. This gimmick was written into the contract at the suggestion of Melvin Cunniff, then a member of the union, now a seat-holding member of the New York Stock Exchange itself. Talent on Wall Street gets promoted.

What makes the whole arrangement so extraordinary is the fact that employees of the exchanges have no control or even effect on the volume of business done. A volume bonus to them is a like a nice-day bonus for employees of the weather bureau. On Wall Street, however, everybody gambles, whether he wants to or not.

4

Wall Street, as everybody knows, is the home of Mammon, which presents to the lay preachers of New York a glorious opportunity. They do not miss it. Every day at lunchtime there appear on the streets two or three or four neatly dressed earnest missionaries with soapboxes, American flags and Biblical texts. Sometimes the texts are most elaborately illuminated on cloth and draped over the podiums, and out on to the sidewalk. "Now careful, gentlemen, please, not to step on the Holy Writ." These preachers are regular fixtures, and the knot of men that gathers about them is equally regular—agnostics whose lunch would be incomplete without a cheerful round of comment, answered with equal good humor. Occasionally outsiders, wild-haired and nervous, itinerant reverends, make fleeting visits to the Street; and before each of the important holidays Salvation Army units come round at closing time to serenade the parting souls.

More established religion, too, is active on Wall Street. Trinity Church stands facing the Street at its head, open all day for those seeking a moment's quiet. Trinity's organ concerts, talks and services break the day. Two blocks away, on the corner of Pine and William, stands a new, red-bricked Catholic chapel, where Mass is said and confessions are heard, and surprising numbers of women stop for a moment's prayer on their way home from work.

This new Catholic church is a symbol of the decline in Wall Street's social prejudices—thirty years ago there would have been little reason for such an institution. Then, too, there were "Jewish" firms—Lehman Brothers; Goldman,

Sachs; Kuhn, Loeb—and anyone of Jewish origin who wanted a job on Wall Street was well-advised to inquire only at their doors. Today Kuhn, Loeb employs more Christians than Jews, and there are religious barriers at only a minority of the important firms. A few houses, under pressure from the New York State laws, are even making an effort to eliminate the previously rigid bar against Negroes.* Though the Wall Street community is still three-quarters White Protestant, in a city nine-tenths Catholic, Negro or Jewish, the proportion is gradually but perceptibly moving toward a more logical balance.

5

Wandering in and out of the towers is a large and powerful Fourth Estate—the newspaper and magazine reporters, the public relations people and the men and women who dig for the various stock-service and bond-rating organizations. They have a special place on Wall Street because the financial market eats pheasant or spaghetti according to the volume of business done by the public. When Walter Winchell touted Pantepec Oil, his listeners sent in overnight orders for 357,000 shares—the largest block of stock ever put together on an Exchange. Public interest in the stock market is the first condition for the existence of a stock market; and the elaborate financial pages of the nation's dozen or so largest newspapers provide the market with advertising that money could not buy.

The progress of the market as a whole is charted by these journalists rather than by the professionals inside. The *New York Times* has a fifty-stock index, the New York *Herald Tribune* a hundred-stock index, laboriously compiled every day to show the high, low and closing average prices of these fifty or one hundred stocks. More important is the Dow Jones Index, printed in more than three thousand newspapers, showing the average daily price for the stocks of thirty industrial corporations, fifteen public utility corporations and twenty railroads, all traded on the New York Stock Exchange. Fourteen hundred stocks all told are traded on the New York Stock Exchange, but when a man asks "What did the market do today?" he is really asking about the sixty-five stocks in the

* 1959: There is now an entirely Negro firm which sells mutual funds to the Negro community.

Dow Jones Index.* If those sixty-five go up, and the other thirteen hundred go down, "the market" is said to go up. It happens; "the market" was described as "rising" in 1951 and 1952, when the majority of stocks declined. Even in the great bull market of January-June 1959, 799 stocks declined and only 550 advanced on the New York Stock Exchange.

The Dow Jones Index is calculated every hour, the *Wall Street Journal* published every business day and *Barron's* magazine every week, by Dow Jones & Company, which also runs the Dow Jones ticker, third largest news wire service in America. The *Wall Street Journal* alone has 22 news bureaus in key cities, plus 370 full-time and part-time reporters working outside the bureaus. Its circulation is approaching 625,000 (more than 90 per cent in subscriptions at twenty-four dollars a year), and it is printed separately in New York, Chicago, Dallas and San Francisco, with local news added on the spot, financial quotations set on the linotype machines by remote control from New York. It is a complete business newspaper, but the name is Wall Street and headquarters are only a block away from Wall Street, in the eight-story Dow Jones building a hundred yards from the New York Stock Exchange.

"This company was founded as a financial bulletin," says Bernard Kilgore, a quiet, short man who rose in twenty years from a forty-five-dollar-a-week fresh-from-college reporter to President of Dow Jones & Company. "They started the news ticker when tickers were invented. That is *the* Wall Street news service. I don't think the Street could get along without it. We give the prices of everything, and how much, plus every piece of news at all related to finance, including what the President says at his news conferences—and we're as fast as the AP, all the time." The ticker machine itself is far neater than the usual press service teletypes, which are ordinary automatic typewriters, printing in black on yellow paper. Dow uses a whirling disc instead of typewriter keys, blue ink and narrow white paper; the result looks somehow more reliable and makes less noise in the printing. "Up to the thirties, anyway, the ticker was the largest part of the business, because there were so many brokerage houses that needed it and the

* 1959: A new index, compiled and published by Standard and Poor, has become a ponderable rival to Dow Jones. It measures the movements of some 500 corporate securities, and is significantly less volatile than any of the others.

newspaper never got above sixty thousand circulation. Then the newspaper went up and the brokerage business went down, and today the ticker is definitely second."

When the decision was made to make the *Journal* a general business newspaper, and to advertise for circulation ("Men Who Get Ahead in Business Read . . .") on billboards, in magazines and in other newspapers, the Dow management nervously set up a public opinion poll to find out how people reacted to the words *Wall Street*. "Turned out," says Kilgore, "the effect is neutral." More important than name or advertising has been the increasing liveliness of the paper itself, which always carries a long page-one story about some business oddity, and then fights to be readable all the way through. Kilgore is proud of his boys. "Our contract salary scale," he says, "goes up to two hundred dollars. Two hundred dollars is cheap for a good man. We spend a lot of money on the staff, and we subscribe to AP, UP, INS and Reuters—though we usually supply more news to them than we take from them. Sometimes I even do a little reporting myself, because people will tell me things they wouldn't tell a reporter. They shouldn't do that, but they do."*

There are few newspapers in the world on which the publisher is a former member of the editorial staff; the boss usually comes from advertising, or circulation, or (most commonly) bookkeeping. Kilgore does not consider his rise too surprising, however, because reporters on Wall Street are highly trained people, and they learn a lot about business. They keep their quality as newspapermen by their incomes (which are not particularly high; and it is unwise to take a reporter's tip on the market), their membership in one or another newspaper union and their own particular club, the Financial Writers Association. Its big effort is an annual

---

* 1959: The contract minimum salary scale has now gone up to $240, and INS has died. And the *Wall Street Journal* has given remarkable public proof of an old-fashioned sort of journalistic integrity by publishing drawings of the designs General Motors planned to use for its next year's automobile models. These designs are supposed to be secret, and the methods by which the newspaper secured them have never been revealed. GM denounced the *Journal* for spying rather than reporting, and withdrew its advertising. Kilgore in reply announced that the reporter responsible for uncovering the designs had been given a bonus and encouraged to try again next year, and that the *Journal* would continue to prosper without General Motors advertising. Scenting a public-relations catastrophe, GM withdrew its complaint and quietly restored the *Wall Street Journal* to its advertising schedule. It was one of the few times in recent years that a newspaper had publicly asserted the old reportorial position that a man who wishes to hold confidential something which is important to the community must keep his secrets to himself.

show, staged before all the greats of finance after a fancy dinner at one of the town's ballrooms. Here the boys get a chance to air all the unprintable comments and complaints that have piled up since the last show—and to demonstrate (since they have to interview these gentlemen again tomorrow) that they really love the Street. Perhaps the most heart-rending of the skits they have presented over the years was built around a little ditty:

In all financial writing you are sure to meet this guy
And in his own opinion he stands supremely high
He knows the bigshots everywhere, the President calls him Sir
He's a very important sonofabitch, he knows your publisher
He is important, tralalalala
Very important, tralalalala
He'll have you know his shirt is stuffed with real chinchilla fur
He's a very important sonofabitch, he knows your publisher.

In addition to the newspapers which service the more or less lay public there are trade journals—*Finance, American Banker, The Bond Buyer, Investment Dealer's Digest*—which spread the news of the business around among the inmates. These journals, and to a lesser exent the financial sections of all newspapers, live off advertising from the Street itself, and there are two large ad agencies within the financial district which handle most of the business—Doremus & Co. and Albert Frank, Guenther Law. Sometimes, of course, these agencies are regarded by an ambitious house as too utilitarian, and help is summoned from Madison Avenue. Gerald M. Loeb of E. F. Hutton, whose book *The Battle for Investment Survival* has been selling 40,000 copies a year for more than a decade, believes that mail-order advertising specialists are the best bet for brokerage advertising. But such firms tend to feel crippled by the legal and ethical restrictions on financial advertising, and their work lacks dignity.

Though all newspaper reporters are wooed by the market, there is one group regarded with even greater solicitude: the reporter-analysts who work for the rating houses, especially *Moody's* and *Standard and Poor's*. Their smile or frown can mean life or death.

Banks and insurance companies are regulated by the state or federal government in the investments they can make; and their investments are supposed to be very high class. Banks and insurance companies are so much the prime customers for new bond issues that large issues cannot be sold unless the banks and insurance companies will buy them. Because state and federal governments have limited research facilities to look into the bond market, they generally take the published ratings as guides: *Aaa, Aa, A* and *Baa* bonds are okay for banks and insurance companies, but *Ba* and lesser bonds are n.g. So the rating that *Moody's* reporters give to a bond will often determine whether or not an underwriter can sell it.

"Many's the time," said a leading partner of a leading underwriter, "I've gone over to a rating house and spent hours with one of their people, proving that something they found in a company's books wasn't really there, after all. Lots of bonds are borderline, between *Baa* and *Ba,* and crossing on the wrong side of that border can mean we go for broke. Many's the lunch I've bought for those bastards; many's the drink."

6

The banks close at three o'clock (though people can sneak in until three-thirty if they know the way), the exchanges shut down at three-thirty. The people who work on the floors of the exchanges, members and employees, go promptly home, and the bank tellers follow when their telling is told. Upstairs, in the banks and the brokerage houses, the accountants, the clerks and the wonderful calculating machines get down to the difficult part of it, figuring out how much cash money was involved in all those verbal contracts made by the men whose word is as good as their bond. Stocks must be delivered and paid for, numbers moved around in the customers' accounts, bills sent out and collected, checks cleared. Meanwhile, the porters are cleaning the litter of paper off the floors at the two stock exchanges, the teletypes are stuttering less frantically in the offices of the over-the-counter dealers. Executives take a last look at the Dow Jones ticker and start heading home to the country, fat brief cases in their hands.

At the brokerage houses the telephones are at last free of customers' calls, and the girls in the wire rooms settle down to long chats with lady and gentleman friends. Stenographers take a coffee break before tackling the two hours' worth of dictation done by the boss in the half-hour since the market closed; these letters must be ready for his signature tomorrow very early, before the market opens. The bright young men pick up lists of closing prices, make obscure marks on little charts, and vanish into the library to check their calculations against the history of the situation.

Five o'clock sounds, the night lines are plugged into the telephone switchboard, and most of Wall Street goes home, lemmings marching to the subway. At some of the larger brokerage houses a part-time evening clerical staff appears to clean up the day; at others the clock ticks off time-and-a-half for the regular help. The stock salesmen and the market spies report briefly into their offices, and a few of the independent dealers and minor executives sit happily down to a few hours' work with no noise from the goddam telephone. The bars sell much liquor to men on their way home or back to work, grabbing a quick one.

Around six-thirty the cleaning women arrive, and the lights flash on in the towers. By eight o'clock they are going off again, and by nine even the busiest of the brokerage houses has its accounts squared away and locks the doors for the night. Now a few selected lights recur, as the young lawyers, having eaten steaks on the expense account, get back to their desks or their firm's library for night work. The presses roar on the bottom floors of the Dow Jones building as the *Wall Street Journal* prints its Eastern edition, and trucks line up on tiny New Street to take the papers away.

At eleven o'clock the young lawyers start packing up for the day to return to their young wives and the children they have scarcely if ever seen; the last telephone call of the night summons home a minor executive of an underwriting house, who has ducked out of a family dinner party to put the polishing touches on tomorrow's deal. By midnight the Street is deserted, excepting only the night watchmen, the special police who guard some six billion dollars' worth of yellow gold in the subterranean vaults of the Federal Reserve Bank, an occasional city policeman, a lawyer or two, the night shift of bank clerks clearing checks, and a few drunks wandering absent-mindedly from their usual haunts, sleeping it off on the cold stone stoops of Wall Street.

Chapter 3

Stocks and Bonds

OF ALL the thoughts hatched from the womb of mind, perhaps the most eternally useful was, "Maybe I can sell a piece of it." Without this original, greedy flash of suggestion, and its embodiment in the corporate form of organization, man's production of useful goods could never have kept pace with his accelerating reproduction of himself. With the corporate form of organization, man, especially the American, has been able to secure for himself a more comfortable and essentially a more decent way of living than has ever been known before. And the corporation itself, as an abstract form, is a creation of art wonderful to behold. Not even man is so well suited to the environment in which he moves; not the most skilled doctor, the most profound philosopher, the most astute banker can place himself in the ruddy physical, mental and fiscal health that glows on the surface of the successful corporation.

A corporation comes into existence when it is needed, and dies when its usefulness is done. It can own property and money and other corporations; it can buy and sell rather eminent men. It can hire lawyers, sue and be sued. It can advertise, buy books, make binding contracts, expand, contract, manufacture all goods, perform all services. It needs no sleep, takes no vacations. It can borrow and steal, and even beg. It is never liable to anyone beyond what it has; if its debts exceed its assets, that is too bad for its creditors. If you prick it, it does not bleed; if you tickle it, it does not laugh. It can scream, however, if taxed or otherwise annoyed.

Exactly what a corporation is, nobody knows; that is one of its beauties. But every corporation must rest on a specific charter from a state, and the ownership of the corporation will be expressed in transferable instruments known as stock. These pieces of paper, and the other pieces of paper which express a corporation's debt, are the stuff in which Wall Street deals. Their valuation and their proliferation are the sum of the work done in the hundred buildings by the hundred thousand people of Wall Street.

2

First there are stocks, and then there are bonds, and then there are many ingenious combinations of the two.

In law and in theory, each share of ordinary—or common —stock in a corporation represents a part ownership of the company that issued the stock. A man who owns ten shares in a company with a thousand shares outstanding is said to own 1 per cent of the company. He will have a 1 per cent vote in choosing the company's directors, in accepting or rejecting fundamental policies. If the company declares a dividend, he will receive 1 per cent of the swag; if the company is dissolved and its assets sold, he will get 1 per cent of the sale, after all debts are paid. If the company goes broke, he owns 1 per cent of the shiny, well-printed stock certificates. No matter how badly the company fails, however, the stockholders in an ordinary corporation (banks are different) never has to kick in more than he paid originally. His risks are limited (in England the corporation title is "Ltd.," which stands for "limited liability company"); his profits are potentially unbounded.

All this is quite true; but in practice the intelligent investor looks upon a stock certificate as merely a proportionate share in a company's future profits. Most of the stock in any large corporation is voted by mail, and the letter which the stockholder signs to register his vote (proxy is the official word, because the vote is actually cast by some designated person at the meeting) is printed by the board of directors whose actions are the subject of the vote. So long as the stockholders are receiving dividend checks they are immensely conservative, and refuse to believe (unless hammered by some tireless piston of a corporate raider) that some other set of directors, some other management policies, could produce still higher dividends. For various and usually sound reasons, corporations since the war have paid out in dividends only one-half of their net profits after taxes; but even here, with possible extra dividends sleeping in the treasury, very few companies have been forced by vote of their "owners" to pay out more than the management thinks is proper. Company managements use this conservatism quite consciously to maintain themselves in power. One shrewd board of directors prints the proxy approving its actions for the year on the back on the dividend check; if the stockholder endorses the dividend check, he endorses the existing management. It is hard to fault this scheme—but the government is trying.*

* 1959: The government has succeeded. This check-endorsement proxy is not valid.

There is a lot of nonsense written and printed about the man who holds one share of General Electric being boss to Ralph Cordiner, and any potential stockholder should clean his head of such stuff before he buys securities. Ordinary concepts of ownership imply that the owner can do something with the thing he owns; all a stockholder can do with his "piece" of General Electric is sell it. He need not always be consulted on decisions that immediately and obviously change the value of his stock; early in 1954 the management of American Woollen announced that it had the power to alter the Corporation's entire financial structure without even asking the stockholders about it. This situation is generally regarded as evil, and crusades to agitate stockholders to their rights of "ownership" leave Grand Central Station every twenty minutes except during the summer. But nothing vital is at stake: boards of directors will in an emergency vote for the stockholders however they are elected. Moreover, Ralph Cordiner is more competent than any stockholder to run General Electric, and his interests (except perhaps in the matter of management salaries, stock options and pensions) are similar to those of the stockholders.

Once the ownership concept is put aside, the real values of the stock certificate stand out more clearly. Basically, they are: (1) a proportionate share in the future profits of the corporation; (2) a proportionate share in the corporation's net assets if the corporation should be liquidated; (3) a proportionate vote on any changes in company policy. The price of the certificate is determined almost entirely by factor (1)—the general expectation among investors as to the amount of the future profits. Factor (2)—the net assets—enters mostly as a calculation in deciding how much profit the company can be expected to make. And factor (3)—the protection of the stockholder's vote—is discarded completely in favor of a judgment as to the quality of the management. Given a certain expectation as to the general state of business in a coming period, the professional investor looking for a place to put his money and the underwriter looking for new securities to distribute both consider the quality of a corporation's management the most important single test of the value of its securities. "If you don't like the management," runs an old Wall Street motto, "sell."

3

Bonds are simpler: they are nothing more or less than loans

made to a corporation by the public rather than by a bank. The loan is broken up into thousand-dollar pieces, and each piece is sold. The corporation then owes a thousand dollars to the man who has purchased the bond, and every six months (or year, or quarter) it owes interest on that thousand dollars. If the corporation fails to pay the interest for a specified length of time, or fails to pay back the thousand dollars when the bond comes due, the bondholders take over the business just as though they were a bank foreclosing on a farmhouse. This result is immensely unfortunate for all concerned; but, as a number of railroads can testify, it happens.

Dividends on stocks can be paid in any amount that the profits justify, or skipped entirely at the discretion of the management; interest on bonds must be paid regularly, in stipulated amounts, no matter how well or how badly (short of bankruptcy) the corporation is doing. In the ordinary course of events a corporation will never buy back its stock; it must, however, pay off its bonds. And if a corporation goes bust the bondholders are entitled to dip into the saleable remains to the full value of the bonds before a single stockholder gets a single penny. Bonds are therefore considered a "safer" investment that stock, and usually (not always) they are.

Some bonds are safer than others. The safest of all—so safe that a completely bankrupt company can still raise money by selling them—are equipment trust certificates. These bonds represent a mortgage on a specific piece of highly saleable equipment, almost always a railroad box car or a locomotive. They are issued to enable railroads to buy new rolling stock, and they are safe because another railroad or a meat-packing house will be glad to buy the box car from the bondholders if they foreclose the mortgage; and because very few managements will be so idiotic as to buy new equipment that does not at least earn its own depreciation. (And because the state keeps bankrupt railroads going, and thus in effect insures the interest on the certificate.) By the terms of the trust certificate the depreciation allowances are automatically used to buy back a certain number of bonds every year. Obviously, this sort of bond can also be used to finance trolleys, buses and airplanes; beyond these vehicles, however, it has been successfully applied to only one commercial property—juke boxes.

Next in safety comes the first mortgage bond, by which the corporation pledges property worth 20 to 50 per cent more than the bonds will cost; if the corporation defaults, the bondholders own the property. The value of this mortgage protection is directly proportional to the saleability or productivity of the mortgaged property—foreclosing on a railroad station, for example, is an unrewarding labor: the thing can't be used for anything but a railroad station, and that for a railroad which is broke; otherwise the bondholders wouldn't have been forced to foreclose. A mortgage on a plant that generates electric power, however, ought to have some value during the hardest times.

Behind the first mortgage bond may come a whole train of second, third or even fourth mortgages on the same property; such bonds are not usually considered particularly safe unless the first mortgage is very small or the property very valuable. Some third mortgage bonds, however, may be as good as first mortgage bonds, because the bonds "senior" to them have already been redeemed. In finance, as elsewhere, the smell of the rose does not depend on the name.

Some corporations do not like to use mortgage bonds at all (some practically can't—mortgages must be registered in the county in which the property is located, and a company like American Telephone and Telegraph would have to spend the proceeds of the bonds in registering the mortgages). Nevertheless, most companies at one time or another need to borrow money from the public. If they don't like mortgages, they sell debentures.

A debenture is essentially an I.O.U.—but an I.O.U. enforceable in the courts. Although most investors look on debentures as somewhat riskier investments, they are often as safe as first mortgage bonds. If there is no mortgage, and the terms of the debenture provide that no mortgage will be made, the debenture stands as a kind of first mortgage on the whole business —holders of debentures will take over the works if the company defaults on the loan. Debentures that are issued behind mortgages—giving the debenture owners second or third grab at the assets if the corporation dies—are of course considerably more nervous investments.

Stockholders vote; bondholders sue. So corporations are far more anxious about arguments with bondholders, and protect themselves against such arguments by placing the enforcement of bondholders' rights in the hands of a single "trustee," usually a bank. Only the trustee can sue on behalf of a bondholder, as an ordinary matter, and the disputes that might provoke lawsuits—descriptions of the mortgaged property, allocations of any money the corporation may collect by selling such property, how many interest payments (if any) can be passed before the bonds are considered in default, how much money (if any) the corporation must pay into a "sinking fund" each year to redeem part of the loan—are negotiated beforehand between the corporation and the trustee. The results of these negotiations are written into a "trust indenture," often longer than this chapter, and the bondholder accepts the indenture when he buys the bond; he puts his rights in the hands of the trustee.

In the old days this arrangement was roundly abused; there was even an "ostrich clause" in the indenture, relieving the trustee of any obligation to act against the company until notified of some default by a third (or even a majority) of the bondholders. Too often the corporation and the trustee were friends, close friends, and the trustee could be counted on to do the bondholders in the eye before offending his friend in any way. In 1941, however, Congress took care of this situation by something called the Trust Indenture Act, a fantastically complicated piece of legislation, and today the trustee is held to higher standards of trustworthiness.

The interest rate that a bond carries will depend very largely on its safety: third mortgages may pay 7 per cent, while equipment trust certificates pay only a little more than a government bond with the same maturity period. Obviously, a short-term loan is safer than a long-term loan, because there is less time for business to go sour; the interest rate on a good ten-year bond will be substantially less than the interest rate on a good thirty-year bond. If the bond will not be redeemed for centuries (there are such bonds, though not many—the West Shore Railroad has a mortgage bond due in the year 2361) the interest on it is likely to be quite high. Actually, this higher rate for the longer term is a fairly recent phenomenon; but it seems permanent today.*

---

* 1959: This turned out to be a wrong guess. The conditions of the money market are such that there is a steady supply of long-term funds, representing the fixed obligations of insurance companies and pension trusts. Because they know the size of their dollar commitments in future years, they need not worry about erosions of value in an inflationary flood. Medium-term investors, however, tend to want their value back, and if they fear inflation they will hesitate to put their money into fixed-price securities. Interest coupons, of course, reflect supply of lendable funds, and recently there have been months when medium-term bonds have carried higher coupons than long-term bonds. In fact, bonds as a whole have been yielding a greater return than common stocks, because the stock customer benefits from inflation and the bond customer suffers. Investors as a group have felt that it is safer to gamble for price increases in individual securities than to gamble

Generally speaking, all bonds are sold originally for a thousand dollars, give or take a dollar or two, and the interest rate reflects the price of money and the safety of the bond *at the moment the bond is sold*. Thereafter, the price of the bond varies according to changes in the price of money and in the safety of that corporation's securities. If the general interest rate goes up, the price of the bond goes down; in other words, when similar new bonds are paying forty-five dollars a thousand, a bond which pays thirty dollars will sink until the return on the new price, including appreciation to date of redemption, is roughly $4\frac{1}{2}$ per cent.

Logic would argue that the price would rise considerably above a thousand dollars if interest rates on new bonds went down—but, as a matter of fact, there is an effective ceiling on the prices for many bonds. Most new bonds are "callable"— the corporation that issued them can buy them back at any time after decent notice is given. The call price is likely to be more than the original price of the bond—say $1,050. But that call price tends to place a ceiling on the amount anyone of sense will pay for the bond.

The safety of a bond is usually calculated by placing the corporation's total yearly interest debt against its total yearly earnings; if the earnings are three or four times the interest, on an average covering good and bad years, then the bond is safe. People who don't want to go to such mathematical trouble can simply look up the issue in one of the standard rating services— *Moody's* or *Standard and Poor's*. If a corporation seems to be skidding downhill the price of its bonds will drop rapidly so that the purchaser gets a higher rate of interest on his purchase price. As an ordinary matter such "secondary" bonds are a bad buy—they simply disappear in a depression. But bonds which have declined greatly in price, for one reason or another, can sometimes be an excellent investment; if the corporation holds off the wolves, it will redeem its bonds at par.

4

Somewhere between stocks and bonds are great, fearsome flocks of hybrid animals—preferred stocks and income bonds; bonds and preferreds which can be converted into common stock at bargain prices if the common goes up; and, queerest

---

against price increases throughout the economy. In mid-1959, the average high-rated bond yielded 7.4% interest, and the average common stock paid only slightly more than a 3% dividend, at current prices.

of all, bonds and preferreds which "participate" in a corporation's increased earnings, if the earnings ever increase.

There is something peculiar about all of these, though preferred stocks have a long and sometimes even honorable history and American Telephone and Telegraph convertible debentures have been found in the most conservative insurance company portfolios. The usual purpose of such issues, nevertheless, is to talk people into buying a security which they wouldn't buy without the added gimmick.

All of these "mongrels," as Professor Arthur Dewing calls them, are "senior" to ordinary common stocks—that is, they receive dividends or interest before common stock dividends are paid, and they have prior rights to the assets if the corporation goes out of business. Beyond this universal seniority, each dog has its own bone.

The preferred stock is the simplest. Its dividend (usually 4 to 7 per cent of its par value), must be paid before anything is paid on the common. If nothing is paid on the common, however, the corporation is not obliged to pay on the preferred. [1959: Most investment analysts despise the straight preferred, which offers, they feel, neither the protection of the bond nor the appreciation potential of the common. Their classic case is the Christiana Securities common and preferred, both issued at $100 a share; the preferred has gone up to 30 per cent over the decades, while the common has gone up to 15,000 per cent.]

The income bond is a first cousin with slightly different habits. The bond itself is an obligation of the corporation and must be paid back when it falls due; the interest, however, need be paid only if it is earned by the corporation during the year. Because of the lesser safety of the interest payments, income bonds and preferred stocks are often upgraded by provisions which make the interest or dividends "cumulative." In a cumulative preferred, for example, dividends that are skipped are still owed to the preferred stockholders, and all dividends on the preferred—no matter how many years have been missed—must be paid up before the common can get a nickel. (This provision is sometimes the subject of hard bargaining between the management and the holders of the preferred. Where a considerable majority of the preferred stock is in the hands of common stockholders, the safeguard may disappear.)

"Convertible" securities are just what the name implies— they can be changed from one of a corporation's issues to another, usually from a bond or a preferred to a certain number of shares of common stock. A typical example would be a debenture selling for a thousand dollars, convertible on demand into fifty shares of stock. If the stock rises above 20, the debenture will sell for more than a thousand. [1959: In the 1920's the usual purpose of convertibility was to put speculative sauce on what looked like a sober investment pudding. But the convertible debenture can also operate the other way, when the company wishes to sell not the debentures themselves but the stock into which they may be converted. A big issue of new stock may be difficult to sell, or may unduly depress the market, while an issue of convertible debentures might attract insurance company money and leave the market in equilibrium. The issuing company hopes and expects that within a few years all the debentures will be converted. It uses the convertible gimmick, not to make its bonds speculative, but to place its full faith and credit behind a projected new issue of stock.

Technicalities of government regulation have made the convertible debenture a prime marketing tool in recent years. "Margin requirements" set by the Federal Reserve system limit the proportion of the price of a stock which a purchaser may borrow in order to buy his shares. The actual percentages vary, depending on the Fed's views of the money market and the stock market, but an average of the post-war period would be something like 30 per cent of the price. Thus a man who wishes to buy 2,000 shares of stock selling at 15 will have to put up $21,000 in cash.

There is usually no difficulty, however, about borrowing 80 per cent of the offering price of a respected new bond. If each $1,000 bond is convertible into 50 shares of common stock, a purchaser can control the same 2,000 shares by taking 40 bonds, borrowing 80 per cent of the price, and putting up only $8,000 in cash. The convertible path is probably trod most often today by companies seeking to find a route around margin requirements in the sale of a new stock issue.]

Least respectable of all these animals is the "participating" preferred or income bond. This twerp of a security supposedly offers the greater safety of a senior issue and the unlimited future of a common stock. The one investor who always loses his money is the man who wants a piece of paper that represents both a sure thing and a gamble; and the vast bulk of "participating" securities have been designed for the sucker trade. Nevertheless, it is notorious on Wall Street that a man selling stock in a gold mine may actually find some gold once the stock has been sold. It isn't an everyday occurrence, but it isn't impossible, either.

5

Looked at this way, straight on, from a purely public point of view, finance is a game—the greatest game ever invented. Any number can play, and each man sets his own stakes. The rules are simple, and the odds change fifty times a day.

But turn the picture around, quickly, and the world becomes suddenly serious. Looked at from the point of view of a corporation, which needs money to produce goods, finance is water, air, fire and stone, the very elements of life. The securities in which the gaming public takes so frivolous an interest are sober matters indeed to the corporation which creates them.

A growing business needs money the way a growing boy needs meat; both corporation and boy can grow up deformed or stunted, or die from malnutrition, if the basic food is wrong. A business now expanding, which needs a million dollars to complete its expansion, can shatter a hopeful future by picking up the money in a way that damages its hopes for further financing, or places unnecessary restraints on its day-to-day affairs.

A million dollars is hard to raise. "If a man walks into my office and says he needs ten million," one of the Street's biggest bankers said recently, "I can tell in about fifteen minutes whether he can get ten million. Either he has a good case for the money or he doesn't. But a man who needs something between half a million and two million—well, he has problems. Nobody ever heard of General Motors going broke, but small and middling-small businesses go broke every day."

The most obvious way to raise money is to walk into a bank and borrow it. Banks, however, are not supposed to be in the long-term loan business (none of them was before ordinary banking dried up like a prune in the thirties). And they are certainly not supposed to risk their money on anything the least bit chancy—they must stand ready to pay off their deposits, in cash, on demand. A man who can raise a million dollars in bank loans to expand an ordinary business is wasting his time; he should be producing movies.

Insurance companies (though they, too, are lending other people's money) are less restricted than banks, but not much less. And they have bad habits of lending; getting money out of them is like pulling teeth out of an enraged water buffalo. They write the terms of the loan themselves (and then make the borrower pay the legal fees on both sides). In cases where any risk is involved the terms usually include collateral up to and including the borrower's family cemetery plots. And from the insurance company's point of view the interest on a million dollars—fifty thousand dollars or so a year, at most—is scarcely worth the trouble.

The corporation can borrow its money from the public— selling bonds or debentures. But just as a bank or an insurance company may not wish to lend money to some corporation, the public may not wish to buy its bonds. In any event, somebody must sell the bonds, and this costs money, too. A small company is a company unknown to the bond-buying public, so an education campaign must accompany the sales campaign. An investment banker must manage these campaigns, and will expect to make a profit on them. Often the only way such bonds can be sold is by investment bankers pushing them on to clients whose names the corporation has never even heard. Such clients are one of an investment banker's prize assets, and for the use of these assets the investment banker will usually charge the corporation a considerable piece of the money to be raised.

The underwriter's fee comes off the top of the money raised by the sale—but the corporation pays interest on the entire proceeds. At this writing the rate for prime commercial names on a moderately long-term bond is 4½ per cent; prime commercial names mean "General Motors." A small corporation that needs a million dollars is no prime commercial name; its coupon is likely to run to 6 per cent and the effective interest, on the money the corporation actually received, will be in the neighborhood of 7 per cent. Meanwhile, the purchasers of these bonds get only 6 per cent on their money, even though the corporation is actually paying 7; the difference has gone into the underwriter's pocket. The enlightened investor knows about this difference, and worries about it; and he asks for a gimmick. At this moment one of the "mongrel" convertibles is born.

Making an issue convertible costs the corporation nothing now; but it can be expensive later on. If the business does well, and more money is needed for further expansion, the existence of convertible bonds casts a cloud over the financial picture. They hold down the price of the common stock, because the holders of the bonds can create new stock at *their* desire, rather than the corporation's. [1959: Keep in mind, however, that many companies think of their outstanding convertibles as stock already issued. To such companies, the following analysis need not apply.] They may also make investors leary of buying new securities of the corporation because its financial structure is now in the hands of outsiders.

(A little arithmetic. The typical convertible might be issued at $1,000, with the right to convert to 50 shares of common stock at any time. The common originally totalled 100,000 shares, paying a $1 dividend and selling for $15. Obviously, the convertible feature is worthless until the price of the common passes 20; which would mean, as an ordinary matter, that the dividend passes $1.20. The corporation is now paying $50,000 in interest on $1,000,000 of convertible bonds; if all these bonds were converted $60,000 would be necessary to keep up the dividend rate. Worst yet, the interest on the bonds is tax-free to the corporation, while earnings for dividends are after taxes, and the basic corporate tax rate is, at this writing, 52 per cent. Some $125,000 in earnings would be necessary to cover the dividend on the new stock created by conversion—$75,000 more than is necessary to cover the interest. If the bonds were not convertible, a $75,000 rise in yearly earnings would enable the corporation to raise perhaps as much as another $1,000,000 to expand its operations further. With convertible bonds, the corporation is stuck.)

Moreover, there can be an embarrassing lack of dignity in the very existence of hybrid securities; and once a corporation begins making a certain amount of profits, it wants dignity.

Raising money by the outright sale of common stock has one advantage over borrowing money by the sale of bonds: there's no compulsory interest to be paid. Fifty thousand dollars must be paid on the million-dollar bond issue every year, or the corporation goes broke; stockholders are "owners," and the corporation need not pay them anything unless the profits warrant the payment. There are, however, three disadvantages for a small corporation trying to expand its common stock issue: (1) the present stockholders' proportion of the future potential profits is watered by the creation of new shares with equal rights; (2) the tax problem; (3) common stock in small, young corporations can't as an ordinary matter be sold at all. A little preferred stock (probably convertible), yes; common stock, no. It may be possible to sell a little common stock by giving the underwriter a quarter of a third of the proceeds; and, of course, some corporations, even small ones, can sell additional stock to those personal friends who got them started in the first place. Without such friends a corporation may find that the price for "venture capital" is high as a gallows.

Under these circumstances it is fairly surprising that small businesses grow; and unquestionably the time of raising new money is a time of anguish in any business. Only an outrageous optimism justifies paying the price for new money that small corporations have to pay; but events often justify the outrageous optimism. And the underwriters who help small corporations issue these securities earn their 10 or 15 or 20 per cent. They pick and choose the corporations whose securities they are willing to recommend to their customers, and because they want to hold their customers they try to pick only the corporations whose securities are worth buying. Every once in a while they gyp the corporations, charging a great deal in commission for securities that will be easy to sell; and sometimes they gyp their customers, building up the romance of the security and playing down the facts. Two-thirds of the thievery and misrepresentation done on Wall Street is committed in connection with these small issues of small corporations, and some firms make from such issues a great deal more money than they should. But two-thirds of the really important work on Wall Street is in this field, too; and in this case, to use a favorite Street phrase, the laborer is worthy of his hire.

6

Large corporations have problems less awful when they need fresh capital, but the number of hairline decisions that must be made is greater. So the anguish is probably even.

Unless the management is considered wholly foolish (there are twenty or so very large corporations into which very few people on Wall Street would be willing to put any money), any corporation that is generally known can sell new securities. It does not have to go begging for underwriters to handle the issues; underwriters will come bidding for the chance to do the job. And it doesn't have to pay for financial services any great proportion of the money to be raised; General Motors paid less than 1 per cent of the total to the underwriters who helped the corporation raise $300,000,000 of new money late in 1953.

Big corporations must be more responsible than small corporations, just as big boys must be more responsible than small boys. A small company sits around for a while, deciding what type of security it wants to sell; then it goes to an under-writer, who tells it exactly what can be sold, and that is an end to the matter. A large company get financial advice on how well the various types of security are selling; then it sits around, with or without its financial advisors, and decides what it wants to sell.

The first question is: debt or equity (bonds or stocks). Up to a point, the government solves this problem by placing bond interest before taxes. But the time may come when a company has too many bonds outstanding, too much of its gross earnings must go into interest payments, and a down-turn in business would mean not the discomfiture of stock-holders (which is normal) but the bankruptcy of the corpo-ration. Moreover, when the debt structure gets out of line, and too high a proportion of the earnings goes to pay off interest, the stock becomes speculative, as so many railroad stocks are today.

(More mathematics. If a corporation has $1,000,000 a year available for dividends and 100,000 shares of stock outstanding, the dividend would be $10 a year. The same $10 dividend would hold, ignoring the tax question, with 40,000 shares of stock and $600,000 in bond interest to be paid before the stock collects. Let the dividend fund go to $2,000,000, however. The payment to the stockholders in the first case goes to $20; in the second case it goes to $35. And a drop in the earnings to $600,000 merely cuts the first dividend to $6, while it kills the second altogether. This second stock has "leverage," and stocks with considerable leverage can become gamblers' playthings.)

For the reasons of dignity and future financial needs, no cor-poration is happy to have its stocks become a kind of roulette wheel. Where a company is regulated in its activities by an agency of government—as all "utilities" are to some degree—the government often sets a ceiling on the proportion of debt as against equity in the capital structure.

The choice between debt and equity will be made only after a prolonged trance and communion with the four spirits—taxes, present debt structure, market conditions and purpose for which the new money is to be used. Now the work begins. Assuming that the Ouija Board has come up DEBT—what kind of debt? Shall we put ourselves in hock to the Metropolitan Life? Shall we issue debentures or mortgage bonds? Deben-tures must carry a higher rate of interest, the market being the irrational creature it is; but mortgages must be registered. If we issue mortgage bonds there'll be lots of legal fees, and the damn lawyers are making too much money out of this company already. How long shall the bonds run? Shall they be convertible? Shall they be callable—or shall they run to the maturity date with nothing we can do about it? They'll be easier to sell non-callable, and the price may be a litttle better; but then we may find ourselves paying 4¼ per cent interest on our bonds when the prime commercial rate is 3¼ per cent, and it would pay us to "refund" (call in the old bonds and issue new ones at a lower rate of interest). Shall we negotiate the sale with an underwriter, or set up the terms of sale and let the underwriters bid for the bonds?

Maybe the Ouija Board reads STOCKS. Shall they be preferred or common? If preferred, what dividend should we propose to pay, and should the dividends be cumulative? Shall the preferred be convertible? If common, should we make sure of our control of the corporation by issuing some special non-voting stock? (The New York Stock Exchange, however, will not list such shabby goods, and the government may make it hard to get out the issue.) There is also something that might be described as convertible common—it comes with a "warrant" that entitles its owner to buy more common from the company at a price higher than the present market. At the time the warrant is issued it is worthless (giving a man the right, say, to buy for twenty dollars something he can presently buy for fifteen dollars); but the warrant may be worth a good deal if the corporation does well and the price goes up substantially. Some of the great fortunes on Wall Street (including that of Charles Merrill, founder and genius of Merrill Lynch, Pierce, Fenner & Beane) have been made through warrants.

The successful conclusion of this trance, however, does not end all worries. Shall the new securities be offered at a discount to the present stockholders, or shall they simply be sold to the public, first come, first served? Maybe we don't really need an underwriter—A.T. & T. sold better than a billion dollars' worth of debentures, with not an underwriter in sight. But that's A.T. & T.; we had better talk to somebody in the finance business and find out what investors want.

A wrong step on any one of these decisions can be unimaginably costly. For example, Continental Baking Company once issued a rather large bunch of 8-per-cent preferred stocks; and from that time until Wertheim & Co. bailed them out of the situation the stockholders of Continental Baking were on the outside looking in—all the profits went to the holders of preferred stock. To keep companies from making such mistakes (and, incidentally, to keep a business eye on the corporation's financial business), investment bankers often sit on corporate boards of directors. Even such august presences from Wall Street, however, are no guarantee that every decision will be made correctly. "A good underwriter," George Jones of Wertheim said recently, "should see to it that companies never get into anything they can't get out of within five years. . . ."

Chapter 4

The New York Stock Exchange (Part I)

ROBERT STOTT was reminiscing in the partners' room at Wagner, Stott & Co., on the twenty-second floor of 11 Wall Street.* This is a very safe place to be, because it cannot be approached except from the seventeenth floor of 11 Wall Street, where the visitor must change elevators to get up into the tower. The building is owned by the New York Stock Exchange, and there are guards all around, answering people's questions.

Stott is a member of the Stock Exchange, a specialist whose firm is charged with maintaining an even market in 33 different stocks, including such as Corning Glass, Gulf Oil, National Steel, Schenley Industries, Glenn Martin Aviation and Union Carbide. He does business only with other brokers, and is as thorough a professional as the Street has to offer. He and Wagner have been partners since 1925, and they never have traded with the public.

"I started specializing in 1917, on the old Curb, when it was out in the street," Stott says, "and during the twenties Wagner and I were specialists in Electric Bond and Share. There was so much volume we used to work to one, two o'clock every morning, just to get all the accounts squared away and everything cleared out for the next day. When we gave up the stock no one specialist was big enough to take it—five firms split it up, each handling a day's work every week."

Stott's desk stands against one corner of a large room with three windows and a very large Oriental rug and dark brown wood panelling. Several back issues of the *Princeton Alumni Weekly* sit sedately on his IN tray. In the opposite corner of the room, about thirty-five feet away, there is a desk for another partner; one of the reasons that Wall Street partnerships stay amicable and prosperous for thirty-three years is that the partners share offices. If one partner wants to know what another one is up to, he merely raises his head and looks.

* 1959: The firm still rents space at 11 Wall, but Stott and Wagner themselves have moved across the trading floor to more modern quarters at 20 Broad Street.

"I came back to the Curb from lunch one day in 1929," Stott recalls, "and I said to Wagner, 'I just bought a seat on the Stock Exchange.'"

"'Really?' he said. 'Do you think they have any left?'"

"I said, 'I guess so.' Wagner bought his seat early in 1930. We both paid about four hundred and thirty thousand dollars for the seat."

It was mentioned that the price of a Stock Exchange seat had not been for some years as much as one-half of that figure. "Oh, that's all right," Stott said airly. "If I hadn't had my money in a membership, I'd probably have had it some place worse."

Stott is a well-built man in his early sixties, with a round, bland, scholarly face, and large eyes accented by thick-rimmed, scholarly glasses. He still has most of his hair, and he looks like a man in his forties: the life agrees with him. His voice is quite soft, so soft that he seems to speak with a slight lisp, and in conversation he emphasizes his points by slowing the words rather than raising the decibels. The glasses are not strong, and when considering a question he will take them off and chew gently on the earpiece as he gazes at some mote in the middle distance.

Toward the end of 1953, a year in which the specialist business was somewhere between poor and fair, an investor came to Stott to sell a block of Union Carbide totalling thirty thousand shares. Stott, who had lost money on his Union Carbide inventory during the year, chewed his glasses for a moment and bought the stock. Union Carbide is by no means a penny stock; the thirty thousand shares cost a large piece of change over two million dollars. "My inventory," says Stott, slowly and earnestly, "is my opinion. . . ."

For Robert Stott, obviously, the years between 1929 and 1958 made little change. He was always honest and pretty nearly always rich; and he has always lived by his opinion. In 1958 he made a lot of money; in 1953, "I was happy to make expenses and a salary"—in short, that's the way the ball bounces. He may complain gently, but he will not gripe.

Stott and those like him (there are never many like Stott in any trade) continue a financial tradition seventy-five years old. They are about the only remaining links to the wondrous days before the big bust—especially in the New York Stock Exchange.

2

Physically, no; physically, the Stock Exchange is just beginning to change. It still occupies three buildings on an oblong block bounded at the long sides by Broad Street and New Street, at the short sides by Wall Street and Exchange Place. The middle building, which is the longest, is eight stories high with an elaborate Classic-Revival front, and a filthy, black rear—like the Italian Navy, the Exchange polishes only the part of the ship that the public sees. To the south was a rather badly beat-up nineteen-story office building, which is now vanishing to make way for an insurance company's skyscraper,* and to the north a somewhat more modern twenty-two-story building topped with the tower in which Stott has his offices.

The main trading room is behind the fancy front. (An annex—an extension of the main trading floor known to its occupants as The Garage—sits on the foundations of the twenty-two-story office building.) The main room is 140 feet long and 115 feet wide and five stories high; and here the stocks of most of the nation's largest corporations are bought and sold from ten in the morning to three-thirty in the afternoon, Monday through Friday.

Large open telephone booths, ten phones to a booth, line the hardwood floor, which is always littered with papers of all kinds (except cigarette-smoking is forbidden). On the floor itself are twelve horseshoe-shaped counters about three feet high, wide enough for clerks to sit within them back to back on opposite sides of a center post, long enough for four pairs of clerks. Above the counters, supported on narrow poles, are signboards connected with each other to form a high, flat horseshoe of their own. Three pairs of these horseshoe counters back gingerly on to each other in the center of the floor; the other six are set symmetrically on the two long sides.†

Stocks are neither bought nor sold over these counters, which are simply convenient desk-space for clerks and specialists. All the trading occurs outside the horseshoe, along the rim, in front of the signboard which identifies the stock. Each

---

* 1959: This undistinguished structure is now a fact. The insurance company owns the mortgage, not the building.

† 1959: One of these horseshoes has disappeared, replaced by a flat electrical signboard. If this new electronic device works well, all the horseshoes will eventually be replaced.

of the fourteen hundred or so stocks traded on the Exchange is assigned to a single counter, or post, and can be traded only at that counter, right below its signboard.

The New York Stock Exchange, like all the other stock exchanges in the United States, is an auction market, and the auction runs two ways. Nobody sets a price. The price results from competitive bidding on both the buying and the selling side. The buyer "bids" at a certain price; the seller "offers" at a certain price, and when these two prices are the same a sale takes place. Obviously, such a market can work well only when there is a constant stream of buy and sell orders coming on to the floor, and when large numbers of people have ideas about how much the stock is worth. For this reason (and others), the Stock Exchange allows on to its trading floor only corporations with large issues of securities outstanding and large numbers of security holders.

Although most trading at the Stock Exchange involves money and securities in the hands of the public, all the actual buying and selling is done by members of the Exchange. By the constitution of the place, only members may do business on the floor, and if a member is not present and prepared to do his own business he must turn it over to another member—his clerks and other employees cannot trade for him. There are fewer than 1,375 members. The membership was fixed at that number up to 1952, when it was decided that business wasn't good enough to support all those people in the style to which they were accustomed, and the Exchange adopted a plan, not yet completed, to retire fifty seats. Memberships are called "seats" because at one time each membership actually did represent a chair in a small trading room; those days are gone the better part of a century now, but the name sticks. As a matter of fact, most of the real "seats" on the trading floor are clerks' stools, and a member can have a hell of a time finding a place to sit down and take the load off his feet.

Something less than a thousand members and a slightly larger number of clerks, reporters and runners work on the floor of the exchange every day; they just about fill the place. When business is slow they saunter, and when business is fast they speed (they may never actually run, because running is forbidden; but they can walk pretty fast). The lighting is not particularly good, since the electric fixtures are old, a heavy gold curtain (replaced in 1952 at a cost of more than eighteen thousand dollars) blocks the high east windows and the fifty-story bulk of 1 Wall Street keeps all light out of the west windows.* The members dress as they please and wear white badges of identification; their employees mostly wear cream-colored cotton jackets, plus yellow badges; and the Stock Exchange reporters wear grey jackets and an offended look. Whenever any of these denizens feels the need for a cigarette he steps off the floor and on to the marble floor of the entrance hall; when he feels the need for liquid refreshment he darts across tiny New Street to one of the convenient bars.

Life on the floor is animated and interesting, because nobody ever stands still waiting for work. If business is bad, there is always politics or baseball, photography or model railroading or sports cars or high-fidelity; and the talk is kept pure by a rigid exclusion of women from the trading floor (for the usual reason: no ladies' room). So that clerks may summon members from these conversations there are large, black annunciator boards, high on the walls at both ends of the room. The clerk pushes a button which posts a member's number on the board. The card bearing the number slaps loudly against the board, at which point everybody is supposed to look up and say, "Hey, Joe, the office wants you." Sometimes this system works, and sometimes it does not. When it doesn't, the clerk will begin slapping the card against the board in rhythm—crack-crack, crack, crack-crack, crack—until finally the errant broker awakes.

Despite vigorous opinions to the contrary, nobody on the floor of the Stock Exchange is so lacking in the sap of humanity that he doesn't have a friend somewhere on the floor; nobody so lacking in spirit that he doesn't have an enemy. The pattern of life on the floor is dictated as much by these personal relationships as by any consideration of pure business. "I'd as lief pray with Kit Smart as anyone else," said Dr. Johnson; and there are brokers far madder than the unlucky poet, who can find defenders richer than Johnson, if not quite so eminent. And "I'll never do business with that sonofabitch again" is a slogan as old as commerce. Nevertheless, when it comes to executing a customer's orders the broker on the other side of the transaction is merely a white badge and a name; membership in the Stock Exchange is very genuinely a guarantee that a man will live up to the letter of his financial obligations, even though these obligations have

* 1959: New lighting fixtures have greatly improved visibility on the floor.

been made merely by the three words "I'll take it," uttered in the midst of a confusing situation on a confusing day. It is a remarkable, and in most ways a very admirable, way to live.

3

When the Stock Exchange explains its operations to visitors, or writes about itself, it always uses the same example. A man in Portland, Oregon, has come into possession of some six thousand dollars (possibly by cracking a safe), and he wants to invest his money in American Industry to earn Dividends and support Our Way of Life. He decides that what he really wants is a hundred shares of stock in the United States Steel Corporation. At the same time there is a doctor in Portland, Maine, who has been captivated by a fancy Chris-Craft and must make it his own. He needs six thousand dollars, and he happens to own a hundred shares of U.S. Steel. So he decides to sell his hundred shares at the same time that his opposite number across the country decides to buy.

The man in Oregon calls his broker and asks to buy one hundred shares of Steel "at the market"—at whatever price the stock is presently selling. Meanwhile the doctor in Maine calls his broker and tells him to sell one hundred Steel "at the market."

The broker in Oregon and the broker in Maine call their New York offices, from whence the order is promptly relayed to the floor of the Stock Exchange. The clerks at the business ends of the telephones jot down the order and push the buttons to clap their members' numbers on the annunciator board. The members trot obediently to the clerks and receive the orders; then they trot to the post at which U.S. Steel is traded. As they arrive one of them calls to the specialist in the stock, "How's Steel?"

"Eighty-nine, one-quarter," says the specialist, which means that somebody has already offered to buy at 89, somebody else to sell at 89¼.* Both of these brokers have orders "at the market," which means that they are supposed to execute the orders damn quick, at the best available price. Eighty-nine is not available to the buyer, because somebody has already bid it, and bids are treated in the order in which they arrive; 89¼ is not available to the seller, for the same reasons. Since the only prices allowed by the rule are those which can be ex-

---

* 1959: It is worth noting and pondering that the figures in this example have been raised sixty per cent from those used less than five years ago.

pressed in eighths, there is just one possibility left. The two brokers do not think this thought; they know it automatically. So the seller calls, "I have a hundred Steel at 89⅛." And the other broker says, "Take it!"

The two brokers look at each other's badges and note down the specifics of the deal; then they go back to their telephone clerks, or send a message by runner, and announce the consummation. The clerks call the New York offices, which call their respective branch offices in the two Portlands, which call the customers, who now know for sure that they have bought/sold one hundred shares of U.S. Steel at 89⅛, plus/less commission to the broker (and, in the seller's case, taxes. There is a federal transfer tax and a New York State transfer tax, running between two and ten cents a share, depending on price. This tax is always paid by the seller.) The seller's broker must deliver one hundred shares of U.S. Steel within four days (the rules allow that much time); the buyer's broker must pay $8,912.50 within four days. How the brokers collect these shares and this money from their customers is their own business; and they have made a deal whether they collect or not. A customer's failure to deliver is not an excuse for breaking the contract.

When the brokers had spoken their piece, in good, loud voices, a Stock Exchange reporter stepped over to a nest of pneumatic tube connections in a rack between the horseshoes, and dropped into a cylinder a piece of paper noting the trade, the number of shares involved and the price. He slugged the cylinder into one of the tubes, and it shot under the floor and then up through the walls to the ticker room. Twenty to twenty-five girls (the exact number depends on the volume of business) are sitting in the room, waiting for such notes. The cylinder is promptly emptied, and one of the girls punches a tape to read "X 89⅛." "X" is the ticker symbol for U.S. Steel, and since the sale was in the minimum round lot amount of one hundred shares there is no need to specify the amount sold. Somewhere between ten and thirty thousand transactions are made every day on the floor of the Exchange, and nearly all of them get punched on to tape. All the tapes from all the girls are then fed into a central machine which prints "X 89⅛" on some 3,000 ticker tapes all over the country, and flashes the information on to six large screens on the Stock Exchange floor itself (four in the main room, two in The Garage).

If either the burglar or the doctor is sitting in his broker's

customers' room (the S.E.C. calls these rooms "funeral parlors"), he will see the record of his transaction printed on the
tape at about the same time that he receives the confirmation
of his order. And the total time elapsed, from order to print,
is rarely more than three or four minutes.

4

So runs the theory—and often the practice, too. Many of
the transactions on the Stock Exchange (perhaps as many as
15 per cent) work in just this manner. The others are more
complicated, more ingenious and more interesting. Although
the first group is the purpose of the Exchange, the second
group makes the whole business possible: it would be simple
(for the genii of I.B.M.) to design a machine that would take
care of the Oregon burglar and the Maine doctor, but the rest
of the work of the Exchange requires human judgment.

When the two brokers arrived at the post they found U.S.
Steel quoted at 89 bid, 89¼ offered. These bids and offers
were not set upon the trading floor by God; they came from
some human source, and they made possible the quick execution of a sale "at the market." They could have come from
lots of places.

For example, there were people who wanted to buy U.S.
Steel, but not at this price. They sent in "limit orders" rather
than orders at the market. One wanted to buy at 89, and
others were willing to buy only if the price went lower still.
Trailing behind the top bid of 89 were dozens, possibly
hundreds of other bids—at 87¾, 86½, 85⅞. The top bid
alone counts in the auction; the other will play a part only if
the price declines to the point where they are highest. The
same logic holds on the other side: only the bottom offer,
89¼, plays a part in the auction. Above it are many other
offers, from people willing to sell their shares of U.S. Steel
only when the price goes to 90, or 91⅛, or 91⅝. If the price
rises, these offers to sell at higher prices will become effective;
until then they are as dead as Queen Anne.

It is not to be supposed, however, that a broker given an
order to buy U.S. Steel at 86½ will stand around the post
(vainly calling "86½!" as a herring-gull cries at a ship) until
the price comes down. He may drop over to the post to find
out what the price is; but then he goes somewhere else, where
he can do business. The customer, however, has placed an
order, and it is not in a broker's competence to laugh in a cus-

tomer's face or kill a customer's order. The order cannot be executed and it cannot be killed, so somebody has to hang on to it and be ready to execute it if it ever becomes effective.

That somebody is the specialist in the stock. There are 350 specialists on the floor, and each specialist (or one of his partners) is constantly on duty near the signboard under which his stock is traded. He is at the least a witness to all transactions, and he or his clerk takes care of announcing the bid and offer. For each stock in which he specializes he keeps a "book," which is absolutely private and may not be shown to anybody on the floor. In the book he lists all bids and offers which are presently "out of line" with the market, and as the price moves to bring them in line he turns the pages of his book and presents the order to the market. All the orders in the book are placed by other brokers, and the specialist never does business directly with the public. When he executes an order out of his book he acts as the broker's broker, and he gets paid with a cut out of the broker's commission. His work costs the customer nothing.

Specialists will hold and execute another kind of order—the stop order. In this case the customer wants to *sell* U.S. Steel at 86½, and orders his broker to sell when and if the price ever goes down that low. At first flush the stop order looks silly, because the customer could sell right now at 89⅛, and it seems foolish of him to take a $262.50 licking just for the fun of entering a stop order. In fact, however, the stop order is serious business. The customer presently owns one hundred shares of U.S. Steel, and he bought them because he thought the price was going up and he could make some money selling them at the higher price. But he recognizes (probably from sad experience) that his judgment is not infallible, that U.S. Steel may go down instead of up. If his guess was wrong, he wants to limit his losses. So he sets a price which he believes is the minimum to which the stock could sink if his judgment is correct and the trend is really up. If the price goes below that point he is willing to admit stupidity and take his licking like a man. In this case the customer believes that the stock shouldn't go below 86⅝; if it does, he wants out. His order to sell becomes effective the first time the stock sells at 86½. If the market is dropping rapidly, there may be no sale at 86½—a sale may be made at 86⅝, and then the next highest bid is 86⅜. The specialist will not leave the stop order hanging at 86½, however; he will execute it at 86⅜. In short, the stop order then becomes an order "at the market," at the best available price.*

5

To get back to the burglar, and change the situation slightly. In this case he was picking up the telephone to call his broker when the police broke down the door. He had just time to say, "Buy one hundred—" when strong hands dragged him away from the telephone. The customer's man at the other end has heard the words "Buy one hundred—" but nothing more. Since he doesn't know what to buy, and all he hears over the telephone is strange sounds, he hangs up. The doctor's order to sell "at the market" arrives on the floor with no matching order to buy.

As before, the doctor's broker asks for the quote, and gets it. As before, he calls "I have one hundred Steel at one-eighth." But now there is no answering call, nobody willing to buy at 89⅛. The broker waits to hear a call, then sadly says, "Sold one hundred at eighty-nine."

Who bought the doctor's stock?

Another broker with a buy order at 89 may have bought it for his customer. (Since the buy order was close to the market, the broker decided to stand around for a while and see what happens rather than turn the order over to the specialist and lose part of his commission.) The specialist may have bought it, executing an order out of his book. Or—and this is vital—the specialist may have bought it for himself, to have and to hold until he sells it.

A member of the Stock Exchange becomes a specialist in a stock by applying for it, and once his application is approved he is obliged to maintain a "fair and orderly" market for that security. A "fair and orderly market" in U.S. Steel means a market that does not bang up and down like a yo-yo between 86 and 95 every day, opening and closing at 89. If the highest bid in the book is 87, therefore, and the lowest offer 91, the

* 1959: Personal finance companies recently found an ingenious subsidiary use for the stop-loss order. Because they are not under Federal Reserve System regulation, they need not respect margin requirements. They offered to lend clients up to 85% of the price of a stock, provided the clients at the time of purchase entered a stop-loss order at 5% below the going market. The stop-loss order protected the finance company's loan, and the company could then collect its 12% interest charge with an untroubled mind. To prevent such abuses of the stop-loss privilege, the New York Stock Exchange in the spring of this year forbade the entering or execution of certain stop-loss orders.

quote "89¼" may represent the specialist at both ends of the spread. He is "making the market" for U.S. Steel.

When the doctor's sell order came in, he bought the hundred shares at 89. A few minutes after that, the burglar escaped from the police and hurried to the corner drugstore, where he called his broker and ordered one hundred Steel at the market. The burglar's order came to the post after the doctor's order had been executed, and the specialist was still quoting the stock at "89¼." So the specialist sold at 89¼ the hundred shares he had just bought from the broker, making $25, less $9 in transfer taxes of nine cents a share. Twenty-five such transactions would bring a day's profit of $400, which would be very nice indeed. On the floor this action is known as "turning around"; down in Washington, at the offices of the S.E.C., it is known as "clipping quarters."

As a matter of fact, however, the specialist has performed a function which is worth money. If an I.B.M. machine were keeping the book, the doctor's stock would have been sold at 87, and the burglar would have bought at 91; both are far better off for the specialist's work. An auction is by its nature discontinuous in time; the specialist supplies continuity. When the specialist gets greedy, however, the cost of continuity can climb fairly steeply. Robert Stott sometimes turns over Union Carbide for an eighth of a point, making of profit of $2.50 (the transfer tax runs $10); but, as he says, "not many people can afford to do it." A quarter of a point seems reasonable, and three-eighths, or even five-eighths, may be justified in an inactive stock. When the specialist starts quoting "89–90⅛," however, making $112.50 just for standing around the post, the price is getting out of line. Such specialists soon develop a bad odor on the floor; brokers do not recommend their stocks to customers, and the volume of their business falls away. If the situation gets to the point where the odor can be smelled upstairs, in the Exchange's executive offices, the stock may be taken away from this specialist and given to another. It is almost possible to count on the fingers of a foot the number of times such action is taken; but it happens.

Sometimes maintaining the market takes a vigorous application of money and intelligence. The doctor's order to sell may be followed not by an order to buy but by another order to sell. The specialist is still quoting the stock at 89¼; so he buys another hundred at 89. Still another order to sell comes in, and he buys it again at 89. At this point he may decide that there is selling pressure on U.S. Steel, and the stock may be overpriced at 89. He drops his quote to 88⅞–89⅛; and another order to sell comes in. This one is filled at 88⅞, and the specialist drops his quote again. The price, in short, goes down.

It has to go down, because all the orders are to sell. If the specialist kept his quote at 89¼, he would not be maintaining the market, he would be rigging it. The auction must be responsive to public feelings about the value of the security, and so far all the public feeling is negative at a price of 89. A drop in the price may bring in people who want to buy U.S. Steel at some price under 89, and discourage the sellers. The bid on the quote now goes to 88¾; and the offer may go to 89. Here, however, the specialist may widen his spread to three-eighths, quoting 88¾–89⅛, to protect himself on the stock he has bought at 89. If the selling pressure continues, however, he will keep lowering both ends of his quote, because he doesn't want to keep buying U.S. Steel indefinitely (he doesn't have all that money), and he badly needs some buyers to take the weight off his scalp. Under these circumstances (or their reverse, with the specialist selling into a rising market), the specialist can lose money on his day's operation. This is not just theory, either; it's a rare (and bad) specialist who doesn't find himself out of pocket for a day's work every once in a while.

When and how much to lower the quote against selling pressure is within the specialist's discretion, subject to a Stock Exchange rule that no price below 20 may move more than one point between sales, and no price above 20 more than two points, without the consent of a Governor of the Exchange. The specialist will try to figure out the cause of this rush of sell orders, and the significance behind the cause. It might be that Russian spies have just blown up the company's two biggest factories, but unless his office is completely staffed with nincompoops, and everybody else on the Exchange floor hates his guts, the specialist will know such a fact just as quickly as the public knows it. He reviews the present case of the company's operations and its plausible future prospect, examines the way the market is moving in other steel stocks and in the other leading corporations, and feels with psychic feelers that grow inside from his forehead to determine how much these sell orders represent a public whim (to be matched always immediately by a buying whim) and how much they represent a trend. This decision is an immensely difficult one to make, and the specialist's own money is involved. If he lowers his quote to meet a public whim, and the buying whim sweeps over the stock, he will be selling at a lower price than he was buying, losing money hand over fist. If he decides to maintain his quote and the public genuinely feels that U.S. Steel is overpriced at 89, he may be forced to buy so much U.S. Steel that he will eat it for months. The decision requires experience and much delicate judgment in the making, and one factor that must influence the specialist is how much he stands to lose on his own inventory in the stock. To keep this factor at a minimum, and see to it that the specialist never panics, the Stock Exchange specifies that each specialist must have at least a certain amount of capital behind him.

Some specialists try to make these decisions strictly on their "feel" of the market, on the same sort of second sight that enables a professional bridge player to guess correctly the location of the Queen of Spades. "This job," one specialist says of his work, "is a ticket on a trolley car. When I feel the trolley car starting up I get aboard: when I feel it slowing down I get off." Such specialists as Stott and Ira Haupt and John Coleman see this attitude as wholly improper. "I've got a responsibility to the market and to the company," Stott says. "I try to know as much as I can about the company, I try to know the people who run it. I think it's wrong just to play numbers." Haupt says, "I call the treasurer of the company every month to find out how last month's business was—any stockholder can do it, and ought to do it. I try to work closely with the company, and I think we help them. The better a market is for a security, the more friends a company has." The specialist's judgment of the company's real worth, however, cannot be his only criterion; it's the public judgment that counts. Haupt and Stott must "feel" the market, too; the difference is that they are maintaining a fair and orderly market, while the trolley-car rider is simply gambling.

He gambles, moreover, with a great asset—the tool of the Book. One of the ways that a specialist feels the market is to see how the orders stand in his book—what sort of support a stock has in the form of limit orders at lower prices, what the dangers are in the line of stop-loss orders. A specialist in a stock selling at 89, for example, may have a buy order for fifteen hundred shares at 86 tucked away in the book; he knows, therefore, that there is an effective floor under the price at 86. On the other hand, he may have a stop-loss order to sell fifteen hundred shares if the price goes down to 86, and this is one of the reasons the book must be secret. Knowing about this stop-loss order, a trader could force the price down from 89 by repeated selling, and then pick up at 86 all the shares he has sold at the higher prices. This little trick (which might yield the enterprising trader two or three thousand dollars for five minutes' work—dirty work) is known as "gunning the book." A man may do it once and get away with it. He'd better not try it twice.

Every few weeks the Exchange calls on a specialist to supply the full details of every trade in which he has been involved for the preceding week. This data are computed and by an involved statistical formula turned into a rating for the specialist's work. His percentage of trades against the market (buying when the market is falling, or selling when it is rising) is worked out, and so is the proportion of his trades for his own account against the total volume in the stock. (A good specialist will be on one end or the other in 15 to 20 per cent of all sales made in his stock.) A specialist of Stott's quality and responsibility trades against the market between 80 and 90 per cent of the time. This figure is a little artificial, because each turn around, or quarter clipping, will count as a trade against the market. But it is impressive, anyway. His fellow members, many of whom trade for themselves without the specialist's responsibility, will be riding with the public on the trolley car, almost every time they trade.

Here is another person who might have bought the doctor's U.S. Steel at 89—a member of the Exchange trading for his own account. On the floor every day are about twenty men who get in and out, round and about, so fast and so often that it is cheaper for them to own seats than to pay commissions. They are mostly wealthy, and they have good connections with banks if they need extra money to finance a deal. Basically, they try to turn their money over very quickly and profit on the short-term fluctuations of the market; and statistical studies have shown that they usually work by following and reinforcing the existing market trend, making short-term fluctuations more extreme. They may scent, for example, that the selling pressure on U.S. Steel is merely a whim, and that buy orders will come rolling in later in the day. Their obvious course is to sell U.S. Steel when the public starts, at 89; and then to buy it back at 87½, just before the buy orders restore the price. If this activity involved only the twenty floor traders it would be interesting but not particularly serious; the problem is that many members who do a brokerage business are also, on the side, trading for their own accounts. Moreover, there is some reason to believe that when the public doesn't co-operate in making the market fluctuate, the traders will set off the fluctuations on their own.

"Take Graham Paige, back in '45," says an S.E.C. officer. "It was a real dog, selling around two points, with three or four hundred shares traded every week. Not every day— every week. Then, one fine morning, the stock opens with a five-thousand share block, and there's a frenzy of activity, sales back and forth.

"All over the country people are sitting in funeral parlors, watching the ticker on Trans Lux screens, and suddenly they see GP, GP, GP, appearing over and over again. They go over to their customer's man, and they ask him, 'What about it? Why all the activity?'

"Now, no broker can ever afford not to know the answer to a customer's question. If he doesn't know the answer, it's sure the broker across the street does. The customer's man has been noticing the tape himself, and wondering about it, and guessing. So he makes up an answer. 'I've heard that there's a rumor in New York about a merger with Ford,' he says in his most secretive voice. The public comes roaring into the market to buy Graham Paige, because it's merging with Ford. The price soars, the floor traders sell out at the top for big profits, and the price and activity in the stock slowly settle down to what they were.

"A lot of money has been made on the floor, and a lot of money has been lost by the poor dupes in the funeral parlors. And there never was any reason for it at all."

In 1945 the Division of Trading and Exchange proposed that the S.E.C. issue an administrative ruling to abolish floor trading (trading by members for their own account). The Commission held hearings on the matter, and representatives of the exchanges came in and offered to set their own houses in order with new rules, restricting the activity of floor traders. The Commission agreed not to issue the ruling its Division had requested, and the exchanges promulgated stern rules of their own. Then, almost every year, the exchanges withdrew one or another of the rules they had agreed were necessary to control floor trading. Early in 1953, with a new administration in Washington, the New York Stock Exchange withdrew all but the last of the restrictive rules. ("We don't like the word 'compulsion' around here," says former Stock Exchange Chairman Richard Crooks.) The floor traders are now pretty much on their own, though there is a rule that public orders must always take precedence over orders for a member's own account. The S.E.C. is studying the trend of floor trading under the new old rules, but it doesn't have the money for a complete study—and the Commission now has an anti-compulsion majority.*

One other person might have bought the doctor's stock— an odd-lot dealer. All of the securities for which the Stock Exchange is the major market (in about half of its listed securities it is only a secondary market, and the important trading is carried on elsewhere) are traded in hundred share lots; and if a customer orders fewer than one hundred shares his order does not participate in the auction. If it is a market order (almost all of them are) it will be filled at the price of the next round-lot sale. The broker on the floor never even sees the order, which is noted by his telephone clerk and dropped into a pneumatic tube, to reappear at the post where the stock is traded. A Stock Exchange clerk opens the tube and time-stamps the slip in an I.B.M. clock, then hangs the order on a hook at the rear of the post. An odd-lot dealer takes the order from the hook, and at the moment of the next sale fills it for the customer (selling out of his own inventory or buying for his own account). The customer's broker pays for executions of round-lot orders by a specialist, but the customer himself pays for the services of the odd-lot dealer—one-eighth of a point if the price is under 40, one-quarter of a point if it is 40 or more. Under current commission rates, however, all but the smallest customer receive a reduction in the broker's commission for an odd-lot sale.

The odd-lot dealer himself is usually not an entrepreneur; he is employed by an odd-lot house, almost always Carlisle & Jacquelin or DeCoppet & Doremus. (There is another firm of odd-lot dealers, V. C. Brown & Co., but they operate at only one post.) For executing the order, the individual member gets from the firm which employs him about 2½ cents a share as a piece-work salary. Odd-lot trading will run about one-sixth to one-quarter of the round-lot volume on the Exchange, which means odd-lot firms must make fairly considerable round-lot purchases and sales to keep their own accounts in order. Hence, the chance that an odd-lot dealer may have bought the doctor's stock.

---

* 1959: Nothing came of the study, but it has not been abandoned. The role of the floor trader in certain recent remarkable stock maneuvers is part of the S.E.C.'s current study of manipulation in 1958-59.

6

As anybody knows who has ever nodded sleepily in a furniture warehouse or scratched his ear at a yearling sale, auction markets are complicated operations. There are more edifying subjects of discussion, to be sure, but some of the ingenuities developed to handle the problem of the auction are worth a quick look in themselves.

For example, the beginning: every day presents a new market. Orders have come in overnight to buy or to sell, and cannot be presented to the auction until the market opens at ten o'clock. The market opens noisily, as the overnight orders are paired off against each other to get the auction started. Since the orders will rarely match exactly, the opening price will be set to some extent by the specialist, who must absorb or supply the excess sell or buy orders. He sets the price by his feel of the market, and this feel had better be accurate. "We expect," says an Exchange officer somewhat grimly, "that the specialist's opening price will stand up well as the auction develops"—that is, the Exchange does not like to see the specialist open the stock at 92 and the public then push it down quickly to 89; the specialist should have sufficient judgment to guess the meaning of the overnight orders.

When news affecting the company's operations has appeared overnight, and orders reflecting the news have flooded the market, the specialist's feel is chopped away with an axe, and a new situation appears. The price is not supposed to represent an expert's evaluation of the news—it must show the public's reaction. Overnight orders, however, are not a complete reaction: lots of people may be waiting to see how the market opens before they move. An oil company, for example, may have announced the discovery of a new oil field, and the announcement may have brought in ten thousand shares' worth of buy orders overnight. The specialist, confronted with this monster of a buy order and no sell orders to match, asks (and receives) permission to hold up the opening on that stock. Bid and offer prices are printed on the ticker tape in the hope that the new, higher prices will tempt some stockholders to sell and discourage some potential buyers. The specialist and a member of the Board of Governors of the Exchange examine the response to this print on the tape, and decide on a fair opening price. Sometimes the print will bring little response because investors like to see a real sale, an honest-to-God fact, not this bid-and-offer business. "Often," says Stott, looking into space, "we wait for sell orders against a buying rush, and they don't come in. So we open the stock, and then, once they've seen the record of a sale, sellers come pouring in to catch the higher prices. Usually they could have done better by hitting the bid when it first appeared on the tape. But they never learn; it's public psychology."

In any auction, it's the first man to make the winning bid who wins the prize; but the Stock Exchange is a continuing auction and after a few sales it would get hard to keep track of when Joe showed up with his 89 bid. The rule therefore reads that each sale clears the floor; if Joe was the first man in with the 89 bid, and the stock sells at 89, Joe buys it. But possibly Harry got there first, and Joe second, and Gus third. Harry buys his stock because he has priority, and that sale clears the floor. Joe and Gus now stand on a level, and Joe might as well have stopped off for a smoke and got there after Gus. If another seller appears at 89, Joe and Gus will decide who buys by tossing a coin. A second rule also affects priority: a rule of size. Harry has a buy order for one hundred shares. Joe also has an order for one hundred shares, and Gus has an order for two hundred shares. Aloysius now appears with a sell order for three hundred shares. Harry buys his one hundred because he was first; but now Joe doesn't even get a chance to match. The only brokers who can match are those with orders big enough to absorb the full order on the other side. The order on the other side, after the sale of one hundred to Harry, is two hundred shares. Gus can absorb it and Joe can't. Joe should have stood in bed.

While Joe was waiting for misfortune at the U.S. Steel post another customer of his ordered two hundred shares of Diamond Match. The order was relayed to Joe's clerk, who started slapping Joe's number against the board. Joe was busy, however, waiting to buy his one hundred shares of U.S. Steel at 89. The clerk had instructions to cover this situation; he clapped on to the board a new number, which called a friend of Joe's, an independent floor broker, to the phone. There are about 150 of these independent members of the Exchange; they make their living trading and executing orders for other members, who are too busy or too lazy to do the job themselves. These independents receive somewhere between $1.25 and $5.00 a hundred shares (depending on the price of the stock) as a "give-up" commission. They call themselves $2 brokers, partly because until 1919 the rate actually was $2 per hundred shares, and partly for a less dignified reason.

Joe's friend took the order from the clerk, went to the

Diamond Match post and executed it. When Joe, having sold his U.S. Steel at last, returns to his telephone to find out why the clerk had been paging him, he learns that he has to pay friend floor broker $6.50 of his $65 commission on the Diamond Match order. At this point Joe screams a piercing scream and goes across the street for a slug of Scotch to fortify him for the coming hour.

Actually, life on the floor is all this informal, or more. Large, beefy gentleman holding a rolled-up newspaper strides vigorously to post and calls, "How's Monkey?" (Montgomery Ward).

"Forty-six," says the specialist in a bored voice, "one-quarter."

"I have six hundred Monkey at one-eighth," says the big broker.

"I'll take two," says a timid little broker to one side.

A floor trader, observing the scene, intervenes. "Ah," he calls to the large broker, "you're such a pain in the ass."

The large broker strides forward with greater purpose, lifts the rolled-up newspaper above his head and brings it down with moderate force on the head of the floor trader. "Just for that," he says, "you'll take one."

"Okay," says the floor trader, rubbing his head.

The specialist waits a minute for another bid, then says, "And I'll take the other three at forty-six."

A minute later a man in Minneapolis learns that his six hundred shares of Montgomery Ward have been sold for $27,637.50, less $252.19 commission and $60 in transfer taxes. Now he can go out and blow himself to a good dinner.

7

One place where the auction market always gets in trouble, with propagandists for and against, is in the matter of the short sale. Actually it is simple enough; sometimes the suspicion arises that the question has been made confusing just for the sake of confusion.

Take, for example, a man who owns five hundred shares of U.S. Steel; to put the matter in Street terms, he is "long" five hundred Steel. He is happy owning five hundred shares of U.S. Steel; he feels it's a sound company. But he also feels that the steel business is going to be lousy for the next six months, and that the stock will drop from its present price of 89 down to 83 or 84 before business turns up again. He sells his five hundred shares of U.S. Steel at 89, then sits down and waits. When the price goes down to 83, he buys back his five hundred shares. Six months after he sold out he once again owns five hundred shares—plus $3,000 cash that he hadn't owned before.

This astute citizen sold "long"—he had owned the five hundred shares he sold. By the rules of the auction market, he could also have sold "short"—without owning the stock he sold. Instead of delivering his own stock he would borrow somebody else's stock and deliver that. Then, when the price went down, he would buy at the lower price, repay the stock he had borrowed, and pocket his profit.

The mechanical process of borrowing is usually simple, and rests on two facts. The first is that the short seller does not get the money proceeds of the sale until after he buys at the end of the transaction; the money goes to the man who loaned him the stock. The second is that a large part of exchange business is carried on with money borrowed from banks, and banks in valuing a borrower's collateral can give him credit, at this writing, for only ten per cent of the market value of his securities. A man with one hundred shares of U.S. Steel can borrow no more than $890 against them from a bank; by lending the stock to a short seller he borrows $8,900. So there are always people willing to lend stock. Sometimes, when the demand to borrow stock is slight, they pay interest on the money they receive for it; sometimes, when the demand is high, they get the money interest-free and even charge a premium, so much a day, for lending the stock.

There are few differences between long selling and short selling, but the few are important. The long seller is out of the market; if the price goes up, all he does is curse himself for a ninny. The short seller, however, is very much in the market; and if the price goes up he can be in horrible trouble. There is practically no limit to the money he can lose, and short selling is one of the world's easiest ways to go broke.*

About 90 per cent of the damage done on Wall Street has come from short selling, the most famous example being the Northern Pacific corner of 1901. Here the Morgan interests and the Harriman-Kuhn, Loeb interests were competing for control of the Northern Pacific Railway. Between them they owned almost all of it; and the remaining shares in private

---

* 1959: Fred Schwed, in his book *Where Are The Customers' Yachts?* points out that it is far easier to go broke with margin buying than with short-selling, but that psychological factors make a customer fear a rise in price of a stock he owes more than a fall in price of a stock he owns.

hands could give either group control. The two groups bid up the price from 112 to 149 in one day; and people who knew that Northern Pacific wasn't worth $149 a share (but didn't know that two giants were duelling at each other in the stock) began to sell short. Soon the public had sold more stock than existed, and the price shot up to $1,000 a share. The short sellers panicked (with reason), and began to dump on to a frightened market everything they owned, raising money to meet Morgan's terms on the day when they would have to admit that they didn't own the stock they had sold him. There followed an economic crisis which took jobs away from people who had never even heard of Morgan or Harriman; and Wall Street was the villain.

The short sale was also commonly used as a manipulative device to drive prices down. Essentially, the public is gypped with equal certainty when prices are driven up by manipulation; but driving them down has always carried a greater onus. There are reasons for this attitude: one is that driving prices down is easier, since people are more likely to sell on rising prices (taking their profits) than to buy on falling prices (endangering new money in an obviously unstable stock).* Another is the native and usually justified optimism, the desire to be bullish rather than bearish, backed by the knowledge that the bull is a more useful animal. Bulls have stolen at least as much money as bears, but they have created an atmosphere of prosperity and progress in which money gets spent and jobs get created and the economy rolls smoothly to progress. The bears' contribution is technical only, and benefits the market alone. The public has a right to its greater rage against them.

To meet this rage, and the Exchanges' inability to police this situation themselves, the S.E.C. added to its general rules against manipulation a special rule about short selling. The rule provides that a short sale can be made only at a price higher than the last different price paid for a stock—can be made, in market language, only on an "up-tick." If U.S. Steel sells at 88⅞, and then at 89, it can be sold short at 89; if it sells at 89⅛ before it sells at 89 no short sale will be allowed. All orders to sell must be marked "long" or "short" so that the broker may apply the rule. Its effect is to keep short sellers from driving the price down, since they cannot sell short into a declining market.

* 1959: The experience of the last four years is contrary to this apparently logical argument.

The short sale today cannot possibly do damage to the market, but it still has a bad reputation—and for a strange reason, too. The reason is that the Stock Exchange explains it badly.

Essentially, of course [says a recent pamphlet] short selling is a normal business transaction. . . . Let's say, for example, that you select a living-room set from your favorite department store. The salesman says: "We haven't that set in stock, but we'll deliver it in three weeks." You say, "Fine, deliver it as soon as you can." The store has made a short sale. . . . A magazine publisher sells you a three-year subscription to a monthly magazine for ten dollars. That, too, is a short sale.

Now, neither of these transactions is a short sale. They contemplate the *production* of goods; if the goods aren't delivered the money will be refunded. (Try that on a short sale some day.) A short sale is a gambling operation, as purely a question of gambling as a bet on the relative merits of five cards containing three Queens.

The Stock Exchange gets into trouble here all the time, because it insists on drawing a semantic line between "speculating" and "gambling." "Gambling," writes broker Edgar Scott, "is risking your money on blind fortune, pure chance, the turn of a wheel. Speculation is taking with your money a calculated risk because you have studied it and have decided that it is a promising risk whereby you may profit." By this definition a man who plays roulette on a system, or drops a card under the table in gin rummy, or bets horses from a form, is a speculator; and anybody who calls him a gambler is un-American. (Recently the Stock Exchange tried another definition: "The gambler . . . has absolutely no control over the outcome of his wager. The speculator in securities, though . . ." It is hard to see why the Stock Exchange, of all people, should wish to support the popular notion that speculators rig the market.) There is a distinction between speculation and gambling, but it doesn't lie here. Buying the stocks of new companies or small but growing companies, in the hope that these enterprises will become large and famous and highly profitable, is speculation; so is putting money into a company drilling for oil. Selling short, reading tape to hit the daily swing of the market or charts to hit the monthly swing— these activities are gambling, and the Stock Exchange merely gains a reputation for shady practice by denying the fact.

Gambling has a bad name because it is so often crooked,

and even when honest usually supports crooks. But there is nothing morally wrong about gambling itself, so long as the people gambling can afford to lose. And the Stock Exchange does not ordinarily try to draw into the securities market those whose basic savings are not protected in banks or government bonds. So the only question is: Is the Stock Exchange honest?

It is incredibly, self-denyingly, almost absolutely honest. It is honest beyond the imaginings of ordinary businessmen; honest in word, thought and deed. Stock Exchange publicity may get too clever once in a while because it doesn't respect public intelligence. But business is done on the floor, and rules are made by the Board of Governors, in an atmosphere so pure that breathing it is dangerous.

Besides, the Stock Exchange could not operate without such tools as short selling. The short sale, for example, is essential to the operations of the specialist and the odd-lot dealer: both are charged with an obligation of selling to the public, and neither can reasonably be asked to hold an inventory large enough to meet all demands, if in his opinion the market is actually heading down. An auction market would in fact be impossible without short selling, because the purpose of the market is to reflect public judgment of the value of securities. If people who believe the price is too low may buy, then people who believe the price is too high must be allowed to sell, whether or not they own a share of the stock.

Floor trading, which is still under serious attack from within the S.E.C., is also gambling; the floor trader buys and sells to make a profit so short term that in the classic case he is completely out of the market at the close of the day. Nevertheless, the floor trader's gambling is essential to the auction, because his activities make it possible for large blocks of stock to be bought or sold on the floor. The correct defense for floor trading is not that it benefits the public, which is nonsense. Floor trading is defensible because without it the volume of business on the Stock Exchange might drop to a point where the inhabitants would cheat in self-defense.

The Stock Exchange was not always honest, and if the government ever got out of the regulating business there would probably be considerable backsliding. But since 1940 or so the Exchange has been sincerely trying a great experiment in honesty. Before 1940 there never was a securities exchange without manipulation; today there are two in New York.

[1959: These four paragraphs were on the enthusiastic side

five years ago, but easily defensible. Today some of the superlatives ought to be withdrawn. Too many stupid people have been making too much money in the market of late, and when these fish are numerous the sharks multiply. Jiggery-pokery has become more profitable, and the growing decay of the governmental regulatory agencies, begun under Truman and accelerated under Eisenhower, means that shady practice is less likely to be exposed in judicial sunlight. Temptation, in short, has become more difficult to resist, and at least half a dozen once reputable Wall Street firms have succumbed.

Nevertheless, the overall standard of ethics remains remarkably high. Considering the increase in the size of the escutcheon, the greater number of blots on it should not be shocking. In 1954, perhaps half a dozen stocks were being manipulated; in 1959, there are perhaps forty—about two percent of all those listed on the exchanges. They may account for as much as five per cent of the trading, but certainly no more. Of new securities sold, a larger proportion are being sold disreputably (indeed, Reynolds & Co., the sixth largest brokerage house in America, was recently penalized by the S.E.C. for illegal selling procedures), but most of the knavery is being done on a small scale by small houses, and those not engaged in it are appalled by it. These paragraphs are written, in fact, partly at the request of partners and officers of Wall Street houses, who feel that the public has in recent years become too trusting of the financial market.

So let the superlatives stand. A rich diet of prosperity has made honesty flabby elsewhere in the economy, and the ethics of Wall Street have kept most of their muscle. Indeed, it could be argued that finance has taken admirably little advantage of the plenary indulgence offered by a "businessman's government" and a somnolent community.]

Chapter 5

The New York Stock Exchange (Part II)

THE NEW YORK STOCK EXCHANGE spends between eight and ten million dollars a year just to keep the doors open, and employs eleven hundred people. Its employees begin their work before the beginning of every transaction, and are still working long after the brokers involved have drowned all memory of the sale. Though they have no direct connection with the public, most of their work is for public benefit rather than for the member firms who own the Stock Exchange and therefore pay the salaries.

It is Stock Exchange employees who decide whether or not a stock or bond shall be listed for trading on the Exchange. (The Board of Governors officially makes the decision, but it does what the employees tell it to do.) Only 1,300 corporations are listed, and only the securities of these 1,300 (often more than one to a company) may be traded on the floor. It is not an easy grade to make. Before a company can have its securities listed it must be a "going concern" with "substantial assets and demonstrated earning power." There must be sufficient national interest in the corporation and its securities to guarantee a certain minimum flow of bids and offers, and enough stock outstanding to ensure that nobody can corner the market. The stock itself must be fully engraved from three different steel plates, to prevent forgery, and the corporation must agree to keep a transfer agent in New York to cancel sold stock and issue new certificates.

"There are certain rules of thumb on all this," says Phillip West, Director of the Department of Stock Listing and a Vice-President of the Exchange. West is a slight man with sandy hair and a short, pointed nose; he has worked for the Exchange all his working life, starting thirty years ago as a runner. He commuted from New Jersey then, and he commutes from New Jersey now. He sits in a huge, home-like office with the high ceiling characteristic of all rooms in the center building which houses the trading floor itself. Outside his office is an immense bull pen with eight desks in it and a carpet on the floor; at the other end of the bull pen are glassed-in private offices for other officers of the Department.

Altogether some forty people, including ten examiners, work at deciding which corporations are large enough and famous enough to justify listing on the New York Stock Exchange.

"Four out of five of the companies that come in here," West says, "don't qualify. We insist that their stock have a market value of seven million dollars, with net assets of at least that size—excluding good will—behind the stock. There have to be at least fifteen hundred stockholders, and we don't count people who hold odd lots. Then there must be 300,000 shares of the stock outstanding, over and above any large, concentrated holdings. And earnings before taxes have to run at least a million dollars.*

"Now, we can't list any security unless the company applies for it, and agrees to abide by the S.E.C. rules and our own rules about reporting information to stockholders. As a general matter, we insist that they make quarterly earnings reports, unless the business is so seasonal that quarterly reports would give a false picture. When they apply, they have to supply copies of their charters, and financial statements complete with the notarized signatures of the accountants. We'll check with their competitors and look around to see how much interest there is; if we don't like the accounting procedure, we may raise some questions about that, too. We want to know about their financial policies, and what they expect to do in the line of raising money in the near future. We feel that we're listing a company as well as an issue of securities. But we're also listing the issue, and we may refuse an issue by a company that already has another issue listed."

Almost all of West's work is done on an informal basis, because the Exchange doesn't like to put companies in a position of having been rejected for listing (sometimes the news leaks out, however, as it did in 1953 in the case of an application for the American shares of a Dutch company). West will gather the company's statements and look into them, then render an informal opinion as to whether a formal application would be worth making. If a company is accepted it pays a listing fee, and for fifteen years an annual fee per 100,000 shares. In return for this payment it receives (it hopes) the strongest and most public possible market for its securities, plus the invaluable publicity of constant appearance on the ticker tape and in the newspapers which report transactions. The fee, however, is not the only payment for listing, because

* 1959: Now market value of eight million, with four hundred thousand shares outstanding.

S.E.C. rules about proxy solicitation, reports to stockholders and "insider trading" (buying and selling of a company's securities by the company's own officers and employees) are far stricter for listed corporations. "Last time we looked, though," West says cheerfully, "there were fewer than 150 corporations we would list that aren't listed now."

These fewer than 150 are not considered eternally beyond the pale; as a matter of fact, West will go some distance out of his way—to Seattle, say—to talk to the officers of these companies about the advantages of listing. About a hundred companies apply for listing every year, and somewhere between twenty and thirty of them get on the floor. There are more new issues than that, of course, because already-listed companies are always coming out with some new and acceptable piece of paper in their financial structure.

In addition to the listing department, there is a Department of Member Firms, which descends on brokers without warning to make sure the books are in shape, examines and approves all customer's men, passes on applications for new membership and looks into complaints against members, from the public or from other members; there is also a Department of Floor Operation, which does what its name says and employs all the clerks, reporters and runners who work for the Exchange itself on the floor. The rest of the employees work for one of the Exchange's three wholly owned subsidiary corporations—the Building Corporation, which takes care of the real estate; the Stock Clearing Corporation, which handles the actual receipt and delivery of money and securities that change hands between brokers as the result of sales on the Exchange; and the Quotations Corporation, which serves the market itself.

For example, a customer may want to know exactly what price he is going to pay for his U.S. Steel. The ticker tape will usually tell him only the price of the last sale, and he wants to know what the spread is right now. His customer's man in New York thereupon picks up a telephone which is on a direct wire, and dials a number.

If he dials a two-digit number, he gets one of seventy-plus girls who sit in a very long, narrow room upstairs in the old office building. On each of the long sides is a teleregister board, and on one of the two boards is the bid and offer for every listed security. The customer's man asks for and receives the spread, then relays the news back to the customer. Until a few years ago, there were ninety-five girls and all quotes went out through them; but now the 251 most active securities are quoted by machine. A series of forty-two magnetic drums hold five-second "recordings" of a reporter's voice from the floor, and the customer's man by dialing a three-digit number plugs his telephone automatically into the channel of the drum that holds the information he needs.

The same reporters feed quotes to the girls and to the drums, and also to the ticker girls. Most sales change the bid and offer, and after each sale the reporters ask the specialist for the new quotes, then step to an intercom mounted in the post. By pushing one button they plug themselves into the proper position on the magnetic drum, and simply say aloud the bid and offer. The push on the button erases the previous "recording" on the drum, and the spoken words produce a new one. If the stock involved is not one of the 251 most active the reporter pushes one of another set of buttons, which connects him with a girl sitting behind the teleregister board up in the quote room. The girl listens and pushes buttons of her own, changing the bid-and-offer shown on the board.

Since brokers pay for this quote service in the form of leased wires and yearly fees, they like to use it. There are only ten- to thirty-thousand round-lot transactions a day on the floor, but the quote room and the drums supply nearly 100,000 quotes.

The Stock Clearing Corporation, the Quotations Corporation and the Building Corporation all pay their own way, and even produce a little profit; the rest of the Stock Exchange is supported by listing fees, membership initiation fees of $4,000 each, membership dues of $750 a year (bringing in nearly a million dollars) and an assessment on members of 1 per cent of their net commission business (more than $4,598,000 in 1958). One of the reasons the Stock Exchange is so expensive to operate is that nobody ever knows what the volume of trading will be tomorrow; and the Exchange likes to be prepared for the three-million-share days that mean prosperity. Since the average day will probably run under two million shares (trading climbed over that figure in 1954, for the first time in years), the place is pretty badly overstaffed.* All sorts of ways to make the operation more efficient are investigated every year. Telephone company engineers and I.B.M. special-

---

* 1959: During the last year four-million-share days have been frequent, and three-million-share days little better than average. The staff has been busy.

ists are always prowling one part of the building or another, looking for ways to cut costs, but the Exchange is reluctant to talk about these matters until final decisions are made. Nearly all the proposed changes turn out unworkable in one way or another.

"I remember," says Fred Reiniger of the Public Relations Department, "stumbling into a stockroom one day and facing up to a real monstrosity. I couldn't figure out what it was, and after getting up courage to look at it again I began calling around. Turned out it was a two-tier post, built with the idea that maybe it would speed up clerical work on the floor. They'd got so far with the idea that they'd actually built one of the damn things out of molded plywood; but once they got a look at it they forgot about it as fast as they could."*

The man who supervises the work of this staff of eleven hundred, and represents the Exchange in public, is G. Keith Funston, President of the Exchange. Before coming up to Wall Street Funston was a corporate executive and then president of Trinity College; his present job pays $100,000 a year. At the time he took it he probably had no idea of the anguish that went with the salary.

"I've got to lead," he said recently, "as far as I can. The membership is the boss—they're the Exchange. I am the chief executive officer, in charge of all the operations of the Exchange. Of course, I devote less attention to certain areas than to others—questions of discipline and the admission of members are handled by the Board of Governors."

This Board of Governors, which is the ruling body of the Exchange, is elected by the membership under various complicated formulae. It consists of thirty-three men in all—fifteen members of the Exchange, fourteen "allied members" (partners in member firms, but not actually members themselves), three representatives of the public (well, not exactly the public; in 1959 the three men were John D. Biggers of Libby-Owens-Ford, Thomas B. Watson, Jr. of I.B.M., and Courtney C. Brown of the Columbia Business School), plus Funston. The Board meets twice a week. The public representatives receive one hundred dollars per meeting attended; the other governors settle for twenty dollars a throw. The Board passes on all applications for membership or listing, all disciplinary actions, all changes in Exchange rules and in the constitution

* 1959: A less elaborate experimental post is now actually in operation on the floor.

of the Exchange. Changes in the constitution, however, require a vote of the membership.

In 1952 Funston, disturbed by the pitiful cries of the small commission brokers, appointed an informal committee to inquire into the costs of brokerage and to see whether they justified an increase in the commission rates. The committee reported back that costs were astronomical and rates should be increased. Then a formal committee was appointed and it presented a formal report, which was endorsed by Funston and sent to the Board of Governors, which liked it fine. The suggested rise in commission rates was then presented to the membership, and the membership unceremoniously voted it down.

"I was in Los Angeles the day the votes were counted," Funston recalls. "You might say I was amazed. Sometimes it's very difficult to assess what the wishes of the membership really are." The committee went back to work and made changes in the new plan, and presented it again. This time it squeaked through.*

"I told everybody who asked me that I was in favor of the changes, the first time and the second time," Funston says. "A lot of people told me I was foolish, that I shouldn't take sides. But I can't see that I'd be doing my job any better if I didn't express my opinions."

When Funston first came to the Stock Exchange, in 1950, he was one of the handsomest young executives in America. He carried himself proudly, and though he knew nothing of the securities business, he had considerable confidence that he could learn it. He had learned other businesses, just as complicated, before. Apparently, nobody had told him about the snake pit in which he would have to stand, twelve months a year, to earn his $100,000.

Of the 1,300 active members of the Exchange, about 650 are specialists, $2 brokers, traders and odd-lot dealers. The other 650 do business directly with the public. This neat balance presents an interesting problem, because the broker who does business with the public has an entirely different attitude towards life from the man whose working existence is spent entirely in the company of his friends on the floor.

---

* 1959: Since then, there have been two further increases in commission rates. Combined with the increased volume, these higher commissions have made brokerage extremely profitable. The average income of a Stock Exchange member is up at least 75 per cent since 1954. In 1958, employee bonuses equal to three months' salary were not uncommon.

As a matter of fact, they disagree on 80 per cent of all subjects. Recently a specialist who is also a member of a commission house was asked his opinion on a question of floor procedure. "Now, you know I can't answer that," he said. "As a specialist I've got one opinion, and as a broker I've got another."

So Funston came down to the Street with his little lamb behind him, and the two factions of the Exchange joined together to murder the lamb. Since then they haven't been together once. Every time Funston asked somebody for advice, somebody from the other party popped up the next day and said, "You know, I wouldn't be talking to Joe if I were you. Looks like you're taking sides." He was able to get a little help from members of his staff, but they, too, have political problems. Finally he was reduced to asking questions out in public, at meetings of the Board of Governors. After a while a general decision was reached that this was a waste of time, and Funston was sent off around the country to make speeches.

Business was good in 1954, and some of the pressure was relieved; but the strange speculation in blue chips which made the bull market of 1954 was nothing on which a man could base his future.* Funston has never given up trying to do his job. He gives straight answers to questions, and says he doesn't know the answer when he doesn't. Everybody likes him, but nobody has helped him much. Even his own staff has on occasion taken the pleasure of bamboozling him; not long ago he approved and talked through a Board meeting a change in the rules governing member firms' finances, with the understanding that it was a relaxation. The next day a few members were in his office, speaking in voices that could be heard in the coal mines of South Wales. "But, gentlemen," he said finally, "this new provision *eases* the rules." "The hell it does," said a member violently, and showed chapter and verse. Funston checked back to find that the staff had taken advantage of his ignorance, and the habitual inattention of the Board, to get through a pet proposal.

No president of the Exchange has ever been happy in the job, or has ever got much done with it. Even the redoubtable William McChesney Martin, now Chairman of the Board of Governors of the Federal Reserve System, could stand only so

---

* 1959: This analysis was completely wrong. The bull market of 1954 was the calf that became the bull market of today. And Funston was in fact just the man the Exchange wanted as its representative before a community which was anxious to believe in the essential simplicity of financial processes.

much of the politics and granite attitudes of the old-timers, and left as soon as he decently could. In the past, after all, it was a show job; to show the government that everybody was behaving, and the public what a fine place the Exchange was. Today, however, the problems are more serious.*

2

Basically, the problem of the Exchange is that it is no longer the major market in half the listed issues. The Bond Crowd, currently stuck into a corner of The Garage, may know the end of the story.

The Bond Room once occupied the back half of the first floor of the old office building on the southern end of the block, and went around a corner to take up part of the front half. At one time the whole huge room, perhaps a third the size of the main trading floor, was occupied by busy brokers executing orders for bonds. The Bond Crowd, they were called. By the time the Exchange decided to tear down the old building, the end around the corner had been blocked off, the Crowd had scattered, and two-thirds of the length of the room had become a large, unlit cloakroom for thirty brokers and fifty or so clerks who worked around four card files near the door. The visitors' gallery, which once rivalled the gallery above the main floor in the number of people taking in the show, was locked; the appearance of a visitor was rare enough to make members look up questioningly from their work.

Something like three-quarters of all the new financing done by corporations since the war has been done in bonds, and most of these issues were large enough to get listed on the Stock Exchange. Lots of them did. And one of the rules of membership in the Exchange is that no member may trade in listed securities off the floor of the Exchange. And most (not all) of the larger firms in the financial market are members of the Exchange.

Why was the Bond Room moribund?

Because firms which are not members of the Exchange found it possible to make a better market than the Exchange could make. Suppose, for example, a bond is selling for $1,019, and the commission for executing the trade is five dollars. The buyer will pay $1,024; the seller will receive

---

* 1959: This statement and the comments which follow are still true, though the structural weaknesses here described are now hard to see beneath the speculative gloss of the current market.

$1,014. Suppose, now, a man sets himself up in business and gets properly registered with all the authorities, and says, "Behold! I will buy this bond from anyone for $1,016, and I will sell it to anyone for $1,022." Both buyer and seller can now save themselves money by trading off the Exchange, which they promptly do.

At this point the member firms of the Stock Exchange find that their customers are going to others to do business, and they come to a membership meeting and say, "Look, boys, we're honored to be in the club and all that. But we've got to do business in these bonds, and we can't do it here any more because the price is wrong. So let's release bonds from this rule about trading in listed securities off the floor of the Exchange. Huh?"

Today a member must bring an order to buy or sell bonds into the Bond Room only if the order is for fourteen bonds or less. If the order is for more, he need not show his face. And even if the order is for less, he may do his trading off the floor if he can get his customer a better price off the floor.

Now, bonds are partly a special case, and partly an illustration of the market's weakening position. They are a special case because the individual bondholder is gone; top-rate industrial and utility and railroad bonds pay only a little more than government bonds, and the individual is far better off in the more negotiable and safer governments. And a general redistribution of the national income has placed more and more money in the hands of people who put their savings "in a safe place." The ownership of bonds, therefore, has passed into the hands of institutions—banks, insurance companies, trust funds of various sorts. This situation is symptomatic because the ownership of stocks has also been passing into the hands of institutions, plus mutual funds, pension funds and the like. Such people can trade in an auction market only with the greatest difficulty, because they bid and offer in large blocks. Unless the market is very active, it simply cannot absorb or supply all the stock or all the bonds the institution wishes to trade.

But a man with a telephone can get on it and call the other institutions until he finds one that wants to buy. So the institution with bonds to sell calls an over-the-counter dealer who does business with it on the spot, immediately, for cash, and at a price usually better than the price that could have been got by throwing a large order into an auction market.

That's bonds; today something like 98 per cent of all high-grade bonds are held by institutions. But preferred stocks turn out to be the same. They are legal investments for savings banks, and to a bank (or most other corporate buyers) they have a great advantage over bonds. Bond interest is taxable income to a bank; but preferred dividends, because the issuing corporation has already paid a tax on them, are 85 per cent exempt from federal taxation. (This exemption applies only to corporations; individuals pay full income tax on both interest and dividends.) Trading in preferreds became concentrated in groups, and went off the Exchange, and again the brokers came to meeting with a demand. (This is one of the reasons brokers and floor people hate each other.) As a result, there is now a list of two hundred "exempt preferreds" in which a member may freely trade off the floor of the Exchange. These exempt preferreds are no cowsilk securities, either—they include such companies as General Motors, du Pont and Dow Chemical.

And now the process is repeating itself in common stocks. Mutual funds are growing rapidly, pension funds rising at the rate of three billion dollars a year. New York State's savings banks have been permitted to invest in common stocks—and as though they weren't big enough separately, they've formed a joint fund to do their investing for them.

How can such blocks of stock be handled on the Exchange? First, by specialists like Stott. There are maybe six such specialists, and fairly large proportions of mutual fund holdings are concentrated in the stocks in which they specialize. In an ordinary market, however, the other specialists can do no such business as thirty-thousand-share blocks of a sixty-dollar stock. "Most of those guys," an over-the-counter trader says scornfully (and he a partner in a member firm, too), "you show 'em a thousand shares and they back away."

Often a large block will be taken off the market by the floor traders, acting together to get rid of the guillotine. And sometimes the large gamblers will go into action on word from their brokers that big pieces are available. The final method is some kind of "secondary offering," by which the rules of the Exchange are relaxed in one way or another to keep the business for a member firm. These secondary offerings apply only on the selling side, and most of them operate under gimmicks such as the seller's paying the buyer's commission.

Essentially, of course, all these transactions are over-the-counter deals consummated within the walls of the Exchange; and as such they are profoundly unnatural. The specialist does not have public or institutional customers; his customers are all on the floor, fellow members albeit brokers. The floor trader, too, has no desire to carry large inventories, and no place to dispose of them unless he's lucky with the market in the stock. And Exchange secondary offerings are much less satisfactory than similar dealings off the Exchange. "Why should I get listed with a secondary?" a mutual fund manager said recently. "I can call Blyth and get a price, and sell the lot over the telephone. With a secondary I have to wait and see if the offering is a success, and there's all the publicity. And the price I wind up with is probably worse than Blyth would give me." [1959: The inflexibility of Exchange commission schedules has been especially painful in this area. Under these rules, each round lot makes a separate transaction, no matter how many round lots are actually included in a single order. Commissions on a single transaction diminish as a percentage of the price when the price goes higher—that is, the customer who buys 100 shares at $100 each pays less than three times the commission paid by the man who buys 100 shares at $10, though his purchase involves ten times as much money. This quantity discount does not extend, however, to the purchase of several lots. Thus, though the same difference in outlay is involved, the customer who invests his $10,000 in 1,000 shares at $10 each pays precisely ten times the commission that he would have to pay on 100 shares at $10 each. Now, the over-the-counter dealer does not need 200 times the Stock Exchange round-lot commission to sell 20,000 shares of something. He can undercut the broker easily and substantially.

The Exchange has never faced up to this situation, probably because its public-relations emphasis on the "little man" leads it to fear any action which seems to increase the already considerable commission advantage of the big speculator. (In fact, the Exchange has tried to persuade corporations with high-priced stock issues to "split" their stock, making the price of a round lot less prohibitive to the less-rich investor, but also increasing the commission take-out on equivalent purchases and increasing the over-the-counter dealer's advantages.)

Funston's one serious effort to stop this leak of business away from the floor was a campaign to persuade the big over-the-counter houses to give up their block business in return for the honor of membership in the Exchange. To facilitate the entry of these dealers, the old Exchange rule against corporate organization of member firms was abandoned. Funston bought a number of people a number of lunches before he realized that the heads of the over-the-counter houses did not value Exchange membership quite so highly as he did. The campaign has now been abandoned, which has made life that much less amusing on the upper levels of the over-the-counter market.]

Meanwhile, there is the problem of the capital gains tax, which many members would blame for all the troubles of the Exchange. It certainly plays a supporting role.

Income is what a man gets by working at his job, skill or profession. Income is also what a shopkeeper gets by buying cheap and selling dear. But a man who buys a share of stock and holds on to it for six months or more, and sells out at a profit, gets something that is called capital gains. The tax rate on capital gains is one-half of the tax-rate on income, with a maximum of 25 per cent. In Britain and elsewhere, there is no tax at all on capital gains.

The capital gains tax has two effects on the stock market. It paralyzes people who have made profits on stock they have held less than six months; by holding it until the six-month period is up they can cut the taxes on these profits by one-half or more. "These guys ought to stop moaning about capital gains," a Washington Democrat says. "That's the tax everybody wants to get in under." Nevertheless, by luring people to stay with what they have, the tax discourages trading, which is the oxygen and blood of the Exchange. It also damages judgment by setting up an arbitrary time before which a profitable buy should not be sold; and the arbitrary time makes buying more risky.

Even worse than the arbitrary time is the punishment meted out to the man who has gone with stock as far as he thinks it can go, and wants to switch. He bought the stock at 40, and it has doubled in price over a two-year period. If he sells it at 80, he must pay a capital gains tax of $10 a share, which means that he must now find stock worth, in his judgment, more than his present $80 stock—but presently selling for $70. Since the market is not entirely lunatic, such bargains are only rarely available. The man does not switch and two commissions are lost to the Street; the stock goes down, and everybody loses.*

* 1959: This sympathetic statement of the Exchange's case does not imply advocacy of abolishing the capital gains tax. Here as elsewhere, considera-

The income tax itself enters. Interest on municipal bonds is tax-free, because it is public policy that cities and states and their subdivisions should be able to raise money for public works at less than the prevailing interest rates. By making the bonds tax-free Congress vastly increased their appeal, and as a result public works can be financed at rates not much more than half as large as the rates for corporate borrowing. For a man in a 70-per-cent tax bracket, a 3-per-cent tax-free municipal gives as good a return as a stock paying 10 per cent—and much more safely, too. Thus, much of the risk money that used to play around in the market has gone to build schools instead. [1959: Some of it has since come back on the wings of the inflation psychology.]

Sidney Smith once pointed out that it takes a surgical operation to get a joke into the head of a Scotsman; and as a general matter devices of similar complexity are necessary to introduce new ideas at 11 Wall Street. Nevertheless, the Stock Exchange has been up and about recently, looking for solutions to its problems. Between the Klingenstein Committee, which held a full-scale investigation in 1952-53, and the advertising agencies, dozens of projects are somewhere in the works.

Along the major battle line, the Exchange in 1953 set up new "turn-around" commission rates, which give the short-term gambler a reduction of nearly 50 per cent on one commission, provided he sells (or buys to cover a short sale) within thirty days after the first transaction. The idea is to set up a partial counter-balance to the capital gains tax and encourage the in-and-out trader.

The rules restricting floor trading were relaxed to help short-term gambling by members, and the Federal Reserve was persuaded, briefly, to reduce margin requirements. "Margin" is the proportion of the price which a customer must put up in order to buy securities; his broker lends him the rest. (This is not wholly a service; the broker borrows the money from a bank, and charges the customer a percentage point or two more than the bank is charging him.) During the twenties, margin was customarily 10 per cent; to buy ten thousand dollars worth of securities a customer had to put up only one thousand dollars. This factor, more than

---

tions of social justice make an overwhelming answer to questions of business efficiency. Nevertheless, the Exchange *does* have a case—despite its usual inept presentation of its arguments.

any other, extended the crash to its amazing bottom; and quite early in the depression Congress gave the Federal Reserve System the duty of regulating margins on securities exchanges and setting limits on the loan a bank could make against the collateral of registered securities. (There is no margin over the counter—but also no regulation of bank loans against over-the-counter securities.) These margins have varied between 40 per cent and 100 per cent, and in really irrational moments brokers tend to place the whole blame for the market's problems on this one little item. Early in 1953, the Klingenstein Committee report "On Broadening the Auction Market of the New York Stock Exchange" demanded a reduction in margin requirements as a first essential in restoring vitality to the market. One of the main duties of the president of the Exchange has always been to protest against increases in margin requirements. On these occasions, it is *de rigueur* to point out that broker's loans account for only a tiny fraction of the total value of listed securities. It is less usual to mention that "margin trans-actions" make up a full half of each day's volume.

To meet competition from municipal bonds the Exchange has proposed, and the present administration adopted, a plan whereby stockholders would have the right to deduct from their taxes 10 per cent (or even more) of their dividends, which is better than tax-free money. This proposal met rough seas in the 1954 Congress, and the percentage was halved, but the boys keep coming back for more.* It is an example of the Street's old tendency to act against its own interests, and the interests of the economy, for the benefit of a tiny majority of very wealthy men.

Double taxation of dividends is partially justifiable as a license fee for the riskless corporate way of doing business; but a fee which takes 52 per cent of corporate income before dividends, and then 20 to 90 per cent of the dividend check for personal income tax, is practically a prohibition. There is a strong case for allowing *corporations* to claim income tax credit for the dividends they pay to stockholders, as the Exchange originally proposed, when this amendment was first considered. Such a law would encourage corporations to pay higher dividends and retain less of their profits. It would

---

* 1959: The Senate voted this June to eliminate the "dividend tax credit," which is currently four per cent. The credit was reinstated, however, by the House.

benefit Wall Street by taking away from the corporations some of their present power to initiate new projects from their own funds, without consulting investment bankers. It would benefit the economy by putting more money in the hands of consumers, especially consumers in the middle-class brackets. Most important of all, it would redress the tax arguments which now force corporations to overload their capital structures with debt securities.

Allowing *individuals* the tax deduction means an easing of present pressures on corporations to pay higher dividends, and thus their greater independence of the financial market. It retains the pressure to issue new bonds instead of new stock. It means little to the small taxpayer, and much to the man in the high brackets, who has a greater tendency to save. Instead of putting money into the economy, its net result might well be the removal of money from the General Stream, setting up a backwater in a body already tending to stagnation.*

Then there is the Monthly Investment Plan, which went into effect in January, 1954, and is presently falling on its face. The Plan was prompted by an Exchange-sponsored survey indicating that fewer than seven million Americans owned shares of stock, and the idea behind it was to make investing easy, convenient and painless for several million more. Since the Plan, though heavily advertised, produced fewer than thirty thousand customers in its first full year (and not all of these new customers), it may be assumed to be dead. This seemly death mitigates its unfortunate creation, since the reason for the fiasco can only be the admirable common-sense of the ordinary citizen.†

The aims of the Plan were sound and even rather noble.

---

* 1959: In fact, the tax deduction has had no discernible effect on corporate dividend policy. I would no longer maintain the highly Keynesian description in these sentences, though I stick by the proposition that in 1955, despite appearances to the contrary, the American economy was tending towards stagnation.

† 1959: The admirable common-sense of the ordinary citizen probably played little if any part in the relative failure of M.I.P. Much more important was the fact that mutual funds were offering much greater commissions and much lower selling costs to the brokerage houses which would peddle their shares. Commissions paid by mutual funds to dealers, on the sale of their own stock, ran well over $100,000,000 in 1958, and the profit rates on such business is excellent. As a result, only those houses which did not handle mutual funds put any considerable effect behind M.I.P. More than half of all the plans sold to date have been handled by one firm—Merrill Lynch. And M.I.P., despite my obsequies, is still alive. Further information on this point is given at the end of the chapter.

There are many people who do not own stocks, who should. They can afford the risk, they would enjoy the dividends and they would strengthen American capitalism by broadening its base. At the same time (and this thought did, of course, occur to the innovators), they would be helping the Stock Exchange out of what may be a nasty corner—and the Stock Exchange is a valuable institution. There is a great need for some investment plan which would enable ordinary middle-class people to afford stock certificates. Unfortunately, M.I.P. was sold on a highly indiscriminate basis, mostly to people who were not in position to make financial judgments or take risks (*Barron's,* urging its discontinuation early in 1955, labelled it as an attempt "to lead the lamb back into Wall Street"). Still worse, the plan made buying stocks so expensive that nobody could really afford it.

The commissions were ruinous. A man who came with $1,200 to buy stock on the New York Stock Exchange paid his broker $14.85; under the Monthly Investment Plan his commissions were $67.92 (plus, in both cases, the odd-lot fee). He paid this extra $53, not for the use of something he didn't wholly own (which is the case with instalment buying of automobiles and such), but simply for the privilege of letting his broker take his money twelve times a year instead of once a year.

To the customer, these commissions mean that:

(1) If his stock paid a 6 per cent dividend and remained stable in price, he would have to be in the plan *two and one-half years* before the dividend payments caught up with the commissions he had paid. For those two and a half years he would have been better off putting his money in a mattress;

(2) If the price of his stock went up *15 per cent*, by regular stages, he would wind up his first year owning stock worth less than the cash he had put into the Plan;

(3) Unless the price of the stock went down violently, he would have been better off borrowing money on an unsecured personal loan (at the highest legal interest rate) and taking the lump in to his broker than he was if he bought the same stock under the Monthly Investment Plan.

Behind these facts lies no Machiavellian desire to cheat the public, but an earnest attempt to fit a new idea into the regular Stock Exchange commission rates. Filling a large order costs little more than filling a small order, so commissions have always been calculated as a high proportion of a small purchase and a low proportion of a large one. The breaking up of an annual investment into separate monthly pieces therefore produced an enormous increase in the customer's commissions. What was just a little reprehensible about the scheme was the advertising, which did not point up for the prospective customer that he was paying heavily for the privilege of membership in the Monthly Investment Plan.

It cannot be too strongly stated that the Exchange believed the Plan to be a good one; Funston was deeply hurt when someone suggested to him the possiblity of a dishonest motive. M.I.P. was a mistake and nothing worse. R.I.P.

[1959: As indicated in the previous footnote, M.I.P. has refused to die. About as many new plans were sold in 1958 as in the first year of the venture. In total, about 170,000 Plans have been purchased, of which roughly half continue technically in effect, though less than 70,000 are still active.

Members of the Exchange have lost on M.I.P., because the average customer continues his Plan only half a year, and high as his commissions are, they do not amortize the cost of opening his account. The market has risen so drastically, though, that most of the individual customers have probably made money on their little flyer, despite its costs.

These facts do not, to my mind, justify M.I.P. Indeed, I would argue that they more than justify my original criticisms. The extremely short duration of the average Plan demonstrates conclusively that the program has attracted people whose social or psychological orientation was such that they should not have gone into the market. Meanwhile, the Gresham's Law of mail-order advertising (all Stock Exchange ads have coupons, and their success is measured largely by the quantity of the coupon response) has made the selling program more and more irresponsible.

M.I.P. has cheapened and partially discredited the New York Stock Exchange and those member firms which have most vigorously supported it. But no other result could have been expected from an allegedly commercial project which was actually political in origin.]

Chapter 6

The American Stock Exchange

THERE is another stock exchange in New York, one block up Wall Street and across Trinity Church graveyard to Trinity Place. It can be seen from Broadway, a few steps away from the members' entrance to the New York Stock Exchange; and on Broadway a short time ago a member of the bigger Exchange stood, looking across the headstones and statuary to the modern, white façade of the American Stock Exchange.

"They got a real policing problem over there," he said sorrowfully. "It's real hard to keep that Exchange honest—a lot of members there, five thousand dollars is a lot of money to them."

This comment was cupped in two hands and carried respectfully to Edward T. (for Ted) McCormick, President of the American Stock Exchange and until 1951 Commissioner of the Securities and Exchange Commission. In the words of *Business Week,* McCormick "has worked both sides of the Street."

He is a very small but solidly built man, and he moves with quick, nervous energy. His hair is turning grey slowly and at a speed that is proper for a man of forty-seven. He comes from Arizona, a blend of Irish and Spanish that could come from nowhere else. He has the happy Irish grin, and a fleck of the Irish temper. The fleck showed when the comment was disclosed to him.

"You go back and tell that guy that this is the best-policed Exchange in the United States—the members here picked for their boss an ex-commissioner of the S.E.C. I investigate all complaints personally. Last Tuesday I went all the way to the Chrysler Building—by subway—to listen to a man who thought he'd been gypped. It was a misunderstanding, which was a very good thing for the people he thought had gypped him."

McCormick's major problem is not honesty, of which the A.S.E. has neither the monopoly nor a marked deficiency, but the listing of securities to be traded on the floor.* For decades

---

* 1959: McCormick might moderate his boast today. The slight lowering of standards already noted has been more severe at the A.S.E. than elsewhere,

the Curb Exchange (the name was changed to American Stock Exchange in 1952) was a "seasoning" exchange—it took the stocks of corporations not large enough or national enough to qualify for listing on the New York Stock Exchange. When the corporations grew, they moved over to the big board. The A.S.E. now believes that it does a better job for corporations than the bigger Exchange, and it hopes to put an end to the moving.

"While you're at it," McCormick said, "ask your friend why they don't have the liberal delisting provisions we have. A corporation can delist from this Exchange, and move over to the New York Exchange, by a management decision. Over there, you've got to have a vote to delist by two-thirds of all the outstanding stock, and even then you can't get off if 10 per cent of the stock votes to remain. There are quite a few corporations over there that I think we could service better than they do—and the corporations think so, too. But the management doesn't want to risk a proxy fight about it, and you can't blame them."

The A.S.E. has much easier listing requirements than the bigger Exchange. Only five hundred stockholders must be on the books, and only 100,000 shares outstanding. While the Stock Exchange demands earnings of one million dollars a year, the A.S.E. will take corporations which have practically no earnings at all, provided that they are going concerns with sufficient financing to do the jobs they set out to do. Kaiser Motors (then Kaiser-Frazer) was listed before it made its first automobile, because public interest in the issue warranted an auction market. McCormick believes that volume of trading, the number of bids and offers, is not a good criterion for a stock's suitability to an auction market. "So long as there's general agreement about the value of the stock—and the bid and offer are consistently close together—you can trade it on an auction market."

The biggest part of McCormick's job is hunting out new listings. Under the Securities and Exchange Act of 1934 a corporation listed on an exchange must perform certain services for stockholders that other corporations need not do. Reports on trading by insiders, regular earnings reports and honest proxy forms are required from listed corporations only.

---

and a regrettably large proportion of the recent startling increase in A.S.E. trading has been due to stock manipulation. Only a small minority of A.S.E. members are involved, of course, but it is significant that McCormick has been unable to police the situation effectively.

Companies presently traded over the counter, therefore, must assume certain burdens when they list their securities on an Exchange; and not the least of these burdens is the pacification of the over-the-counter dealers, who not only trade the securities but may also have inventories representing a substantial piece of ownership. Even small, local dealers can make large, local problems.

The A.S.E. is a national organization, with nearly 1,500 tickers in 140 cities in thirty-nine states. It owns and operates its own ticker network, which it is currently expanding with all possible speed, to place itself in a better competitive position against the bigger board. Each ticker entered is also another argument for listing.

Actually, more than one-third of the stocks traded at the A.S.E. are "unlisted" and do not have to meet the S.E.C. rules. Before 1934 the Curb Exchange did not require a corporation to request listing before stock could be traded; if brokers wanted to trade in the stock, and could prove public interest in it, the Exchange would accept it for trading on their request. Many of these corporations are still traded on the A.S.E. floor, and few of them have seen any reason to list, which would subject them to stricter regulation and also cost them money (the A.S.E. does not charge any annual fee, as the Stock Exchange does, but there is an initial fee of one thousand dollars). So long as the law does not require all corporations of a certain size to abide by the S.E.C. rules the Exchange sees no reason to play St. George. In fact, Congress at one time debated the advisability of banning unlisted trading, but decided against it. Two reasons have been offered—one, that there was a strong desire to keep all retroactive features out of the law; two, in the words of an over-the-counter dealer, "because it would have killed the New York Curb Exchange probably." Recently a sounder approach, sponsored by the S.E.C., the A.S.E. and Senator Frear of Delaware, tried to make all corporations with more than three hundred stockholders and three million dollars in assets subject to the S.E.C. rules which now affect listed corporations only. The law was introduced a few times, but never got out of committee. [1959: Rechristened for Senator Fulbright, the law is still around—still in committee.]

Although McCormick has had considerable success weaning American corporations away from the obscurity of over-the-counter trading, the most important new listings of recent years have involved foreign companies. Nearly a hundred Canadian corporations are now admitted to trading on the American Stock Exchange. During the twenties many European corporations sold stock in the United States, and the Curb Exchange joined with the Guaranty Trust Company in setting up American Depositary receipts, which gave the securities roughly the same standing as shares in American companies. Some of these are still traded on the A.S.E., though currency restrictions have made them difficult to manage. There are about 170 foreign issues traded on the A.S.E., which puts it, in one category anyway, far ahead of the New York Stock Exchange.

The other side of the listing war is keeping on the A.S.E. corporations large enough to qualify for the big board; and here McCormick must try to redress uneven odds by sheer force of personality, intelligence and golf game. Often the opposition is simply too strong for him. The executive offices of the New York Stock Exchange, for example, have the air of established wealth. They are austerely simple in Georgian furniture, with soft carpeting, white walls and enormous rooms; the open spaces remind a visitor of the Great West. The A.S.E., on the other hand, is distinctly *nouveau riche:* Oriental rugs, wood panelling and furniture that is too heavy and too ornately carved. Though its lesser offices are all efficiency, and sometimes even a little threadbare, the Board of Governors room, the president's office and the other show places are entirely too showy for a suspicious corporation president.

But McCormick makes full use of his personal initiative and understanding of the financial market. "He'd have been a hell of a salesman," one Stock Exchange member said a trifle wistfully. "It's a pity he went straight." Although his entire experience before assuming the presidency of the Curb was as an accountant and a public servant (he also has a scholarly background, and holds an honest, not an honorary, doctoral degree), he has a shrewd sense of retailing, employee and public relations. His major coup so far has been the lengthening of trading hours, which were once ten to three and are now, at his insistence, ten to three-thirty (this also enabled the exchanges to stay closed on Saturday, which helped labor relations all around the business). He pioneered this change in 1952, and it was the first time the junior exchange had ever led the way in any important forward step on Wall Street; when a reporter called the New York Stock

Exchange for comment on McCormick's original announce-ment, he was told in a choked voice, "There is no comment and there will be no comment." Nevertheless, the senior ex-change followed McCormick's lead only a few months later.

"He has an even bigger bomb ready to go off if his member-ship can ever be talked into it," says one of McCormick's closest associates. "One of these days he's going to keep the A.S.E. open until nine o'clock Thursday nights, just like a department store. He feels—and he's right—that the ex-changes are in a merchandising business, and ought to keep the store open for customers." The New York Stock Exchange does not regard itself as "in business" at all; the phrase is too vulgar for such an institution. But if McCormick ever carries out his plan, the Big Board will follow tamely enough.

While the New York Stock Exchange was launching its implausible Monthly Investment Plan in the winter of 1954, McCormick was promoting a far more enlightened scheme—the Investment Club. There are several hundred of these clubs —including a "Finest Investment Club" in a New York police precinct headquarters, and a "BAD Investments Club" in the Business Administration Department of the University of Michigan—and they provide a hearth for the small investor. The ordinary man with savings to invest doesn't have the time to investigate any substantial number of the investments open to him; he may look at one or two pieces of literature, and then he buys a blue chip. Moreover, he pays the high costs of investing on a small scale.

By banding together in Investment Clubs, customers can pool their money to get the lower commission rates, and can farm out in manageable pieces the job of looking for good investments. "Groups of people with a common interest—they're all members of the same P.T.A., or they work in the same office—get together and agree to put up so many dollars a month," McCormick says. "A broker sponsors the group, but they make their own investment decisions, and they be-come students of our economic system. People become en-thusiastic, too, and relatives and friends of members put up about ten times as much money as the members themselves by the time the Club is rolling.

"They really learn, too. The president of a local corporation may come to a meeting to tell members about his company, and often the Club will put a good deal of money into local enterprises, which it can watch and help. I studied a group of clubs in the Detroit area, and nearly 90 per cent of their money was in local industry. The bookkeeping is so simple they can do it themselves. All the plan costs them is the kind of brokerage that a big investor pays." McCormick went out to Detroit in 1953 to speak at a convention of the National Association of Investment Clubs: "You," he said to them, "not Wall Street, have found a practical answer to selling shares in our future."*

"I work very closely with Mac," says John J. Mann, the florid, moon-faced specialist who is Chairman of the A.S.E. Board of Governors. "But that doesn't mean I agree with everything he does." Another broker, overhearing this, commented: "Sure. But Johnny, like everybody else around here, is only scared somebody's going to come along and buy Mac away with a better job."

2

Basically, business is done in the same way on the New York Stock Exchange and the American Stock Exchange. The A.S.E. is smaller, handling a volume of transactions only about one-quarter of that on the senior exchange. ("Remember, though," McCormick says, "that they've got all the trouble with the big blocks. We're expanding.")† And the average price per share is considerably lower, so that the A.S.E. handles only a tenth as much money volume as the big room at 11 Wall. Bond trading, which has suffered at the N.Y.S.E., has practically disappeared at the A.S.E., though during the twenties it was so heavy that members considered turning the place into a Bond Exchange.

The building which houses the A.S.E. is twenty years newer than the Stock Exchange building, and the trading floor is a trifle larger. There are twenty-one posts instead of eighteen, the posts are octagons instead of horseshoes, and there is no high signboard around their rims. Only five hundred or so people work on the floor, and there are only 499 members (and the price of a membership is far lower. "But remember," said an officer of the A.S.E., "that price over there includes a share in their Gratuity Fund—which amounts to a free twenty-thousand-dollar life insurance policy for every member.") Specialists rather than odd-lot firms handle the odd-lot business. ("And it's better that way. Over there, the specialist

---

* 1959: An investment banker of an older school objected strongly to the praise of Investment Clubs on the grounds that "I never heard of a committee making a good choice of stock-market purchases."

† 1959: The proportional volume would now be closer to one-third, but not entirely for the reasons McCormick foresaw.

doesn't know how the odd-lot trade is going. Here, he has the whole market to see, all the time.") Instead of the noisy, ugly clapboard the A.S.E. has an electric-light system which lights a member's number when he is wanted. But the most immediately noticeable difference is in the seven tiers of telephone desks which rise in stately measure along the whole length of the east wall and half of the west wall. Clerks sit at these desks and relay messages to the brokers on the floor by means of hand signals, which makes the A.S.E. as much as a minute per transaction faster than the New York Stock Exchange.

These hand signals come from the old days of the Curb Exchange, when it actually was out in Broad Street, in the open air, and clerks leaned out the windows of the office buildings to wig-wag messages to the members. For their part, the members wore odd, colorful hats which would identify them to their clerks and did business—shine, rain, snow, heat or biting cold—on the unguarded pavement. The Curb Exchange moved indoors thirty-five years ago, but the hand signals were kept, for the sake of speed and also to keep clerks off the floor, where they get in the way of the members. Another part of the system has been kept, too: just as second-floor windows cost more than third- or fourth-floor windows when the market was in the street, desks on the lower levels rent today for more than desks on the higher levels. Only the east wall desks are used (or ever have been used); the west bank is dark, kept in reserve for that blessed emergency when one wall of desks will no longer hold all the clerks.

The signals themselves are elaborate but commonsensical. The leading automobile stock, for example, will be expressed by the motion of two hands clutching and turning a wheel; the leading aviation stock by the quick take-off of a hand. Prices are expressed by cutting motions of one hand against another—and the signals go down as far as 1/64th of a point. Executions will be signalled by fingers up or down. All the motions are made vigorously, so that a broker signalling a confirmation to his clerk nearly always looks mad at the world, though he has just committed the act by which he earns his living. A busy afternoon at the A.S.E. looks like the annual convention of the deaf-and-dumb section of the Anti-Vivisectionist League.

At present only 130 or so commission brokers work on the floor, and they are substantially outnumbered by a floor citizenry of 150 specialists and forty floor traders. The balance is redressed, however, by associate members, who send in many of the orders which keep the Exchange busy and split the resulting commissions with the brokers who execute the orders. These associate members are not, like regular members, part owners of the Exchange, though they pay the same annual dues of five hundred dollars; the purchase price of an associate membership is only 10 to 15 per cent of the regular membership price—five hundred dollars for every five thousand dollars or fraction of five thousand dollars paid for the last seat sold. They have a strong voice in the management of the Exchange, however, and the A.S.E. constitution provides for their representation on the thirty-two-man Board of Governors.

The A.S.E. has only three hundred employees, and women work on the floor in clerical capacities. A little decoration is encouraged; at Christmas time the people who work at the various posts hold a competition for the most attractively got-up octagon in the Exchange. The Stock Exchange, conservative in all things, puts a large tree in the middle of Broad Street; the A.S.E. dresses up its windows with imaginative lights. There is nothing at the A.S.E. like the Stock Exchange Club; the A.S.E. restaurant is open to the public and privately owned, and it serves somewhat better food.

The Stock Exchange employs more people than it needs, looking for the big day, but the A.S.E. holds down its expenses and everybody works a little harder. Martin Keena, for example, the A.S.E. Vice-President in charge of the Stock Listing Division, has a smaller office, a smaller staff and a good deal more work than Phillip West, his opposite number at 11 Wall. Keena came to the Curb Exchange in 1920, just before it moved indoors, and he has held the same job all that time. "With different titles," he says. "When I first arrived there was an indoor office, one small room at 25 Broad Street, and all the administrative personnel was in the one room. I was twenty years old, and it was my second job— I'd worked for a company that made scientific instruments. I was called the 'listing man' then, and my duties weren't much different from what they are now. Except, at that time we were our own boss, there was no S.E.C.; we would just announce we were admitting to trading the John Jones Company, and then make an auction market. In those days the proportion was about sixty-five—thirty-five, with the unlisted on top; now it's the other way around."

One of Keena's more delicate jobs is to determine what is

called the ex-dividend date for securities traded on the A.S.E. When a corporation declares a dividend, the form of announcement is always, "payable on such-and-such to stockholders of record on so-and-so"; A.T. & T., for example, announces a "regular quarterly dividend of $2.25 a share, payable on October 15 to stockholders of record on September 20."* A man who buys A.T. & T. in mid-September will get the October dividend only if the ownership of the stock has been transferred to his name on or before September 20. Now, all stocks bought or sold "regular way" must be paid for and delivered four days after the trade itself is made (there is also a "cash" sale, with delivery the same day, and a "deferred" sale, with delivery at some stated time in the future). A man who buys A. T. & T. "regular way" on September 16 will receive the October dividend, but the man who buys on September 17 will not. Consequently, on September 17 all bids in the specialist's book are automatically reduced by 2¼, the amount of the dividend, and the stock is said to "go ex-dividend." On the New York Stock Exchange this ex-dividend date is invariably the third day before the books are closed for that dividend; the Stock Exchange demands that every listed corporation maintain a transfer agent in New York, right near the market, and any stock bought on September 16 can be transferred immediately to the new owner when it is delivered on September 20. The A.S.E., however, does not demand that any but the most actively traded corporations maintain transfer agents in New York, so the ex-dividend date must be set back by the time required for registered mail to go from New York to the corporation's transfer agent in Potowatamie or whatever. This ex-dividend date is quite a serious matter, because a man who sells ex-dividend and then doesn't get the upcoming dividend has been gypped by the automatic reduction bids. To some extent Keena is at the mercy of the United States Mails in setting these dates, but he has learned how to handle the problem. "It's much easier now," he says. "Back in the twenties it was catch-as-catch-can to get information from unlisted companies about when they were going to pay dividends. Now we have them all pretty well educated."

Nor is there anyone at the Stock Exchange quite like the A.S.E.'s Ed Kelly, a Dickensian gentleman in a wide pin-stripe

---

* 1959: This seemed eternally valid at the time of writing, A.T. & T.'s $9 dividend having survived the crash and the inflation. Now the dividend has been raised and the stock split. *Ave atque vale.*

suit, Secretary to the Committees that deal with new members and the conduct of present members, and the resident expert on questions of discipline. "Ah, ha! Yes!" says Kelly, who has been with the A.S.E. for thirty years, "discipline! Everyone loves to talk about discipline. Expulsion! There's been only one expulsion in the last eight years, but the procedure is definitely fixed. The expelled member's seat is transferred to the Board of Governors, which sells it for him. He receives the money—but if he owes anything to the Exchange or any member, that debt is deducted first. The Board says, 'Behold! We order you to pay this money to so-and-so. We are a court of competent jurisdiction.' The Board tries to sell the seat at the price of the last sale, Article Four, Section 7, Subsection D. If the seat isn't sold within two weeks, the price is reduced by one-eighth of the difference between the original price set and the money the expelled member owes the Exchange. Every two weeks I walked down and posted a new price, and all the members would look at me and I could see them wondering whether they should buy it now or hope it would go cheaper. If nobody does buy the seat at a price higher than the expelled member's debt to the Exchange, the Board of Governors buys the seat for the Exchange itself, and the seat is retired. It's all set out in the constitution!"

This constitution is a marvel of legalistic draftsmanship, several times as long as the Stock Exchange constitution, and adminstering it takes more time from the Board of Governors. ("Over there," said a broker encountered at the A.S.E.'s annual Christmas cocktail party, "they just do whatever the staff tells them to do. Over here, we work like dogs. I'm a member of both exchanges, and I've sat on the Board at both, and I know.") The commission rates set forth in it are far more complicated, and work on a different scale: it costs more commission to do a small transaction on the A.S.E., but considerably less to do a large one. [1959: A.S.E. commission rates have gone up far less sharply than N.Y.S.E. rates in recent years, which probably accounts for some of the A.S.E.'s gains in relative volume.]

This elaborate formal organization is a kind of making for lost time; during the first seventy years of its existe Curb had scarcely any rules at all. Until the turn o tury there was no limit on membership; any play. Then they fixed a number.

It was observed that fixing a number m

cult. They were out in the street, and the street was a public thoroughfare. What was to keep a man from putting on a fancy hat and talking deaf-and-dumb language to the sky, and trading securities with members?

"I don't know," said Keena. "They went indoors soon after I came."

"There must have been some way," said Kelly thoughtfully. "They didn't wear badges, the way they do now, I know that."

The question was put to Thomas Hockstader of L. F. Rothschild & Co., head of the A.S.E. Committee on Public Relations. Hockstader, a tall, thin, youthful gentleman with black hair and a slightly querulous expression, scratched his head and moved over to the next post to talk with a grey-beard in a cream-colored cotton jacket. He came back grinning.

"He says you knew members because you knew them. Everybody started as a clerk, or was introduced around and worked under a member's wing for a while before he went out on his own. You recognized the people you traded with, and you also recognized members you wouldn't trade with. There were some people to whom you'd sell stock for a sixteenth less—and there were others you'd charge a sixteenth more, a sort of insurance premium to cover the risk that you'd never get paid."

It was healthier then, too; the year-round open air kept members physically trim. There were more people out sick during the first winter indoors than at any time in the history of the Curb. But they're indoors for good now, there's a new name and you can do business with everybody—a broker's membership in the Exchange is a guarantee that he meets his obligations. For such a change in atmosphere health is not too large a price.

Chapter 7

The Brokers

SOME years ago an officer of one of the many semi-official organizations that help police the financial market was sitting in on a Merrill Lynch cocktail party at an investment banker's convention. He was sipping a drink and listening to the cheerful sounds about him, and suddenly he felt a finger tap on his shoulder. He turned around.

An anonymous minion was standing above him. "The boss wants to see you," the minion said.

The officer rose and followed to the top floor of the hotel, where a dozen men were standing around the living room of a suite, smoking and talking in hushed voices. Every once in a while the bedroom door would open and somebody would come out, move over to one of the men and nudge him toward the bedroom. Finally it came the officer's turn. He walked into one of the best bedrooms that could be offered by one of the best hotels in the state of Florida, and Charles Merrill was sitting on the bed.

"What do *you* want?" Merrill said.

"I don't want a goddam thing," said the officer somewhat irritably. "All I know is, one of your people told me that the boss wanted to see me, so I came up."

Merrill grinned. "Sit down, young man," he said. "Sit down." The officer sat down and Merrill said in his best Southern manner, "I just wanted to tell you that I like the work you're doing. And if you ever need any help with anybody, just let me know. I'll follow your orders."

"Thank you," said the officer, sincerely.

"You know," Merrill said reflectively, "there isn't a single trick in this business that I don't know." He stopped, and grinned. "And the reason I know them is, I've pulled every one of them m'self. Now that I'm an old man, I don't want to see anybody pulling them on me."

It will be understood that Merrill was giving an explanation, not a reason. Although nobody in government or finance is so fanatically devoted to honest practice, most people on Wall Street believe that anyone who tried to gyp Charlie Merrill would get his business throat cut in short order. Merrill is a sick man and has been for ten years, but whatever it is that has weakened his heart has by no means taken the force from his personality.*

He is the first authentically great man produced by the financial market in 150 years. The Drews and Goulds, the Cookes, the Morgans and the Livermores—these men existed in a tight little island of their own making, where the public was sheep to be shorn. They made the alleys of Wall Street dark and dangerous places, and they kept for themselves as much as possible of the benefits that came from the system which produced their fantastic riches. Merrill brought in the public, not as a lamb to be fleeced but as a partner in the benefits. Today a man who loses his shirt in the market is a victim of his own stupidity or greed, not of the machinations of insiders.† The climate of the thirties helped, the laws helped and many individuals helped; but the prime mover was Charlie Merrill.

Originally a Floridian, the son of a doctor, Merrill came North to go to Amherst and worked his way through two years of college, then quit and returned to Florida and a short stint as a newspaperman. He tried law school and ordinary business, then found his full scope on Wall Street. Merrill made his first fortune as an underwriter, specializing in chain stores; he took stock warrants as part of his underwriting profits, and as the stocks went up he cashed them in. In 1914, at the age of twenty-nine, he was a millionaire; and the course has been up ever since.

He was one of the first to see the coming crash, and wrote an article in 1928 telling his customers and everybody else to get out before the house came down. "We think you should know," he wrote, "that with few exceptions all of the larger companies financed by us have no funded debt. . . . This is not luck. . . ." In 1930, when prosperity was supposed to be just around the corner and the prices of seats on the Stock Exchange were climbing again, Merrill Lynch went out of business, so immensely solvent that it was able to supply five million dollars in new capital to the firm that took over its commission customers and most of its employees. Merrill himself, at forty-five, retired; three marriages and a constantly

---

* Merrill died in 1956, but the section has been left unchanged.

† 1959: Despite the comments inserted on previous pages about the slight decline in Wall Street ethics, this sentence still holds true. Nobody tries to take advantage of the sort of customer who has a sensible attitude towards the market.

growing fortune are experience enough for any man, and he wanted to brush up on his tennis before it got too late.

In 1940 he came back. He is a modern man, but by no means a radical; he was disturbed by the trend of the economy and economic thinking, and he thought the time had come to prove that capitalism could be profitable for the many. A specialist in chain stores, he opened a super-market of a brokerage firm. Though Edmund Lynch was dead, Merrill wanted to keep his name in the firm. The original letterhead read Merrill Lynch, E. A. Pierce & Cassatt: the next year it became Merrill Lynch, Pierce, Fenner & Beane.* A merger of four large firms, with a hypodermic of new capital from the Merrill fortune, it was from the beginning the largest brokerage house in the world—called by outsiders "The Thundering Herd of Wall Street"; by the insiders, cleverly, "We the People."

2

Fifteen years is a longer time than most people realize; it is, in fact, an accurate measure of a generation. In fifteen years today's first-grade schoolchildren will be getting out of college, and the freshest crop of college graduates will be executive vice-presidents. In fifteen years the temper and manner of an industry can change so enormously that even the old-timers have difficulty remembering how it was fifteen years ago.

Fifteen years ago in the brokerage business the central institution was the "customer's man." He had a following of rich clients, and he split brokerage commissions with his employer; the best customers' men could get 40 per cent. If the month had been slow, the customer's man might call two large customers and switch one of them from Radio to Motors, the other from Motors to Radio, getting himself 40 per cent of four commissions. After all, customers' men have to eat, too.

Charlie Merrill paid his salesmen (he called them "account executives," and the official name all over the business now is the wonderfully dignified "registered representative") a flat salary; their income was not to be determined by the amount of business they could churn up. Eventually the New York Stock Exchange set up a rule that all registered representatives should be paid on a salary rather than a commission basis. The rule was honored mostly in the breach (there

---

* 1959: As of January 1, 1958, the name became Merrill Lynch, Pierce, Fenner & Smith, giving much work to stonemasons and makers of gilt lettering.

was nothing in it to say that a man's salary had to be the same every month), but its very existence was a tribute to Merrill's revolution. The revocation of the rule, in 1954, was tribute of another kind.*

Fifteen years ago a man who wanted information got advice, which is an entirely different matter. If a customer demanded a complete report on a situation, his broker would supply it. And charge him for it. There were charges for rendering monthly statements of a customer's account, for maintaining an inactive account, for holding a customer's securities in a broker's vault, for executing legal transfers.

Charlie Merrill set up on a no-fee basis. Any customer (or potential customer) could write in or call in and get a research report on any stock that interested him. He could also get, free, the firm's little magazine, *Investor's Reader,* which comes out bi-weekly with more information than can be found in a full year's subscription to *Forbes,* or some of the other business magazines.† The customer, it was decided, would be advised to buy a stock or sell it only if he asked for advice. And his certificates would be kept for him without charge. Almost everybody followed; Merrill Lynch did it first. And when brokers started restoring the old charges, Merrill Lynch waved its banner even higher.

Fifteen years ago each brokerage house kept its business a dark secret, often with reason. How well or how badly a firm did was its own affair; its customers had no right to know anything. A firm might be touting a security it owned, and never tell the customer; it might be next door to broke, with the customer's account in danger, and he would never know about it. The profits might be fantastic, based on exorbitant service charges, and the customer could never find out.

Charlie Merrill kept the doors open, so everyone could "see what makes the eggs stand up." He printed an annual report of the firm's operations, and made it available to any-

---

* 1959: This comment was somewhat unfair. Merrill's system, as expressed in the firm's "statement of policy" was compensation "on a salary and bonus basis rather than a straight commission basis." Obviously, a man who handles a great volume of business—especially new business—will be paid bigger bonuses than the man in the next cell who is just plodding along with his routine accounts. The Stock Exchange rule promoted hypocrisy as much as honest dealing, and there is always a strong argument for the repeal of regulations which are admirable in purpose but irrelevant to reality.

† 1959: Malcolm Forbes has objected strenuously to this statement, and a casual look at his magazine would seem to support him. But *Forbes,* it seems to me, is angled towards opinion and advice rather than towards information, and the distinction is a real one.

one who asked for it. He saw to it that every report on every stock carried a complete disclosure of the firm's holding in the stock and the holdings of its individual partners.

Fifteen years ago young men could come down to Wall Street only if they brought their fathers' business with them; there were no vacancies for boys whose only recommendation was ability. Consequently, there were no young men, and the Street today suffers from a really drastic shortage of talent in the thirty-five to fifty year group.

Charlie Merrill started a training program for young men, and more than thirteen hundred have already been graduated from it. They are the firm's greatest single asset, and a few of them are already partners. By example, Merrill forced the rest of Wall Steet to throw the doors open to talent—in fact, to comb the woods for it. Today there are dozens of training programs, and Wall Street is the best place there is for a bright young man who wants to make a mint of money.

But the most remarkable contribution of all came from Merrill's insistence that the public is intelligent. The hot water in which Wall Street habitually bathes flows from its disrespect for the public. Fifteen years ago brokers never advertised, partly because it was undignified, partly (bigger part) because it cost money, but mostly because they felt that the public couldn't understand sensible ads, anyway. Those that did advertise used the pattern now used by people like investment adviser Major L. L. B. Angas: "OUR CUSTOMERS HAVE YACHTS."*

By and large, Wall Street thought the public was a sucker; Merrill thought Wall Street had suckered the public. He refused to believe that people who could make money were incompetent to invest it; he advertised respectfully to them, and to do his advertising and public relations he hired no less than the managing editors of *Business Week,* best of the business magazines. (This ex-managing editor, Louis Engel, is now a partner in the firm.) One day a full-page newspaper ad appeared, eight columns in type so small it was barely legible, explaining the central facts about stocks and bonds. The ad ran first in the *New York Times,* then in other newspapers all over the country, finally as a three-page slice of *Time* magazine. There were two theories behind it: that the public wanted to learn, and that only those who were willing to do

---

* 1959: The implication here is most unfair to Major Angas, who—stock-market considerations aside—has been an *economic* analyst of great force and originality.

a little work should be encouraged to become investors. There is no way of telling how many of the firm's 400,000-plus customers came in through that ad; but they are the best customers a firm could have.

Finally, Merrill announced that he would keep commissions low. (The minimum commission that a broker may charge his customer is set down in the constitution of the Exchange, and the members may raise or lower this minimum by majority vote.) Merrill has always thought that brokers ought to cut their costs rather than raise their commissions; he has fought every proposed increase. Though the only one he ever beat came back in modified form and triumphed, he has made it difficult indeed for the boys to soak the public.

Fifteen years ago, despite all the laws and all the agitation, the stock market still hung from riggings. Today the exchanges, and practically all the rest of Wall Street, stand four square as a free market. No matter what factors an analyst counts in, a great slice of the credit must go to Charlie Merrill.

[1959: In nearly all respects the firm has carried on Merrill's tradition. The 1959 annual report warns against "the current era of financial exuberance"; deplores "the rash tips and rumors" and "the crescendo of inflationary language in many financial ads"; denounces "the increase in fraudulent stock promotion." Nevertheless, involvement in the Monthly Investment Plan, undertaken while Merrill was still alive, has led the firm down a few dark alleys.

One Merrill Lynch pamphlet on M.I.P., for example, ended with a table of figures "prepared at a university." The figures showed the progress of a man who had invested a constant sum of money, in representative stocks, every year from the 1929 peak to the next time that peak was touched, in the early 1950s. Even though the market was at exactly the same place on the chart, this hypothetical fellow had made a lot of money on his purchases.

Now, these statistics will not do at all. Ignoring the question of whether our mythical customer had constant funds to invest each year through the depression period, the table at best merely asserts the known advantages of "dollar averaging" when prices go down and then back up. Assume you put in a thousand dollars a year in a stock which sells in Year 1 at $10, Year 2 at $8, Year 3 at $5, Year 4 at $8, and Year 5 at $10. You buy 100 shares the first year, then 125, then 200, then 125, then 100 again. Your $5,000 bought you 650 shares now worth $6,500, though the final price is the same as the first price.

What the table did *not* point out was the fact that dollar averaging works *against* you if prices go up, then down. To return to our example, let us assume that the $10 stock goes to $12.50, then $15, then $12.50 and back to $10. Your $5,000 buys you only 427 shares, and you have lost $730 even though the final price is the same as the first place.

"Dollar averaging" is, in short, a dishonest sales argument—so much so that the S.E.C., in better regulated days, forbade its use. Perhaps the greatest condemnation of M.I.P. is that it has led firms as reputable as Merrill Lynch to the dissemination of such frowsy stuff.]

3

Merrill's monument is a brokerage house so big that it does one-tenth of all the business done on Wall Street. Its gross income, from commissions, underwritings, dealing and trading, reached $45,650,000 in 1950, then swarmed to $73,314,000 in 1954 and $115,000,000 in 1958. In 1950 the profits to be split among the partners, after payments to the employees' profit-sharing plan, hit $12,544,000; in 1954 they were $19,-267,000; in 1958, $27,000,000.

It costs $265,000 a day just to open the doors at Merrill Lynch, because 126 doors must be opened in 126 different offices in 114 cities in five countries. There are more than seven thousand employees, nine hundred teletypes, one hundred and ten thousand miles of leased wire, 7,900 feet of conveyor belt in the third-floor wire room and two hundred leased I.B.M. machines (including two of the big model 705 electronic calculators) in the I.B.M. room.*

Everything must be said a little slowly about Merrill Lynch. It is the largest securities broker on every exchange of any size; the largest commission broker in every commodity futures market; the largest over-the-counter dealer; in 1958, the fifth largest underwriter of corporate securities and the seventh largest manager of syndicates to sell corporate securities. It is always expanding, and it has no prejudices; if Merrill Lynch likes the deal it will go in on anything, with anybody.

---

* 1959: Five years ago these figures were $145,000, 116 offices, five thousand employees, six hundred teletypes, ninety thousand miles, 5,450 feet, seventy I.B.M. machines. Boy!

The home office is at 70 Pine Street, the third tallest building in the world, and occupies the bottom six floors. Escalators connect the floors, which saves time waiting for elevators, and saves the management of the building from the strain of hiring new elevator operators to replace the dead ones every three days. More than 240 people work in the research department, which prepares reports on securities and answers 120,000 letters a year. Two and a half millon dollars is spent for advertising, a million for leased wires. Two repairmen from A.T. & T. and one from Western Union are always on hand to keep the telephones and teletypes working; three repairmen from I.B.M. keep a weather eye on Mr. Watson's fantastic creatures. Down in the main room (which is like every other funeral parlor, only so big that people in the back use binoculars to see the board) sixty salesmen and four vice-presidents handle orders involving more than one million dollars every day. Eight directors are members of the New York Stock Exchange, and six of them work on the floor; but Merrill Lynch is the largest employer of $2 brokers. In 1958 some four dozen members of the New York Stock Exchange collected nearly $2,500,000 in commission from Merrill Lynch, Pierce, Fenner & Beane.

4

Four hundred thousand customers can send in a lot of orders in a single day. Where a medium-sized brokerage house might have three or four clerks at telephones, relaying orders from customers' men to the floor and confirmations from the floor to customers' men, the Merrill Lynch wire room takes up half a floor of a building, and the time of a hundred clerks. The downstairs board rooms relay their own orders to the trading floors, but all orders from the branches come to the wire room on some fifty multi-channel teletype machines. Since Merrill Lynch must be competitive with other brokers, and process a hundred orders in the time it takes a small broker to process one, all the ingenuity of a machine-minded management has been flung into the communication system and the spacious preserves of the wire room.

Basically, the wire room is organized as an assembly line, complete with conveyor belts. The belts are used to carry slips of paper from one location on the line to another, and above each compact set of belts is a series of narrow rails set so close to each other that a piece of paper dropped on its end on to the belt will balance between the rails and ride jauntily on to its appointment with destiny. These appointments are made very simply: a clerk who is processing or confirming orders stuffs a small rubber sponge between two rails, and all the papers riding that belt bump to a halt against the sponge. There are six sets of these belts, feeding into each other up and down, round and about the huge room, and a clerk dropping a slip on to a belt sometimes cannot see its destination. To indicate the routes and stopping places of the belts, the rails above them are brightly colored, each color signifying a place and a purpose. The bright colors, the long rails and the papers bouncing gaily around corners give the room the look of a very rich child's nursery, with an immensely complicated set of electric trains.

Clerks sit at teletypes and small switchboards on narrow tables beside the turning belts, and immediately process orders MKT (at the market) and limit orders GTD (Good Today Only) for stocks traded on the New York or American Stock Exchange. The clerk simply rips the order off the teletype and hands it to the telephone operator, who calls the Merrill Lynch telephone booth on the floor nearest the post at which the stock is traded. (There are six Merrill Lynch booths on the floor of the N.Y.S.E.) When the clerk on the floor calls back and confirms the purchase or sale, the operator hands a notation to the clerk at the teletype, who confirms to the branch office, then drops the executed and confirmed order between the red rails. Red at Merrill Lynch is the color of money; slips dropped between the red rails ride to the end of the belt and plop off into a metal basket called the cash box.

Orders for commodities traded on the Chicago Board of Trade come into the New York wire room only for the purposes of record; they are received on totally enclosed teletype machines in a corner of the room and are automatically retransmitted to the Chicago office, which will execute them. Orders for cotton, coffee, sugar, hides and other commodities traded in New York, orders for odd-lots on the New York exchanges, "open" orders at limit prices (orders which are good this week, good this month or good till cancelled—GTW, GTM, GTC)—these will appear on the clerk's teletype with the "market" orders, and then zip away on the longest belt—128 feet, the distance from home plate to second base on a regulation baseball diamond—to someone else. Orders for unlisted securities ascend via another sandwich-type belt through a hole in the ceiling to the over-the-counter trading department, two floors above.

All this neat efficiency is fairly recent: it was only half a dozen years ago that the wire room looked like a mechanized steam laundry, vintage 1910. The conveyor belts then rode bare and exposed to the elements, high above the heads of the clerks, who had to rise up and attach their order slips to a kind of clothes-peg. The belts swung around exposed pulleys in the corners of the room, and clattered and clacked; moreover, a good part of the work was done by runners, small boys and girls in their late teens darting between peoples' feet and sweating.

Now the runners are used only to empty the cash box, and they walk, carrying heir precious cargoes all of five or six yards at a trip. On the other side of a door sit sixty-four women working at key punch machines, transferring the information on the executed order slips to holes on rectangular I.B.M. cards. The holes on the cards will signify the customer's account number, the name of the stock, the place where it was traded, the number of shares bought or sold and the price; and this is enough information to satisfy the I.B.M. machines. From this point on the customer is untouched by human brains.

First the cards are fed into one of the three electronic calculators, Model 604, for which Merrill Lynch pays I.B.M. a rental of six hundred dollars a month, each.* The electronic calculator is a black box so big that two tall, fat men could stand inside it. Its face is a glass panel behind which can be seen hundreds of tubes, blinking incomprehensibly on and off. When the card arrives here, it expresses only the number of shares, the price of each share and certain details of the sale. When it leaves here it expresses the net amount of money which the customer owes on a purchase or is to receive from a sale. In short, the machine calculates the total amount of money (multiplying the price by the number of shares), the commissions (by whatever formula applies), any taxes, postage or registration fee, and finally the net amount of the trade from the customer's point of view. Having calculated this, the machine pauses to consider, and goes over the whole business again to prove it was right. Four times the machine feels over the card, to figure and check figuration. Because it must go over the card four times, the machine can do only

---

* 1959: Two even more elaborate 705 calculators have been installed. Their rental is $81,616 a month, each.

twenty-five transactions a minute. This is too bad, but maybe I.B.M. can perfect it one of these days.

The punched-over card that finally emerges from the electronic calculator is the master posting card, and it will be used for lots of purposes. It will be copied (in a special machine), and another machine will print in English across the top the information in the holes. After all, there are still some dowdy, old-fashioned people who can't read I.B.M. cards by the holes. Another machine will arrange and collate the cards by security, office of origin, etc. A special keyless typewriter will transmogrify the cards into daily lists of securities traded, and monthly statements for customers. Before the monthly statement goes out, however, there must be the bill.

The master cards, arranged by office of origin, are now fed into what is probably the most incomprehensible of all machines. Nine of these squat monsters stand in the wire room itself, each digesting a pack of I.B.M. cards and punching new and mysterious holes in a long roll of colored tape that feeds out its rear end. The color of the tape is different for each machine, so a culprit can be isolated and repaired if it starts punching cockeyed data. When the machine finishes a batch of cards representing the trades from one office, the roll of tape is detached and carried to a teletype. It feeds through the innards of the teletype, which merrily clacks out its message, printing customers' bills on another teletype in the originating office. All the customer's local office need do is address the bill, slip it in an envelope, run it through the postage meter and mail it.

The operations of these mechanical genii, and their attending staff of eighty regular and twenty-five part-time employees, are supervised by Charles Duncan, a forceful, middle-aged former bookkeeper. The staff includes one technician and four supervisors familiar with all the operations affecting their individual units. "The rest," Duncan says, "are people we have trained ourselves, people with no particular technical background, though we like them to have a high-school education, it helps." As machines take over and bookkeepers become obsolete, the few surviving bookkeepers grow more and more important. "Somebody has to tell the machines what to do," Duncan says, "and the only person who can plan that out is an experienced bookkeeper, who knows the cashier's operation, the margin operation—all the things he doesn't have to do any more because of the machines.

"We expect," says Duncan, looking over the clicking,

crunching, clattering machines, listening to the Muzak that sounds from loudspeakers all around the room, "great improvements."

5

Every securities transaction breaks into three parts: buyer to buyer's broker, broker to broker, seller's broker to seller. The quick remarks on the floor are the center, and from that center flow activities in each of the three parts. The transaction will not end until the buyer's money has reached the seller, and the seller's stock has reached the buyer.

In the old days the market closed at three o'clock, and the brokerage firms collected all their slips into neat piles, each pile representing trades with one other brokerage house. Runners swarmed out of the offices with the slips, heading for the other offices to make "comparisons" and be sure that everybody had the same idea about what happened in every transaction on the floor. Buyer's broker and seller's broker would confirm the transaction anew in the late afternoon of the day, and arrange for a transfer of money and stock on the fourth succeeding business day. Then they would hustle to get their customers' money and securities into the office for delivery on that day. Since customers very often do not deliver by the fourth succeeding business day, it was necessary to borrow money from banks, and securities from other brokers, in order to "clear" the sale. The securities end of it was easy, since everybody had the same problem; on the money end, however, the clearing operation involved many millions of dollars in bank loans, which means many thousands of dollars of bank interest. Then, on settlement date for a market day with fifteen thousand transactions, it would be necessary for hundreds of runners to make thirty thousand deliveries of securities and cheques (certified checks, too).

By 1920 the labor of clearance had become unbearable, and the New York Stock Exchange formed the Stock Clearing Corporation. (The A.S.E. has its own clearing corporation.) Now a broker merely gets together I.B.M. cards on all his *sales* for the day and delivers the cards to the Stock Clearing Corporation. It takes one boy instead of hundreds. The Stock Clearing Corporation has its own I.B.M. cards and keyless typewriters, and from the brokers' "sell cards" they make up lists of what each firm bought and sold that day. Bright and early the next morning the lists are delivered to the brokers involved, and they check against their own records.

The okayed or adjusted lists are returned to the Stock Clearing Corporation, which feeds the cards back into the machines and comes up with a net balance for each broker in each stock. Merrill Lynch, for example, may have been involved in transactions of 3,500 shares of General Electric; but at the end of the day it may owe exactly 300 shares. Its customers bought 1,600 and sold 1,900, and the Clearing Corporation is interested only in the difference. There is also a net balance in money—with 2,800 transactions, Merrill Lynch may wind up owing $915 altogether. On the settlement date, instead of making 1,400 separate deliveries, and receiving 1,400 separate deliveries, Merrill Lynch need merely send over to or collect from the Clearing Corporation its net balance in each security, and its net debit or credit in money. One boy. The cost of the service is forty dollars a month, plus five cents a hundred shares on each buy or sell list, five cents a balance order and five cents a delivery envelope.

This service, however, merely solves the broker-to-broker part of the transaction; broker-to-customer remains. One part of it is taken care of by the bill or notice of sale, printed on the teletype by the mysterious tape. Then the money must be received or paid, the securities delivered or collected. This is relatively simple when the customer maintains a balance with his broker; Merrill Lynch merely informs him that he has a credit of so-and-so much. It is equally easy on the other side when the customer asks the broker to keep his securities for him, because the securities are right there and need merely be transferred. Often the securities are even in "Street name"—that is, the corporation has them on its books as owned by Merrill Lynch, and only Merrill Lynch and the customer know that the stock is merely being held for the customer's account. When securities are left in the account in "Street name" the broker guarantees their safety and takes care of all the bookkeeping involved in forwarding dividends, proxies, and such. It is something of a mystery on Wall Street why people ask for their stock certificates at all, since they really get nothing but the expense of buying a safe-deposit box in a bank.

Many people, however, want to see the color of their stock; and when they sell they want the cash. The stock certificates delivered to Merrill Lynch, from the Clearing Corporation or other customers, are still made out in the name of their previous holder, and they must be transferred to the new holder; Merrill Lynch sends a boy to the transfer agent, who tears up the old stock and issues new stock in the new name. Then the certificates are mailed to the customer. If the customer has sold stock and wants the proceeds, his broker on the fourth succeeding day will mail him a check for the amount. Meanwhile, the broker hopes and expects to receive certificates from sellers and cash from buyers in time to avert borrowing. A margin customer, in borrowing from his broker to buy stock, gives the broker the right to lend his stock at any time; so sometimes a broker can borrow painlessly from himself.

Several hundred people work at Merrill Lynch clearing sales. It is an immense and immensely costly job. But many people on Wall Street will say that the huge cash balances which customers leave with the firm provide a more than adequate reward.*

6†

There is a story about two men running into each other on Wall Street, and one of them says, "I hear they fired two people at Merrill Lynch yesterday."

"That so?" says the other one.

"Yop. But they had to take the men back. Turned out they were partners."

A partnership the size of Merrill Lynch has problems all its own. Corporations, for example, are chartered in a single state, and pay their corporate income tax in the home state only. A partnership, however, exists in every state in which it does business, and the partners must pay state income taxes everywhere that Merrill Lynch has an office.

Under the federal tax laws, moreover, a partnership cannot carry its profits over from one year to the next. Every-

---

* 1959: This point is worth stressing. Merrill Lynch has customers' credit balances of no less than $300 million, seven times the size of the firm's capitalization. Brokers have unrestricted use of this money, and pay no interest on it; the saving to Merrill Lynch is thus on the order of $10 million a year, at savings bank interest rates. The windfall profit represented by these figures is not only legal—it is required by law. Because bankers cannot be brokers, brokers cannot be bankers, and cannot accept customer "deposits"—just customer money. Carter Glass, who wrote the law in question, surely had no such intention, but 25 years of free use of customers' funds has given brokerage houses the feeling that they have a "right" to the privilege, and they would vigorously oppose any change in the law.

† 1959: This section is now completely out of date, because Merrill Lynch became a partnership as of January 12, 1959. It has been retained for historical interest.

thing except the capitalization must be distributed among the partners at the end of the business year. When Merrill Lynch opens its doors on January 2, therefore, the $145,000 cost of door-opening must be paid out of capital.

And a partnership is an agreement among living persons, existing at the pleasure of living persons. Every time a new partner is admitted, the whole partnership agreement must be redrawn and signed all over again by everybody. The proportions of ownership change, too, since there is only 100 per cent to be split. Charlie Merrill originally put up the biggest chunk of the capital (which is now over twenty million dollars), but over the years he has gradually reduced his partnership interest.*

He has done it in an interesting way. Partnership breaks up because people believe they are getting less than their just share; and perhaps the only way to establish just shares is to split up the profits in proportion to the partners' contributions to capital. As Merrill Lynch has increased in size many partners, who could not contribute to the firm's capital in proportion to their partnership interest, have been brought up from the ranks. At the firm's present size a partner with an interest of one-half of one per cent should have contributed $100,000 to the firm's capital. A new partner might be able to put up only a quarter of that amount; the rest would be supplied by the others—principally Merrill. Such a partner would be expected over the years to put up the other three-quarters out of his share of the annual profits, and ultimately he would own his piece of the partnership free of all obligation. The principle of contribution to capital would be kept inviolate, but the doors would stay open.

Until 1953, only individuals and partnerships could be member firms of the New York Stock Exchange. All partners in a brokerage firm were thereby responsible for all the firm's debts, and if a firm went bankrupt the partners were liable out of their own assets. Corporations, on the other hand, have no call on their stockholders' assets (except to pay back wages to employees); and a corporation may fail while its principal stockholder remains a wealthy man. Merrill crusaded to change the Stock Exchange rule, not to protect himself but to make Merrill Lynch a more manageable proposition. The solvency record of Stock Exchange member firms is

---

* It was Merrill's death, however, and the need to pay inheritance taxes on his estate, which finally forced the conversion from partnership to corporation. The Estate is one of the stockholders.

excellent, and the protection provided by a ban on corporate membership seemed to Merrill unnecessary.

In 1953 the other members agreed, and amended the constitution to allow member corporations. This amendment was proposed not for the benefit of Merrill Lynch (many members of the Stock Exchange would like to see Merrill Lynch and all connected with it sink to the bottom of the sea), but in the rather naive hope that the big over-the-counter dealers, most of which are corporations, would come do their business at the Exchange. None of these corporations has yet made a comment more positive than a horse laugh, however, and Merrill Lynch itself, to its deep regret, remains a partnership.

When the amendment passed, the firm got together with its lawyers and accountants, and found out that the excess profits tax, which penalized new corporations, would hit too heavily at Merrill Lynch & Co., Inc. Then the excess profits tax went off, and the lawyers, consulted again, produced an opinion that under the strictest letter of the law Merrill Lynch would need the signed permission of every customer to change its form of organization. The partners examined this opinion from a distance, looked at their long lists of customers and said, Uh-uh.*

7

The other 86 per cent of the business on the New York Stock Exchange is done by firms ranging in size from the likes of Bache & Co., nearly half as large as Merrill Lynch, down to one-man, one-girl, one-clerk offices. A large underwriting house like Goldman, Sachs may be a member firm, but the individual member works in the office, the customers never look in and all transactions are done by $2 brokers. Wertheim & Co., with two members and a capital of more than thirty million dollars, has a two-man order room calling in orders to one clerk on the floor, and the account cards of all active customers are kept in two little metal filing boxes on the head bookkeeper's desk. To these firms, which make their money elsewhere, the brokerage business is merely a sideline, a service to important customers.

There are still a few firms, however, who do a broker-

---

* 1959: When the heat went on, the lawyers modified their opinion and required merely formal notification of every customer.

age business alone, and one of the most highly respected of them is T. L. Watson & Co., successor to other partnerships more than a hundred years old. The office is approximately half a floor in a building on the southern fringe of the financial market, and all the work of the house is done in this small, efficient space. The service given is intensely personal, and practically all of the firm's income is in brokerage commissions.

The size of a brokerage house can be determined at sight by the extent of its teleregister board, a black wall with yellow numbers which revolve at the touch of a distant key to show the price of the most recent sale. The board is more useful than a mere ticker, because the seeker after knowledge does not have to thumb through yards of tape to find the stock he's after; he merely looks up at the board and sees. Western Union used to run the teleregister service, but sold out to the Ogden Corporation at the end of 1953; whoever runs it, however, the broker pays an installation fee and then a yearly rental based on the number of stocks shown on the board. At Merrill Lynch all stocks of reasonable activity are shown on a concave board occupying about one-quarter of the length of 70 Pine Street; at Watson & Co. a wall of medium-sized bull pen is devoted to a teleregister board which shows the market leaders, the Dow Jones averages and a few commodity prices.

Nine customers' men and five partners sit facing the board, telephones at the ready. When an order comes in they take it and call it back (by phone or by yell) to the four-man order department behind a glass partition at the back of the room. The order department calls it to the floor, where the firm's member executes it (floor brokers are used only when absolutely necessary). The clerical work is done on adding machines rather than I.B.M. machines, and the bills are typed by hand. There are three outside offices, one in New York City, one in Bridgeport, Connecticut, and one in Perth Amboy, New Jersey.

Merrill Lynch is organized to give service to the man who knows more or less what he wants. Though the hundred researchers will recommend portfolios, they do so only on request; and they do it by asking a few crucial questions and pigeon-holing the customer's needs into one of a few general categories. The main service of the research department is the preparation of reports which will be evaluated by the customer himself, not by his customer's man. Customers are advised to submit their portfolios for periodic examination, because securities can go sour as quickly as cream and because a brokerage house makes its living by having its customers sell and buy securities. If the customer does not submit his portfolio for correction or approval, however, Merrill Lynch will not bother him. He had the sense to make the money; he ought to have the sense to invest it properly.

At Watson all is different. A new customer's needs and desires are very carefully investigated, and a custom-made portfolio is drawn up for him. His customer's man will then keep an eye on that portfolio, with the help of the four-man research department which sits across another glass partition from the center room. If the research department, or the movement of the numbers on the teleregister board, or some news development over the Dow Jones ticker seems to dictate a change in one of the customer's investments, Watson's man gets on the telephone and calls the customer. "Chrysler just sold Dodge back to Greg Sherwood," he'll say, "at cost. Better get out while the going's good. You want to keep motors in your portfolio, so I think your best bet right now is a switch to Studebaker." The customer says, "Okay, anything you say, Ethelbert," and the customer's man makes the switch for him.

There is an obvious danger in this system, since it has proved only too easy to switch customers around aimlessly, earning a sell commission and a buy commission each time. A firm such as T. L. Watson, however, has been in business a little too long for that; and its partners are a little too close to the situation to have such thievery by a customer's man go unnoticed or unpunished. Frost Haviland, a dignified, white-haired gentleman who handles special accounts and sits in the partners' room behind still another glass partition, is proud of the profit record Watson has made on switches for its customers. Still, keeping an eye on the customers' investment means a considerable expense of time and energy for each customer, and the job cannot be done for everybody with five thousand dollars who walks in through the door.

Nearly all of Watson's income comes through this brokerage operation, and Watson was therefore vitally interested in the campaign to increase commissions. The war was won because firms like Watson are the last bastion of the Stock Exchange. Confronted with a block of bonds or exempt preferreds, Watson will send the order down to the floor and consult with the specialist and the floor traders until some arrangements are made to execute it; other firms will take the easier and simpler course of calling up some institutional customer and selling the stuff over the telephone. Without income from underwriting, or important profits from speculation for its own account, Watson literally needed the money it got from increased commissions.

There is a principle behind all this. "I think it's wrong," Haviland says, "for a man to be both a broker and a dealer. Supposing he's underwritten some Rio Grande and Western bonds, and he's still got them on his shelf. A customer walks in and says he's heard good things about Denver and Rio Grande bonds, and he'd like to buy a dozen. Is that broker going to sell his customer Denver and Rio Grande—or is he going to sell the man the Rio Grande and Western bonds he owns, on which he makes a clear profit? You know as well as I do what he's going to do, and I say it isn't cricket."

Mr. Haviland does not stand alone in this position; a special committee of the S.E.C., headed by James M. Landis, reported to the same effect in 1936. Essentially, however, the peril is greatest not with the firm that underwrites securities, but with the firm that speculates in the market for its own account. "We all lay eggs in one security or another," Ira Haupt says, "without a capital gains profit we couldn't exist." Watson, however, lays no eggs; and by this avoidance of speculative positions it also avoids the horrible temptations that come to any firm with customers to advise and in private stake in higher prices for certain securities. Even the most honest and upright of brokers must believe that a security he owns is going up; and he cannot entirely eliminate from his counsel to his customers the evil thought that the more people who buy the stock, the more it will go up. Merrill Lynch rids itself of this demon to a great extent by publicizing its holdings, so its customers are forewarned of the broker's self-interest. Watson eliminates the demon entirely by staying out of the market.

Nevertheless, Watson studies the securities which it recommends to its customers just as carefully as a firm like Wertheim, which devotes most of its energies and capital to investing for its own account. Watson even considers the personalities of the management, and passes the information along to its customers.

"I trade in the securities of two small steel companies," says Henry Bruns, who is in charge of Watson's miniscule over-the-counter department, "and I go to their annual meetings every year, and when the meeting is over I go up to the president of the company, and I say, 'How much money are you going to make this year?' Now, the president of one company is a Scotsman; he scratches his head and says, 'Henry, you shouldn't ask no such a question like thut,' and then he says, 'If all goes well, I suppose we'll earn a mickle less than a million dollars.' The president of the other company is an Irishman, and when I ask him the same question, he says, 'Sure, and we'll make a million dollars, anyway.' At the end of the year, the Scotman's company shows a profit of a million and a half, and the Irishman's company shows a profit of half a million. It happens all the time. You've got to know things like that."

You do, indeed.

8

And then there are two firms which do not use the Stock Clearing Corporation but do all their own clearances; which operate on fees less than one-third as large as the ordinary brokerage commissions; and which handle between them close to twice the volume handled by Merrill Lynch, Pierce, Fenner & Beane. They are Carlisle & Jacquelin and De Coppet & Doremus, the odd-lot dealers who execute the small orders; and their operations are a symphony in efficiency.

They are not brokers at all, and they have no immediate dealings with the public. The two firms have about twenty partners, and between them they employ about eighty members of the New York Stock Exchange. At least one partner or employee of Carlisle & Jacquelin is stationed at each of the eighteen posts (De Coppet & Doremus covers only seventeen), and the firm stands prepared at all times to buy from or sell to a broker's odd-lot customers. On prices below forty dollars a share, the fee will be 12½ cents a share; on prices forty dollars or higher, the fee will be 25 cents. The odd-lot firms make nearly all their money from these pieces of eighths and quarters; they carry light inventories (averaging less than thirty shares in each stock—though the total value of the inventory, because of the number of different stock issues, may run as high as $1,500,000) and do not try to make profits on inventory appreciation. The price to the customer is always the odd-lot fee above or below the next succeeding sale price, so that the profit is a pure and immediate eighth or quarter only when the odd-lot dealer himself is buying or selling the next round lot. Otherwise he is dependent on the motion of the market, which can easily wipe out his tiny profit before he replaces his stock or sells his acquisition. What makes the business possible at such a low fee is that purchases and sales partly balance, giving the dealer a quarter or a half for bringing the buyer and seller together and transferring the stock; and where they do not balance the odd-lot public is usually trading against the trend of the market, which means that the odd-lot house can often pick up another eighth or quarter in the purchases or sales which keep its inventory steady.

Even so, it is a tight squeeze, especially tight because of the really incredible amount of pure public service done by the two odd-lot houses. Odd-lot orders are sent from the brokers' floor clerks to the proper post by pneumatic tube, and time-stamped by a Stock Exchange employee when they come out of the tube. They are then supposed to be executed at the price of the next round-lot sale (plus or minus fee); and the odd-lot houses feel that they must be able to prove to complaining brokers with complaining customers that the order *was* executed at the next price. For this purpose there are eighteen deleter tickers in a big barn of a room at Carlisle & Jacquelin, each ticker printing the sales at only one of the eighteen posts. The ticker tape is automatically time-stamped every minute, and the clerks sitting beside the deleter ticker keep exact ledgers with records of the time and price of every sale. If a customer complains, Carlisle can prove him right or wrong; moreover, if one of the dealers on the floor thinks he may have missed something, he can check the facts with the ticker clerk immediately, protecting himself from the wrath of broker or boss.

These records of all sales are useful to the brokers in another way, because every broker has a certain number of limit orders or stop orders in the hands of specialists or floor brokers. If the price of the stock reached a point where these orders should have become effective, the broker wants to know about it. He gets nothing but bad cess by asking a specialist such a question (since the specialist is guilty of lazy misfeasance or worse if the answer to the question is yes), and it would take him hours to thumb through the day's ticker and catch all the prices. A simple high or low will not do, because the order merely becomes effective on a certain price, and need not be executed unless another sale occurs at that price. Carlisle & Jacquelin or De Coppet & Doremus will answer more than 1,500 such questions from Merrill Lynch alone during the fifteen minutes after the close of the market; the total of such queries runs into tens of thousands every day. The two firms are in competition with each other, but the competition is friendly, and most brokerage houses divide their odd-lot business fifty-fifty. Merrill Lynch works two months with Carlisle, then two months with De Coppet, and back again.

The executive offices of Carlisle are in the huge Equitable Building, decorated in the spacious, quality-goods tradition of the Stock Exchange itself, with lots of conference rooms, broadloom carpeting, Georgian furniture and heavy drapes on the windows. In the little entrance hall, across from the receptionist's peephole, stands a corner of the Old Stock Exchange Post 16, where senior partner Charles Samson worked as a specialist from 1908 until the horseshoe posts were installed in (oh!) 1929. Across the hall in one direction is the big room with the big teleregister board and the deleter tickers, and spaces for the long metal racks in which are kept the slips (SOLD TO or BOT OF Carlisle & Jacquelin) which are the primary record of the day's dealings. When the slips are a few days old, and no complaints have been uttered, they will be transferred to a Brooklyn warehouse containing millions of slips just like them.

Across the hall in another direction is the Carlisle I.B.M. room, where the information on the slips is transferred to cards, tabulated, calculated, refenestrated and printed. Finally, there is a stock library, metal library stacks marching in dozens of rows, containing thousands of pigeonholes in which stock certificates are kept in different denominations, just as though they were one-, five-, ten-, twenty- and fifty-dollar bills. Any clearance operation is complicated; the odd-lot clearance operation is horribly so, because of the need to break down and build up hundred-share certificates. Carlisle will make more than three thousand deliveries of money and securities every day, and before those deliveries can be made somebody has to go to a corporation's transfer agent and get a stock certificate in the proper size. If Carlisle wishes to hold down its inventory by selling out what it has purchased from its odd-lot customers, it must carry the little certificates to the transfer agent and get one big one for a round lot. There is a fee for this transfer service; but Carlisle absorbs the fee as part of the cost of business, which also includes salaries to four hundred employees.

Another cost of business arises from this clearing procedure and the fact that customers never get their money and securities in on time. On an average day Carlisle will require seven to eight million dollars of bank credit to carry its clearances; which means interest payments estimated at nearly $225,000 every year. That sum is equal to the odd-lot fee on 1,800,000 shares of stock costing less than forty dollars each; luckily, Carlisle's volume even in weak years runs better than 60,000,000.

Chapter 8

Over the Counter

THIS happened nearly thirty years ago, but the memory of it still burns bright, and the names of the people involved could be printed only at the risk of multiple murder. It is a Real Life Story, however, and it illustrates an important point.

Once upon a time, in the expanding days of the middle twenties, a young investment banker got married, and his bride purchased an eight-thousand-dollar dining-room set. They lived with this sample of furniture for three months, and then decided that they didn't like it, they wouldn't have it in the house, they wanted to sell it. And a few days later, in the course of business, the banker was on the telephone with an over-the-counter dealer. After they had concluded their transaction, he said, "By the way, d'you know of anybody in the market for a fancy dining-room set?"

"Nah," said the dealer. "Market's dead on that stuff. What've you got?"

"You know—the usual thing, Spanish. We paid eight thousand dollars for it."

"How much," said the dealer, "are you asking?"

"Well, I'm willing to take a big loss. I figure I'll get three thousand for it."

"Never," said the dealer, "come near that. My mother sold her dining-room set just a while ago, and she barely got one-sixth what she paid for it. That was a new set, too."

"No kidding?" said the banker.

"Absolutely," said the dealer, "You'll be lucky to get fifteen hundred."

"I'll junk it first," said the banker, considerably disturbed. "The very least I'd sell for is two thousand."

There was a moment's silence. "Don't see how you can hope for that," the dealer said finally. "The best you'll see for it, I'm sure, is eighteen hundred."

"I might take eighteen hundred," said the banker conversationally.

"Good," said the dealer, with the air of a man closing a deal. "I'll send my mother up to look at it tomorrow."

Glancing back over the years, the banker is still unable to work up an ounce of resentment about this conversation, and at the time he delivered his furniture without a quiver. "That man," says the banker affectionately, "that man is a born trader."

2

The over-the-counter market in securities is larger in every way than all the exchanges put together. The best buys are nearly always over the counter, because that is where developing corporations are traded; the safest securities are over the counter, because that is where all bonds and nearly all bank and insurance stocks are traded; and the very worst buys are over the counter, because unlisted trading is a little less honest than listed trading and because nearly all the companies with public stock issues that will become worthless next year are traded over the counter.

There are 4,700 over-the-counter dealers registered with the Securities and Exchange Commission, and the pure type is a small-town factotum who handles the securities of local companies in which there is a local interest and a local pride. The dealer owns or owes a few shares himself, and knows where he can get more when he needs it. He makes a profit on his trading, but if trading is slack he will find some other use for his money. He is the solvent of the local money market: an investor and a speculator, a lender and a borrower, an investment adviser, and an underwriter.

This pure type is very rare in New York, though Wall Street has a third of all the over-the-counter houses. About as close as these houses ever approach to the type is Joseph J. Lann Securities, Inc., which employs a trader of aristocratic mien, two telephone girls and Joe Lann himself. It is a three-room office, with the best view on to a court, and the aim is to keep business as simple as possible. But there are lots of different businesses.

As an over-the-counter dealer Lann will purchase from or sell to his customers any security available anywhere in the world; instead of charging a brokerage commission, he buys the security from another dealer, and adds a sales mark-up, just as though he were running a dry-goods store. Then he will act as an investment adviser to individuals, trustees or corporations, and manage their accounts if they wish. When he has customers for the issue, he will participate in an underwriting, or find money for a corporation that needs it, accepting a finder's fee in return. When business is slow, he will "specialize in my own investments."

Whatever Lann is doing, his telephone never shuts its ugly yap. Lann sits at a truly noble maple desk with rounded edges, placed squarely before a bay window; at one hand is the telephone, and at the other The Sheets, a thick book issued every day and giving the wholesale prices (dealer to dealer) on every security traded over the counter. Standing against one wall is a tall metal box on wheels, with glasses up top and liquor inside. Lann himself is a large, strong, heavy man with dark grey hair and a large grey moustache, wearing a wide pin-stripe suit and a glittering gold-and-diamond ring on his left pinky. He has many talents; he was champion of his golf club in 1953, and it is legendary in the market that only idiots play pool with him for money.

He lives by applying his wits constantly to a capital of $125,000. He makes a primary market in Graham Paige bonds—that is, he owns an inventory of the bonds and stands ready to buy them or sell them at any time. Then he makes use of a special talent, his fluent Spanish, to work in such matters as Philippine Railway Bonds. He receives an advance tip from Manila that these bonds will be called in at a price higher than the present market, and stocks up on them; then he receives another tip to the effect that a certain proportion of the bonds were destroyed by a Japanese bombing raid at the beginning of the war, and that the money appropriated to buy in these bonds will be distributed in three years to the bondholders claiming redemption. So he offers a price somewhat higher than the redemption price, and keeps the bonds alive for trading purposes.

He always has his eye out for new corporations, or special situations in which people might like to trade. He may hear, for example, about a proposed bank merger in Maine. He will get hold of the balance sheets, look them over, and decide whether or not the proposition is interesting. If it is, he will call Maine, talk to the presidents of the banks, to any local dealer and possibly to a few of the larger stockholders. He will buy a few shares of one bank or both, make sure he can get more, and then put an announcement in The Sheets, to the effect that he maintains an interest in these shares, will buy at a certain price or sell at another, higher price. He has made a market, and now a man who owns shares in these banks can sell his shares just as surely as if they were traded on the New York Stock Exchange—and usually gets a price which represents just as clearly public feelings about the value of the stock. If Lann is lucky, people all over the country may get interested in the banks and start trading; Lann will buy a thousand shares at, say, 29, and sell them at 31, and make himself two thousand dollars, less expenses. Any such interest, of course, will bring other over-the-counter houses into the stock, to set up rival markets—"to draw flies," Lann says somewhat irritably. "There are so many leeches around here."

Lann was graduated from the High School of Commerce in New York City, and got a job with a shipping firm that did most of its business in Latin America. In 1918, two years after graduation, he moved over to the securities business, opening a foreign department for an over-the-counter house. He worked mostly in foreign currencies, which were fluctuating at a great rate in those days, then moved into foreign securities, and then into domestic securities. "My experience," he says seriously, leaning back in his swivel chair and touching an end of his luxuriant moustache, "covers every phase of the financial market." So it does; he is the ideally equipped trader.

3

While Lann is making the market in Graham Paige bonds and occasional other securities, the fourteen traders who work for Troster, Singer & Co., are vigorously making markets in some 550 common and preferred stocks. Lann has individual customers and a dozen sidelines; Troster is exclusively a wholesale house, doing business with other dealers the way a Stock Exchange specialist does business with brokers. The telephone bill runs between eleven and twelve thousand dollars a month; eighteen leased wires feed into the shabby (but air-conditioned) trading room; and literature about Troster's securities goes out at regular intervals to nearly three thousand dealers throughout the country. There are 117 employees all told; and 57 of them are needed to do the dull, nasty, necessary job of clearing.*

Colonel Oliver Troster (he was called back to service during the Korean War) started in 1919 with the firm he now heads, working at the office end of a wire to the Curb Exchange. In 1926 the firm abandoned its brokerage business and went exclusively over the counter. Troster still does some

---

* 1959: The expansion of these figures since 1954 is on the order of Merrill Lynch. Five years ago, Troster had only 47 employees, eight leased wires to correspondent firms, two thousand dealers on the mailing list.

of his over-the-counter trading on a brokerage basis, in order to avoid transfer taxes (if a customer buys a security through a broker there is one sale, and one transfer tax; if a dealer buys it from another dealer and sells it to a customer, there are two sales and two transfer taxes). But the vast bulk of his business is the fast turnover of his own positions, buying all day and selling all day.

When a customer calls an over-the-counter firm he does not say, "What are you charging for Cinerama?" or "What will you give me for Cinerama?" He says, "What's the market on Cinerama?" The dealer does not know (in theory, anyway; sometimes he can guess) whether the customer wishes to buy or sell, so he gives both sides of the spread—"One and a half," he says, "three-quarters." Then the customer says, "I have five hundred at 1½"; or "I'll take five hundred at 1¾"; or "Will you give me 1⅝ for five hundred shares?" If the customer is out-of-state, the dealer will try to make sure that the customer, not the dealer, utters the fatal words "I'll take it" or "Sold" because New York State alone has a state transfer tax. If the "situs" of the sale can be established in Connecticut, no state transfer tax need be paid; if the "situs" is New York, on comes the tax. And the "situs" is established by the location of the man who speaks the key words. No dealer has ever been known to admit that he was the first to say "Sold" in such a situation, and for this reason some prominent dealers have suggested that the motto of New York State be changed to read, "Be good, and let who will be clever."

The price quoted by the trader applies only to a certain number of shares. In a low-priced stock like Cinerama it might be five hundred; in a high-priced stock like Weyerhauser Timber it might be one hundred. If the customer wishes to buy or sell more than the dealer's "size," he may have to take a poorer price. Ordinarily the dealer adds to his inventory or sells from it; but Troster does not like to carry heavy inventories or go substantially short in a stock. The acceptance of a large order, therefore, would mean that he has to get on the telephone himself, and find buyers to take the top off his top-heavy inventory, or sellers to rescue him from his short position. This added work is one reason for the customer's poorer price; the other reason is that large orders move prices, on an exchange or over the counter. It would seem on first glance that the over-the-counter customer might be able to sell to one dealer at that dealer's exact "size," then call another dealer in the same stock and peddle the rest of his holding. This can be done, sometimes, if the respective dealers are personal enemies; if they are friends or neighbors, one will call the other and say, "Watch out for Harry; he's got a thousand Weyerhauser."

Troster's fourteen traders sit at opposite sides of a long table which is also an elaborate switchboard. At the sides of the room are the seven teletypes, which feed in orders and requests for information. The traders themselves get work from their telephones and from the man at the teletype, who yells at them the contents of the messages that are being batted out. At the front end of the room is Troster's desk (privacy is very hard to come by at Troster, Singer & Co.), and at the back is a blackboard with the quotes on key stocks. It is even more informal than the Stock Exchange floor.

"Hey!" the man at the teletype will yell. "Nature boy! What are you making on Dumont?"

"Seventeen one-eighth, nineteen one-eighth!"

"He wants three hundred."

"Okay!"

It is very noisy.

"Hey! Nature boy! Now he wants to know if you got any more."

"Not at that price."

"Okay, nature boy. I tell 'im!"

The fourteen traders are not all equal in experience, or in ability, or in the amount of money Troster gives them to play with. Troster sets a figure for each man—it ranges from $15,000 for the youngest and least-experienced to $250,000 for the most professional—and no trader may wind up the day holding more than the allowance, either long or short. If a large block is offered at an advantageous price, the trader may report it to Troster, who will decide whether or not to suspend the rules and let the trader buy it. Otherwise the trader is completely on his own, choosing by himself the stocks in which he wants to make a market, dropping from his list stocks that no longer seem to generate much interest, adding stocks that look promising. Troster checks this end of the traders' work only to make sure that a man doesn't try to deal in more stock than he can efficiently manage.

This one dank room in an office building handles a fourth as many stock issues as are traded on the floor of the New York Stock Exchange, and does one-fiftieth the share volume (much less, of course, in money volume, since many of the

stocks are very cheap). Because of the breadth of the operation, the telephone calls and the teletype messages come in
from all over the country. "There aren't many houses in this
country," Troster says proudly, "with whom we don't do
some business over the course of a week, a month or a year."

4

The size and the scope of Troster's business, and of the
over-the-counter market in general, are made possible by The
Sheets, a mimeographed book of 175 yellow and pink pages
(yellow for bonds, pink for stocks) issued five days a week
by the National Quotations Bureau, Inc. The book goes to
more than 2,100 over-the-counter firms everywhere in the
United States, giving the prices at which some 1,800 dealers
were buying or selling some 8,000 securities at two o'clock
yesterday afternoon. Since the prices do not vary enormously
from one day to the next, a dealer who has never even heard
of a stock can give a customer who is interested in the stock
a roughly accurate idea of its price, simply by looking in The
Sheets. Everything considered, the manufacture of The Sheets
is perhaps the most amazing operation in the financial market
—at any rate, that was the opinion of a group of visiting
Japanese dignitaries. They climbed to the visitors' gallery at
the Stock Exchange and stared politely at the brokers on the
floor; they looked into the Chase National Bank and smiled
at the people they met; they investigated an underwriting
house and remained impassive. Then they were taken around
the old Front Street buildings which house the National
Quotations Bureau, and shown twenty-five men hand-feeding
twenty-five mimeograph machines at the rate of three hundred
pages a minute. Five every second. There arose a cross-
current of Japanese, and then the group turned to Louis
Walker, president and majority stockholder of the N.Q.B.
"*Oo*nique," said the spokesman. "*Oo*nique. There iss nothing
like it anywhere."

Louis Walker is a tall and very erect gentleman in a
cream-colored cotton jacket, somewhere in his high sixties
but much younger in appearance. After brief jobs with an
upstate dairy and a New York bank, he went to work as a
runner for Arthur Elliot's monthly reporting service in 1907.
"There were five of us in those days," Walker recalls. In 1911
Elliott started a daily service in over-the-counter quotations,
and in 1913 the National Quotations Bureau was incorporated.
Today there are three hundred employees.

The Sheets are strictly for the trade; they give the prices that a wholesaler such as Troster charged other dealers, not the prices that the dealers charged their customers. The public may not subscribe, and the wholesale prices that are printed may not be quoted to the public. Walker polices his subscription list very carefully, demanding that all subscribers be dealers registered with the S.E.C., and that all full subscribers show $5,000 in net worth if they are partnerships or individuals, $25,000 if they are incorporated. Every subscriber to The Sheets must give Walker a fairly detailed account of his business and financial position, and this account will be relayed to any dealer who asks for it. In addition, Walker will cut off a subscriber's Sheets if he finds that they are being used improperly.

A subscription to the Eastern and Western editions of The Sheets costs $280 a year; the Pacific Coast edition costs another $66 (Pacific Coast subscribers, however, get all three for $200). This payment simply entitles a subscriber to receive The Sheets; if he wants to list his own bids and offers, he pays $456 for the "full service." He then has the right to put in bids and offers on ten securities every day; he can list in any ten, and change all ten from one day to the next. If he wants to list more than ten, he must pay more. Additional listings are sold in units of five, at a price of $186 per year; Troster pays Walker more than $20,000 a year for his Sheets and his listings.

The Sheets are prepared separately in New York, Chicago and San Francisco, and every morning messengers from the N.Q.B. call on 600 New York firms, 140 Chicago firms and 40 San Francisco firms to pick up their listings. Most out-of-town houses mail in their listings the night before, each security on a separate "ticket," and then bring them up to the minute by telephone or on one of Walker's six teletypes. It would be relatively simple to make stencils and mimeograph these lists of quotes, showing what securities every dealer is interested in. The idea of The Sheets, however, is to be useful, and a list of quotes by dealers would not be particularly useful to anybody. Teams of highly trained clerks rapidly rearrange the tickets according to the security quoted, so that all quotes on Dumont preferred, for example, appear together under the heading Dumont. Stocks are listed in the book by alphabetical order, so all a dealer needs to do is turn to DU and read. Different houses often give different bids and offers on the same security; the dealer merely picks out the house that seems most likely to provide the best price, and dials his telephone.

No quotation is simply reprinted from day to day; if a dealer does not specifically request its continuation, his listing in a security will be dropped. And after he has listed, the dealer has the right to change his quote at any time up to two o'clock in the afternoon (one o'clock for the green-and white Chicago edition). The actual job of producing The Sheets, therefore, cannot start until two o'clock; and it must be finished by five-fifteen, when the trucks leave for La-Guardia Field to load the books on to airplanes. At two o'clock sharp the tickets are passed out to the typists in batches of 125, and stencils start rolling to the mimeograph machines. The men at the machines make 2,500 copies of each page, then boys set the pages into cubbyholes on a wall full of shelves which slope down towards a table; in the collating process the boys need merely run their hands down the shelves to pick up a sixteen-page section in the proper order. The book is stapled and baled and loaded on to trucks; and thank God this day's work is done. Most subscribers to The Sheets will have their copies, complete with Walker's index of over-the-counter stocks (comparable to the Dow Jones Index of listed securities), before nine o'clock the following morning.

On the top floor of the N.Q.B.'s five-story loft building is a neat and spacious library. Sunshine floods in from an old-fashioned skylight on to shelves holding back copies of The Sheets, filing cabinets stacked with the prospectus of the original issue of every security traded over the counter. These files are among the best in New York. "Some of the largest underwriters on the Street," Walker says, "will send a man here to look over the prospectus on an issue. They brought out the issue themselves, mind you—but they've lost all their copies."

Besides the library and Walker's office, the fifth floor holds the glassed-in cubicles in which skilled clerks rearrange and check the tickets from the dealers. On the fourth floor are the typists and the small staff which gathers *retail* quotations on some eight hundred over-the-counter securities. These quotes are passed on to the National Association of Securities Dealers (which pays for them), and then distributed to six newspapers, the Associated Press and the United Press; and it is these prices that are published in financial sections. The third floor is devoted to production, mimeographing and collating, stapling and baling. On the second floor Walker stores six months' stock of paper, partly to protect himself against strikes or shortages, partly because paper must be aged at least two months or else the pages will stick and refuse to be fed into a mimeograph machine at the rate of three hundred a minute.

The N.Q.B. puts out a *Monthly Stock Digest* as well as a daily service. The monthly is a thick, bound, printed book which gives quotes on more than fifteen thousand stocks. On active issues the book supplies the price range during the past month, and then yearly back to 1939; on inactive issues it shows the dealer and date of the most recent available quote. Once listed, a stock will be carried in the pages of the *Monthly Stock Digest* for a full five years after the last quote on it was submitted, and the N.Q.B. will check the old books for a customer to see if a certain stock has ever been quoted. In addition, the book gives dividend information, details on reorganizations or mergers involving the stock, the names of dealers or banks who will take in obsolete stock and issue current certificates. Anybody can subscribe to the *Monthly Stock Digest,* for eighty-four dollars a year, and any dealer can send in twenty-five listings a month for free.

"The prices in the daily service," Walker says doggedly, "represent the prices at which the public did business yesterday, just like the summary of trades on an Exchange. You can call them wholesale quotes, but they're actually what customers were charged." This statement is quite true, usually, because dealers spread their real market (lower their real bid and raise their real offer) when submitting quotes. At first sight it would seem that they thereby run the risk of having a competitor "make a market within their market"—that is, quote both a higher bid and a lower offer. As a matter of fact, however, this spreading of quotes is a necessary protection. It guards against overnight fluctuations that might take the prices well out of line with a printed quote, and it also leaves room for haggling. Dealers love to haggle.

If the wholesale prices in The Sheets represent the real prices at which securities were sold to customers, what is represented by the retail prices Walker's staff gathers and gives to the N.A.S.D.?

"Nothing more than rough guidance," says Don Regan, head of the Merrill Lynch over-the-counter department. "The problem with this market is, the prices in the paper aren't precise. The papers print them with a warning." And even the prices in the paper cover at most only eight hundred of the seven thousand securities listed in The Sheets. The Sheets are private, not available to customers; the prices available to customers are expanded to protect the marginal dealer, or are non-existent. Even this is a great advance over the old days, when the published prices, gathered unofficially from favored dealers, meant nothing whatever. It took the N.A.S.D. five years to set up the present system, and it was five years of hard work. Nevertheless, there still exists a considerable opportunity to gyp the customer, and it is an opportunity of which dealers have been known to avail themselves. This is a nice way to put it; actually, there have been some really shocking cases of robbery in the over-the-counter market.

The most obvious are instances of outrageous mark-ups: a dealer buys a stock for six dollars from a wholesaler, and sells it to his customer for twenty dollars. The S.E.C. has rules against this sort of thing, and other, more practical prohibitions are enforced by the National Association of Securities Dealers, which has also set up an "interpretation" to the effect that a dealer should not charge a customer more than 5 per cent over the price he gets from the wholesaler. It is not a "rule," it is an interpretation, and not always easy to enforce. Still, the majority of dealers accept the interpretation as a fair one and try to stick by it—and those who don't, of course, always run the risk that the customer will check another house and find out he's being rooked.

A different opportunity for thievery arises at those firms which, as a matter of policy or low capital, do their over-the-counter business on a brokerage basis. Instead of buying from a wholesaler and adding a retail mark-up, they buy for the customer's account and charge him a service fee. Under these circumstances the boss has little interest in what his man at the telephone pays for a security, and need not hire a skilled or expensive man to handle the orders. A low-paid employee, executing over-the-counter orders on the telephone, may be subjected to some very considerable temptations. He has a choice of half a dozen or a dozen wholesalers in most of the active issues, and the customer may have no way of knowing what the price for the stuff really is. So a wholesaler can make an arrangement with the employee: "Tell you what—I'll give you a quarter a share on every order you send my way." Whenever an order comes in for a stock traded by this wholesaler, the employee channels it his way. For his part, the wholesaler adds a quarter on to the price he charges;

and the customer pays an extra quarter a share into the pockets of the employee. A quarter a share is twenty-five dollars on one hundred shares, and the average order-executing employee doesn't make more than ninety dollars or so a week.

This problem is not, of course, confined to the over-the-counter market; it exists to some extent on the floor of the New York Stock Exchange, where an ill-paid order clerk may have the power to assign orders to any one of fifteen or twenty $2 brokers, and may reasonably expect a favored floor broker to be properly appreciative. Kickbacks are not unknown in the business world at large, either; but they are a peculiarly direct charge on the customer, and therefore peculiarly nasty, in the over-the-counter market.

And they do crop up; one of them cropped up, in fact, at Merrill Lynch, Pierce, Fenner & Beane. It was cleaned out, and shortly thereafter Don Regan, a handsome Bostonian in his middle thirties, was installed as boss of the over-the-counter department. At the beginning of 1954, in recognition of his work, Merrill Lynch made him a partner, the youngest the firm has ever had.

Although Merrill Lynch makes a primary market in 107 common and preferred stocks, most of its vast over-the-counter business is retail, sent in by the salesmen in the 126 offices. The trading room is on the fourth floor, directly above the wire room, and orders speed up on a special vertical conveyor belt which runs through a hole in the floor. They are examined on arrival, then slapped on a horizontal conveyor belt for delivery to the appropriate telephone. A dozen of the men beside the conveyor belt are traders who can take positions just as Troster's traders take positions; the other two dozen are merely clerks who execute orders on a brokerage basis. Down at one end of the long room are eight men trading in municipal bonds and three government bond traders—all under Regan's direction. Regan's traders are backed by twenty or so subsidiary traders in the branch offices. The prices Regan's traders are quoting go out on the internal Merrill Lynch news wire to all offices, and the local traders are empowered to buy or sell one hundred shares of anything on these prices; if more than one hundred shares are involved, the local man must check back with New York before accepting the order. The volume is enormous.

Regan uses the ever-faithful, incorruptible I.B.M. machines as cops to check prices and executions. All sales slips go to the I.B.M. room, turn into punch cards and finally reappear upstairs in the shape of a neat, complete list of the day's transactions—the price paid or got, the time at which and the wholesaler with whom each transaction was made. Regan sits with The Sheets at one hand and his list at the other. If a customer complains, he calls other dealers in the security and finds out what prices they were quoting at the time the disputed order was filed. Every trader at Merrill Lynch is under instruction to check three markets before making a deal for a customer, and must write the responses on a file card, which is filed. Every week Regan browses through the files to make sure the boys are checking, and with whom. Just routine.

"I'm one of the new school," Regan says with a grin. "I come out of sales and selling." In 1954 his department set new weekly records in volume and profit every week.*

5

In some firms, over-the-counter trading started as an adjunct to underwriting, and then just grew. Of the five giants—Merrill Lynch; Wheaton; Goldman, Sachs; Blyth and First Boston—the last three are primarily underwriters. They do everything else, too, except exchange brokerage (Goldman even does that); but the top executive officers work in underwriting, and the trading department is there only to make money. "We're interested in money," says Edward Ladd, who runs the First Boston trading department. "Some of the houses are always trying to do a big volume. We figure that you make a profit, too, and that's what counts."

Two hundred leased wires run from the First Boston trading room to dealers and banks in New York City alone, and other wires run to the firm's branch offices in Boston, Chicago, Pittsburgh, Cleveland, Philadelphia and San Francisco. The executive offices and the center of all operations are in New York; the firm is named First Boston because it is basically a successor to the sales and trading department of the First National Bank of Boston. In 1933 the Glass-Steagle Act kicked the banks out of the securities business, and the old Chase National Bank buying division joined

---

* 1959: Merrill Lynch does not publish statistics on its over-the-counter operation, because it is primarily a Stock-Exchange house. It is generally believed, however, that the firm's over-the-counter volume has more than doubled since 1954, and may amount to as much as ten per cent of the Merrill Lynch brokerage business.

First of Boston to set up the new corporation. Old-timers on the Street still call the new firm "First of Boston."

Trading at First Boston is broken up into manageable pieces: the corporate sales department, the municipal bond department and the government bond department sit in different sections. Nearly the whole tenth floor of 100 Broadway,* a block from Wall Street, is one wide open space, split into departments by fences and gates and pieces of walls, and the trading room is therefore far less noisy than smaller departments in smaller places. Moreover, there is a carpet on the floor.

A high switchboard with tables attached on both sides runs parallel to the north wall of the room, and twenty-two men sit at the tables on high swivel chairs bolted to the floor like stools at a lunch counter. A Stock Exchange ticker feeds slowly along the top of the switchboard, and a Dow Jones news ticker rattles at one side. By the windows, behind the switchboard, are teletype girls sending out TWX's to the branch offices and to out-of-town customers. Beyond the switchboard to the east is the syndicate department of the underwriting business; beyond it to the west is a huge blackboard giving prices on government bonds, and four traders sitting at ordinary desks, studying the blackboard. Over in another corner is the municipal trading department, with its own little switchboard and four places to sit down.

First Boston will list in The Sheets on more than two hundred securities; it trades industrial stocks, utility stocks (including stocks listed on the New York Stock Exchange), bank and insurance stocks and bonds of all kinds. Twenty traders in New York are empowered to take positions and build up inventories; five more out of town can make small but firm markets. Although the basic business is wholesale to other dealers or to institutions, First National also has a small, cherished list of private citizens with whom it trades. First Boston is not bothered by the N.A.S.D. 5-per-cent policy—"I don't know that there's any situation," Ladd says, "where we'd actually take as much as 5 per cent."

Ordinarily in the over-the-counter market the dealer's quoted price is good for a "size" of one hundred shares, or five hundred on a low-priced security. First Boston's size is usually one thousand shares. A certain amount of the firm's

---

* 1959: First Boston moved in 1957 to 15 Broad Street. The trading floor is now even quieter.

gigantic $22,000,000 capital is allocated to over-the-counter trading by the corporation's "executive committee" and the department uses the money as it best sees fit. "They allow me a 'line,' " Ladd says, "and then I allow a line to the traders. We review a trader's position in a security every month to make sure that too much of the money isn't frozen into an unprofitable place. You have a problem there. If a trader has built up an inventory in a stock, and the stock has gone down, you have to pry him loose from it—he doesn't want to take his loss. If we like a stock, we'll take a large position and hope for it to go up, but essentially we're in the trading business. Thirty days after we've bought something we get it out of the house."

Other houses make markets where they think they can make money, but First Boston has certain securities in which it feels obliged to make the market. If the underwriting department brings out an issue, and there is no other good market for it, Ladd believes he owes it to the firm's customers to trade in the security. If a man wants to sell what he bought, or buy more, there must be a place where he can go—otherwise the security is worth very little to him. A bad market will damage the value of a security, and the underwriting house does not wish to have damaged goods on its record.

As financial adviser to many of the corporations in whose stock it trades, First Boston often finds itself arguing vigorously with itself. McCormick of the American Stock Exchange, or Phil West of the big board, has been up to see the president of the corporation, and he thinks maybe he'd like to list. When the corporation lists, most and maybe all of the trading profit in that security will be gone. First Boston at that moment will take a firm grip on itself and remember that its primary work is as an underwriter and a financial adviser to corporations.

"There are many securities that will have their best market on an exchange," Ladd says. "When we think a corporation has sufficient stockholders, and sufficient interest in the stock, to guarantee a good auction market, we'll advise them to list. So far as we're concerned, the over-the-counter market is primarily a distribution market, getting the stock into the hands of many people. When that job is done, we're not against listing."

Late in 1953, the Boston Edison Company listed on the New York Stock Exchange, and the executives of the Ex-

change congratulated Philip West on a good job well done.
West was modest about it. Although he had been up to see
Boston Edison half a dozen times, he knew that all the time
he was talking they were looking right through him; they
were looking down to New York, and Edward Ladd. When
First Boston thought there was enough interest in the stock to
produce the conditions necessary for an auction market, Ladd
nodded. And when the underwriter nodded, Boston Edison
went on to the big board. It was nothing more than routine
practice; and as such it makes an interesting measure of
where the real power lies in the Wall Street of today.

Chapter 9

The Underwriters

"LET'S take a case," said James Lyles, a quizzical* Vice-President of The First Boston Corporation. "It's just one case, and what was done yesterday may not be the thing to do tomorrow. There's an infinite variety in this business. But let's take a case, the Seaboard Finance Company. They're in the small loans business.

"Seaboard Finance was started in 1927 by Bill Thompson, a young man about thirty years old, with about ten years of experience in the small loans business. It was out West, in Los Angeles, and he opened a small office. He had exactly $2,700, which is not enough money, but he also had a friend with a rich mother, and the mother was going to put up fifty thousand. The day they opened the office, the mother decided that she wasn't going to put up fifty thousand, or any money at all. So he had an office, and $2,700, and a secretary. The secretary became his wife, which consolidated expenses.

"Business was good, and Seaboard expanded, began opening new offices. By 1935 it needed more money than it could get by borrowing from banks, and it was big enough to sell some stock. The boss went over to a local brokerage house, and they put out the issue. The company grew some more, opened up all over the West Coast, and finally, in 1945, it became big enough to buy another finance company, with offices up and down the East Coast. It didn't really buy the other company—the two of them merged.

"Well, the business kept expanding, and soon they needed still more capital, and they went to an Eastern underwriting house which specialized in moderate to small issues. And then, a couple of years after that, the boss and founder walked in through my door here, and we had a talk.

"I must say I was glad to see him—boy, did he need a lot

---

* 1959: Mr. Lyles looked up "quizzical" in the dictionary, and I was embarrassed at what he found. "Drily cheerful" would be the correct phrase. It should also be understood that Mr. Lyles is a man of great personal distinction, substantial enough to have married off two daughters in a single season, traditional enough to be a railroad buff, modern enough to be a trustee of Sarah Lawrence College. Lyles is now a *Senior* Vice-President of First Boston.

of financing! He had a complicated capital structure, bonds here, subordinated notes with a Midwest insurance company, little or none of his stock held by institutions, the whole situation very unstable. And he wanted to expand further. He couldn't expand on a basis of that crazy-quilt capital structure—but at the same time he had to raise money to clean up the capitalization picture before he could go to the public and sell anything.

"I said, 'We'll make a private deal. You can use the money from this private deal to get your finance in shape for a public offering. Right now, we wouldn't put our name on a public offering for your company—but we can go to an insurance company we know really well, and make a deal on your behalf.'

"The next year, Seaboard was still growing, and he came in again. This time we sat down and went over the whole picture of what would have to be done over the next few years. I told him, 'What you really need is more equity capital, more common stock, but you shouldn't sell common stock in Seaboard right now because people don't know enough about it. The earnings picture, though, is good enough, so we can sell preferred stock. We'll make the preferred convertible, and as your earnings improve and your dividends on the common increase, the preferred holders will convert to common. When they've converted that issue, we'll put out another issue of convertible preferred; and then another, and on and on as long as you need new equity capital. You'll be able to sell preferred at a lower dividend than you're presently paying on your common, and we'll be able to sell the preferred more easily, so the underwriting will cost you less, too.'"

Lyles rocked back in his chair, nodded and continued the story in his very level, even way. "Seaboard went in on five convertible preferred financings, one after the other. In 1949 and 1952 and 1953 and 1954 we sold senior debt for them, in 1950 and again in 1952 we refinanced the issue of subordinated notes. In 1953 we sold an issue of straight, nonconvertible preferred.

"When we started with Seaboard there was five million dollars of common stock outstanding; today there's more than thirty million, and the stock is listed on the New York Stock Exchange. There's less than two million dollars of the twenty-two million of convertible preferred still outstanding, and five million of straight preferred. Most important of all, we've raised immensely the level of the investors in the company. When we got into it there was only one institutional holder; then, after a while, we began to get the highest grade of insurance companies, pension funds and investment trusts in the debt and preferred. Today Seaboard is in many of the finest institutional portfolios.

"In seven years," Lyles concluded proudly, "the company grew five-fold and many people of importance became interested in its securities. Today Seaboard's rating is *almost* at the very top of its group; the only one ahead, Household Finance, has been in business about twice as long. It happened because Seaboard is a sound and excellently managed company. But I think we did our part. I don't say we were the only people who could have done it, and it certainly isn't the only company we've done it for. It's just that this company happened to walk in through my door, and I'm familiar with the situation."

Lyle's door opens into a square, rather small office (as Wall Street executive offices go), and a wonderfully congenial personality. He came to finance with an engineering degree from M.I.T., and he must have been a redhead once, because his moustache is still rusty. On one wall of his office is a magnificent relief map of the United States, the mountains poking up through the cloth, dark green and light green and cream and pink and red, with blue depressions where the rivers make valleys. There are half a dozen photographs of railroad locomotives.

Lyles picked up the telephone and called Edward Ladd, boss of the trading department. "Hello, Miss Witherspoon," he said. "This is Jim Lyles. Is the fat boy there?"

Edward Ladd is ghostly thin.

"No? Well, tell him I called, will you, please?"

2

Every year sees a hundred thousand ideas for new businesses, and fifty thousand schemes to enlarge companies already in existence. They all take money, and the money does not exist for all of them; many have been called, but only a few can be chosen. The choice involves the allocation of labor and material to one project rather than another, and making it correctly is the first necessity of a continuing strong economy. The choice is not automatic: somebody has to make it. And in the United States, by and large, it is made by the underwriters.

When an underwriter sells a stock to a customer, the money goes into productive enterprise that never was before. When a stockholder sells his stock on an exchange or over the counter, the money goes, simply, into the former stockholder's pocket. This is why the underwriters are the powers of Wall Street: they do the useful work. Deciding which stock they will sell, they make that choice between alternative projects which sets the direction of the economy.

For example, Seaboard Finance. The incredible prosperity enjoyed by the United States after the war was due first of all to the enormous popular demand for goods and services, especially homes and "big-ticket" hard goods—automobiles, television sets, washing machines. To buy such items the people of the United States borrowed in the first postwar decade, from banks and finance companies like Seaboard, more than *one hundred billion dollars*. Meeting Seaboard's own demands for money, in a way that guaranteed its continuing fiscal health, was an economic service of the first order.

These matters, of course, do not work according to plan; they work by each underwriter's guess at which businesses will be profitable in the years to come. Mistakes are inevitable, constant and costly. The decision that America needed another automobile company proved ruinous to Henry Kaiser and many thousands of his fellow citizens*; and less spectacular errors are made every day. But the free financial market, combining the judgments of industry, underwriters and investors, is the only known way of allocating resources so that successes can be noted and continued, failures recognized and punished. On Wall Street failures are punished quickly and severely; successes are rewarded with yachts, racing stables and diamonds.

3

Underwriting as a profession is, in its present form, fairly new; only a strong pull can stretch it back as far as seventy-five years, to the founding of the Chicago firm of Harris, Forbes. Before that time every new company had a "promoter" who went around raising money, selling stocks to his friends, talking bank presidents out of their cash or governments into land grants, guaranteed monopolies or actual subsidies. If a group of rich men became interested in a

---

* 1959: Less ruinous to Kaiser, who is living very comfortably in Hawaii, than to his fellow citizens.

project, they sent some bright boy to look at it, as John Rockefeller was sent to look at the Pennsylvania oil fields. Sometimes new stock would be sold on a Stock Exchange (secretly, and disguised as old stock) through market manipulators. But most often the promoter would work in an expanding circle, starting with his own immediate friends, until he had picked up sufficient pieces of change.

These methods went out of fashion in the late nineteenth century, when the huge "trusts" were formed by amalgamating small companies under the auspices of a large bank. The men connected with these companies had to be bought in, and the public was willing to pay: there was an excitement in the huge figures, the prospect of one corporation controlling a nation's steel production or oil production or shoe manufacture. Stock salesmen began to appear in large numbers, and above them skilled men who trained themselves to know which stock could and which stock could not be sold to the public. In 1915 Morgan organized the first large selling syndicate, involving many dealers, to raise money for the French government, which had to pay for a war. By that time there were many firms, mostly banks, which specialized in bringing together the company with stock to sell and the man with money to risk.

In Britain, "underwriting" means what it says: the underwriter does not market the stock himself, but guarantees to buy all of an issue that a company cannot sell through its own efforts. This sort of underwriting still occurs in the United States, but only when stock is sold to existing stockholders, who receive new stock, supposedly at bargain prices. The stock that is not claimed goes to the underwriter, who sells it to outsiders. This process is known, for obvious reasons, as a "stand-by" underwriting; and the underwriter receives a fee for standing by, plus a part of the profits, if any, on selling the unclaimed stock.

This is an inconvenient way to do business, because the underwriter must be ready over a period of time to buy an indeterminate amount of securities; his capital is tied up, waiting, and he cannot plan for the future. It would be, and is, more convenient for him to buy the entire issue from the company and sell it to the public, as quickly as he can, making his gross income on the difference between his cost price and his sales price.

There are two separate steps in this process, however—a money step, buying the stocks from the company; and a selling step. Before the 1940's, most underwriting houses performed either one step or the other. One firm would put up the money, and then get together a group of dealer firms, which would sell the stock to scattered individuals on a commission basis. If the stock didn't sell, the money firm was stuck with it. Both the risk and the necessary selling effort were considerable; but so were the profits.

Today, risk, selling effort and profit are all minimal. The risk is split among a "syndicate" of underwriters, each of which buys an agreed portion of the issue. The major customers for new issues (especially bonds, which predominate) are institutions, and institutions buy in large bites, so that the selling effort on a top-grade bond issue may involve as little as twenty telephone calls, a couple of telegrams and a clearing operation. Finally, more and more firms have crowded into the business, drawn by the high profits of former years, and competition among them has reduced the underwriter's profit margin, the "spread" between his cost and selling price, to as little (on the best issues) as one-half of one per cent— or, rarely, even less.

As the spreads went down the pie shrank, until finally an issue produced scarcely enough profit to split between a money group and a selling group. The monied underwriters formed selling organizations, aimed specially at the institutional customers; the selling organizations dug in their pockets and demanded a chance to cut in on the risk. Finally, in the 1950's, the two groups pretty much amalgamated, forming for each issue one syndicate that would put up the money and sell the stock. Though there is still a "dealer's concession," and many underwriters will sell part of an issue through other firms, the separate "selling group" has practically disappeared from the scene.

What a company wants out of an underwriting is money at the lowest possible cost, which means selling the right piece of paper at the right time, with the least possible spread to the underwriter. To achieve such objectives, corporations need very good advice, and those which go regularly to the money market keep a close relationship with an underwriter, who will often sit on the board of directors. In this case advice is easy to get and it is also easy to choose the underwriter who will handle the issue. The "closely acquainted" underwriter new money must be raised. From his experience and his knows all there is to know about the company's business, and he has sat in on the discussion which led to the decision that knowledge of the company's existing financial structure he advises on the kind of paper that should be issued. Then, from his day-to-day intuition of the financial market (and his knowledge of investors' needs) he tells the company what can be sold, which is not always the same thing as what should be issued. After a conference with his sales department he tells the company how much (in his opinion) the public will pay for the issue, and how much the company must pay him to sell it. The atmosphere of friendship will not haze over a little, and there will be some negotiation on both these points. The final price to the public will be left to a last-minute decision, to hit the going market; but the spread—the underwriter's profit margin—has been set. Lawyers will now draw up the terms of the issue itself, the contracts between company and underwriter, and the necessary papers for the S.E.C.; and someone will hire a man to engrave securities.

At this point the underwriter, the business in his pocket, forms a syndicate of which he will be manager. He takes the largest single piece of the risk for himself, and assigns the other pieces to his fellow underwriters: "We're bringing out eighty million in first mortgage bonds for the Wapping Power Company, and we'd like you to take two million. Offering date will be four weeks from Monday, and right now we expect that the price will be 100¼ for a 4⅛-per-cent coupon. Your spread is half a point—may I put you down for two million?" The manager will handle by himself all the syndicate's clerical work, and will find some way to rescue syndicate members who have taken larger "participations" that they can actually sell. For these services (and for bringing in and setting up the business) he receives a flat fee, usually 10 to 15 per cent of the spread, off the top of the entire issue.

This is the classic "negotiated" underwriting, and a company without an underwriter on its board of directors can play the same game simply by picking up its telephone and calling Wall Street. An underwriter will arrive on the next plane. As a way of raising money, it has one great advantage: the company is protected by expert and friendly advice against issuing a kind of security that may prove a financial embarrassment in the years to come. It also has the great disadvantage that the mutual friendship of company and underwriter tends to raise the underwriter's spread, and make each sale more costly than it might be. Personal advice is expensive in any business.

To keep down the costs—or to avoid the responsibility of deciding the price themselves—some companies shop around the underwriting houses, gathering advice and preliminary offers for the securities. Others will remain open to suggestions from rival houses up to the last minute of negotiations with their chosen underwriter. But the most popular method of keeping down the underwriters' spread (especially popular with the S.E.C. and the Interstate Commerce Commission, which regulates railroad issues) is public, competitive sealed bidding. Though detested by the underwriters (because it destroys the useful confidential relationship between company and underwriter, and makes for much narrower spreads), competitive bidding rules today over the public utility, railroad and municipal bond markets.*

In a "competitive" underwriting, the company first calls in a consultant who helps draw up the issue. (A big company, which does considerable new financing every year, may swipe somebody out of an underwriting house and put him on salary, thus eliminating repeated consultants' fees.) Papers are filed with the S.E.C., and it is then announced that at eleven o'clock on the morning of such-and-such a day (it is almost always, for some reason, eleven o'clock) the company will open and examine sealed bids for the entire amount of the issue (each bid to be accompanied, please, by a certified check), and will award the entire issue to the highest bidder.

This announcement is somewhat gloomily received in the underwriters' offices, and a young man is told to examine the prospectus for the issue. He reports back on the state of the company as he finds it, and the officers of each large underwriting firm assemble to examine the entrails. If a firm decides to bid for the issue, its syndicate manager picks up his telephone and starts saying, "Hello, Harry, how's the kids? Good. Look, how about joining us in trying to get these new Wapping Power bonds, which are up for bids three weeks from Monday. I'd like you in the syndicate. May I put you down for two million?"

An hour or so before the bids are to be submitted and opened, the syndicate gets together by telephone or in a large room, and the manager announces what price he believes the public (read "the insurance companies") will pay for the

---

* 1959: It was widely expected that competitive bidding would decline in importance once Republicans ran the administrative agencies that were insisting on competition. In fact, however, the proportion of competitive as against negotiated underwritings has held relatively steady.

issue—and how close to that price he is willing to bid. There is some discussion; occasionally the group will make the manager change his bid and sometimes one or two of the members will drop out of the syndicate rather than risk taking a participation they do not believe they can profitably sell. Usually, however, it is wiser for a house to take its shellacking on an overpriced issue rather than quit the syndicate: a house that quits today may not be invited to join tomorrow.

A syndicate manager can invite anyone he wishes to join his group in a negotiated underwriting; in a competitive situation, of course, he can invite only those firms which have not joined some other man's syndicate. Generally speaking, the big houses scratch each other's backs, and in negotiated situations the manager will give participations to other managing houses according to how much he gets from them in their own similar underwritings. Beyond that, every house has friends, who join with it in competitive syndicates and therefore get first crack at the negotiated deals. If there is local interest in an issue local dealers receive big participations: a small San Francisco house might sell more than a large New York house in an issue by Pacific Power & Light. Finally, certain houses specialize in certain industries, and a pitch up their particular alley is best thrown to them.

Sometimes, inevitably, an issue is so popular, so guaranteed of success, that everybody wants his name on it, and the syndicate manager never has to call anybody. Instead, his telephone rings all day long: "You remember me, Jack . . ."*

However the preliminaries are worked, the end result is always two contracts: one between the underwriters and the company, the other among the underwriters themselves. The first obliges the underwriters to buy the securities from the company at a certain price, and the second binds the underwriting houses into a syndicate for the sole purpose of selling this one issue. The syndicate agreement will last anywhere from thirty days to six months, and its central provision is

* 1959: To show how wrong such expert judgments can be, the biggest sell-out in history, to underwriters and to the public, was the first offering of stock in the Ford Motor Company, in 1956. Within a week, the price of the stock had dropped below the original offering price—supposedly set at less than actual value (by no less an authority than Sidney Weinberg of Goldman, Sachs) to make sure that future issues of Ford stock would be easy to sell. It was not until the big bull market of early 1959 that Ford sold on the New York Stock Exchange for a price as high as that which the underwriters put on the stock.

that everyone will offer his share of the issue at the same price. Anybody who cuts his price without the consent of his fellow members in the syndicate can be sued, and will be kicked out of business by the National Association of Securities Dealers. Moreover, each dealer is expected to sell to legitimate investors, who will hold the securities for a decent length of time; if the bonds allotted to him make a sudden reappearance on the market, he must pay a fine. Occasionally, in stock issues, the syndicate decides to "stabilize" the market in the company's stock, holding up the price of the old stock to make sure that the new weight of supply does not sink the ship. Any such decision must, by law, be publicized.

These contracts have behind them a force of custom which is greater than any force of law. When Otis & Co. backed out on its agreement with Kaiser-Frazer in 1948, a shock wave passed through the entire industry, and the N.A.S.D. began its proceedings as soon as K-F began its lawsuit. Wall Street was not interested in whatever legal defense Otis might find, Wall Street was not softened by the fact that K-F stock was rapidly sinking (despite aggressive stabilization) below the issue price of the new stock, and that Otis would surely have taken a bath on the deal. Cyrus Eaton, boss of Otis, had signed a contract, and if it was a bad contract that was his own fault. "I never liked Eaton," said an underwriter, "I never liked the way he did business. But I never thought it would come to this."*

4

John Pierpont Morgan was a banker, and J. P. Morgan & Co., Inc., was and is a bank. Before 1934 it was also an underwriter, and so were the Chase National Bank, the Guaranty Trust Company, the First National Bank of Boston and many, many others. This seemed a logical way to handle the underwriting business, because banks should know more about credit ratings than anybody else, and banks have depositors who are natural customers for new securities. The actual check that a corporation receives in payment from an underwriter is only in small part the underwriter's own money; the rest represents a loan to the underwriter from a bank, to be repaid from sales to ultimate customers. So the simplest way

---

* 1959: This is the same Cyrus Eaton who has recently, in his capacity as private citizen, exchanged gifts with Nikita Khrushchev and held international conferences on a Canadian estate. He is, in short, a man with an original approach to problems.

of handling new securities was to have the bank underwrite the stuff itself, supply all the financing, all the brain work and all the selling effort.

It was so simple it became a little too simple. In the early thirties the American banking system went broke, partly because it had been underwriting worthless securities, and still had a lot on hand. Notice of this phenomenon was taken in Washington, and in 1934 there appeared a law to the effect that a bank had to decide whether it was going to handle corporate securities or accept customers' deposits. Experience had proved that the attempt to do both kinds of business put too great a strain on both the ability and the morality of bankers.

J. P. Morgan & Co., Inc., like most of its fellows, decided to stay in the banking-and-lending business and get out of the securities business. A number of officers of the bank (and of its sister bank in Philadelphia, Drexel & Co.) thereupon lost their function in the company. Headed by Henry S. Morgan and Harold Stanley, they went out on their own and formed the underwriting house of Morgan Stanley & Co., Inc. In 1941 the Inc. was dropped (it is far easier to say this than to do it); the company reorganized as a partnership to do a brokerage business on the New York Stock Exchange. Morgan Stanley is still trying to expand its brokerage business and over-the-counter business, but it spends more time arguing with The First Boston Corporation for the title of the nation's greatest underwriting house. In 1958, according to the *Investment Dealers' Digest* annual survey, Morgan Stanley managed syndicates that underwrote $1,860,163,000 worth of corporate securities, while First Boston came in second with $1,167,175,000.

The two houses are not much alike. First Boston is a corporation with eight thousand stockholders; Morgan Stanley is a partnership with fewer than a dozen partners. First Boston is capitalized at $22,000,000; Morgan Stanley at $4,500,000. First Boston runs a department store and sells a large percentage of the issues it manages; Morgan Stanley is basically a money house and sells comparatively little. First Boston has about 500 employees; Morgan Stanley, last time they counted, had 95. First Boston has offices all over the country; and Morgan Stanley has one office, at 2 Wall Street, New York.

It is a very pleasant office, too—high in the tower, looking over Trinity Church and the office buildings of Trinity Place, out to the Hudson River, the ships and New Jersey. Most of the partners sit together in one large corner room, with ten high, roll-top desks marching in pairs at right angles to the two long walls. The carpeting is grass-green and the walls are white to reflect the brilliant sun that pours in the long southern exposure. There is no clutter, and no nonsense.

Managing partner Perry Hall is short and chubby, and at sixty-odd he still has his freckles; only the grey hair and the immense, friendly confidence testify to his age and importance. He wears a black suit and vest, in keeping with his dignity, and a Kelly green tie, in keeping with his personality and his carpet. A graduate of Princeton in the class of '17, he went to work for Guaranty Trust (a "Morgan bank")* in 1919, moved over to J. P. Morgan & Co. in 1925 and the Philadelphia affiliate in 1930, then became one of the original officers of Morgan Stanley. Early in 1954 *The New Yorker* ran a sketch of him, calling him "open-faced" and featuring his love of shooting grouse and wild turkey: for three weeks his telephone was occupied by friends calling to rib him about it. Nevertheless, he received another reporter shortly thereafter, and in that reporter's presence made a date to go shooting. He has remarkable courage.

In 1953 Morgan Stanley led First Boston by virtue of a single issue—a $300,000,000 bag of debentures underwritten by Morgan Stanley for General Motors. It was business that Morgan Stanley had gone out to get; in fact, the issue had its origin in a suggestion made by Hall to General Motors, more or less to the effect that GM had been expanding pretty fast and maybe the company could use a little money. This is the highest function of investment banking—solving a company's problems before even the company knows that it has them—and Morgan Stanley richly earned more than its one-eighth of a point management fee, which ran to $375,000. It also earned its management, in 1955, of a $325,000,000 General Motors stock issue. No man is an island.

Usually, of course, the company comes to the underwriter. "Our people," Hall says, "have been trained in the work involved in setting up large issues, and corporations know it. They respect us. They come in and they say, 'We'd like to raise twenty-five million dollars.' We're supposed to be able to make recommendations, tell them what particular kind of financing suits their needs. The expense of making these

* 1959: This year the flip phrase "Morgan bank" became a legal fact: J. P. Morgan & Co. and Guaranty Trust merged to form a single corporation.

recommendations, and preparing the issues, and organizing the syndicate, isn't a great deal more on large financings than it is on small ones. For that reason, we're always most interested in large issues. But Morgan Stanley is interested in quality at all times, whatever the size."

Northy Jones, a partner and the firm's Stock Exchange member,* wandered into Hall's office in a casual tweed jacket. "Sit down, sit down," said Hall cheerfully. "Join the chorus." He returned patiently to his exposition. "Ever heard of the S. C. Johnson Company?"

"Johnson's———" said Jones.

"No, no," said Hall. "Let him guess. Give up? Ever hear of Fibber McGee and Molly—now we have it, Johnson's Wax. Well, they came to us to underwrite an issue. I went home and said to my mother, 'What's the best floor wax?' She said, 'Johnson's Wax.' So I told the Johnson people we'd handle the issue. We sent a man out to Racine, to their plant, spent a lot of time with them discussing their needs. The issue we brought out amounted to only $848,000."

One-half of one per cent of a $300,000,000 issue is $1,500,-000. One-half of one per cent of an $848,000 issue is $4,240. It isn't very profitable to underwrite small issues, and do a good job a it.

Up to 1941, Morgan Stanley did a wholesale business exclusively, selling to dealers who then took a mark-up and sold to the public. In 1941 (which was the first year of compulsory competitive bidding for S.E.C.-regulated public utility companies) the firm started developing retail customers of its own in the New York area. Even today, however, much of Morgan Stanley's actual participation in its underwritings will be sold through dealers, with two profits to come out of the difference between the price paid to the issuer and the price charged to the public. Most of Morgan Stanley's income unquestionably comes from its management fee of seven to fiften cents per hundred dollars on the total amount of the issue.

Usually, the manager of a syndicate takes between 20 and 40 per cent of the issue for himself—that's why he is manager. Morgan Stanley's average participation is ordinarily less than 10 per cent. The firm is chosen by companies to underwrite their securities not because of its financial backing (though Hall could, as he puts it, "lay my hands on twice as much as

---

* 1959: Allan N. Jones died last year.

our capital tomorrow, if I wanted to"), but because of its enormous ability and experience, and its reputation. Everybody likes to think that his name on an issue means a great deal to the sale of that issue; this happy boast is probably more true of Morgan Stanley than of anybody else.

As many as 298 firms have helped Morgan Stanley underwrite an issue; as many as 801 dealers have helped Morgan Stanley sell one. They have accepted the leadership of this rather small firm because the name Morgan Stanley helps them sell; and for this reason also the list of companies for which Morgan Stanley has put out securities reads like a *Burke's Peerage* of American industrial enterprise.

Like *Burke's Peerage*, Morgan Stanley tries to keep its list simon-pure—but sometimes has to admit the bar sinister. Morgan Stanley's outstanding bastard, as noticeable on first sight as a Mickey Mouse in a jeweller's tray of Patek-Philippes, is a land-speculation company called Western Leaseholds; how this little item got in with the collection of tiaras is one of the deepest mysteries of Wall Street.*

5

When the Glass-Steagle Act separated church and state in 1934, one of the big firms elected to give up its banking business and continue as an underwriter—Kuhn, Loeb & Co., founded in 1867, brought to full flower by Jacob Schiff, perfected by Otto H. Kahn and now led by Schiff's great-grandson John Schiff, a graduate of Yale, Oxford and the Bankers Trust Company bond school. Schiff at fifty-five is the handsomest man on Wall Street, very tall and thin and erect, a graceful man. He makes it a practice to come out to the waiting-room himself, and usher a visitor in.

Kuhn, Loeb has its own building on the dark corner of 52 William Street, a block from Wall Street; and the firm occupies the bottom four floors.† On the ground floor it looks like a bank, with barred tellers' windows and a quantity of white marble. The second floor is reached by a small elevator or by a black-marble staircase that winds in the open about the elevator shaft. From the staircase, behind the tellers' cages, a visitor can see a very small army of clerks adding

---

* 1959: This coy comment was, of course, nonsense. Western Leaseholds came out under the Morgan Stanley imprimatur because of a back-scratching arrangement with the firm of Carl M. Loeb, Rhoades. It must be noted, also, that Western Leaseholds was a successful land-speculation company.

† 1959: Kuhn, Loeb has moved.

columns of figures at adding machines that look anachronistic on the old-fashioned, high desks by the walls. At the top of the stairs he will be greeted, firmly, by Donald Beaton, an elderly, kindly gentleman who was private chauffeur to the late Otto Kahn before he became a bank guard. Beaton is hell on messenger boys, condescending to partners.

Underwriting is like riding on a yo-yo; the amount of business that a house does is entirely unpredictable from year to year. In 1951, Kuhn, Loeb managed syndicates that underwrote $99,739,000; in 1953 its total managing of corporate financing came to $984,441,000; in 1958, according to *Investment Dealers' Digest,* it was down to $280,170,000.

"We don't have any trading department at all," says J. Emerson Thors, the partner in charge of the underwriting syndicates, "but we do have a few sidelines. We're advisers to charity funds and pension funds and estates. Most estate money goes to the trust department of a bank, which is always over-protective. We're willing to assure a higher rate of return on the money if we're made the trustees, because we give each account a personal attention. Our business, though, is underwriting and distributing large blocks of securities, and we don't solicit small accounts."

Kuhn, Loeb has no salesmen. "When you have salesmen," Thors says, "you have to split commissions; the salesmen get 40 per cent. At Kuhn, Loeb we have only top people, and top people work on salary. We service 250 institutions, we think they value our advice and they buy the securities we underwrite. We'll run risks, too—we're perfectly willing to underwrite a utility issue of ten or fifteen million dollars all by ourselves. The others won't do it—they all want three or four partners on a five-million-dollar deal."

Nobody in the underwriting business much likes competitive bidding (except Halsey, Stuart & Co., a Chicago bond firm that is co-giant with Morgan Stanley and First Boston) but Kuhn, Loeb hates it most. "When you're hungry," Thors says gloomily, "when you haven't got much business, you'll drive down your spread to make sure you win the issue. Before 1934 you got three, four, even five points on good bonds; now you get a quarter or a half—if you get three-quarters you're getting a lot.* And it's not just on competitive issues either. Your regular clients know what size spread you take on competitive issues, because all the figures are published.

* 1959: Three-quarters would be more common today, and full points are not unknown.

And you can't charge your friends more than you charge strangers.

"Worse, you're responsible under the law for the truth of all the statements in the prospectus for any issue you underwrite. Under the early conditions everybody was very indulgent, and companies ran junkets to look at the dams and power lines and so forth. Today you just can't afford it; you send an engineer out to verify the statements in the prospectus, then you don't win the issue and it's cost you the engineer's fee, for nothing. The company that's issuing the bonds picks a lawyer to answer the underwriters' questions about the issue and assure them that everything is kosher. All the underwriters consult him, but he was picked by the company. And the underwriter whose bid wins the issue pays the lawyer's fee, which is six to eight thousand dollars. You make half a point on the spread, and on what you can't sell yourself you give a dealer a quarter of a point. The management fee, which the syndicate manager receives on the entire amount of the issue, looks very big these days."

Nevertheless, Kuhn, Loeb goes after participations in other people's underwritings nearly as hard as it goes after management fees for itself. There is an organization of selling dealers to be kept alive and anxious to work with Kuhn, Loeb; besides these faithful retainers there are dealers whose help may be necessary in a sticky issue, and who count on Kuhn, Loeb to give them an occasional piece of its participations—"wolves," says Thors dryly, "all following the droshky. You throw them crumbs."

Kuhn, Loeb was founded by immigrants—Jacob Schiff's naturalization papers, dated September 8, 1870, are on display with the portraits in the long, high conference room—and for years the firm maintained an Old World dimension of dignity, remaining entirely aloof (in theory) from the brawling for business done by rival underwriters. Today Kuhn, Loeb brawls, too; but the dignity is still important. "We will accept," Thors says, "participations in any issue of quality, regardless of the syndicate manager, provided we have a place in the ad consistent with our standing in the business."

This question of "a place in the ad" is very serious all over the underwriting field, with a true comic-opera seriosity. Every issue of any size is announced in the *New York Times,* the New York *Herald Tribune* and the *Wall Street Journal* with a "tombstone" ad featuring the list of firms from whom a prospectus, and eventually a stock or bond, may be obtained. The syndicate manager, of course, has top position in the advertisement; if there are several co-managers, they will be listed in a line across the top. After that the firms are listed by their "bracket" in the underwriting—three firms, say, each taking a fifteenth of the issue, seven firms taking a thirty-third; nine firms taking a fiftieth. A firm's position in the ad therefore indicates its importance in this piece of business, and firms will fight for larger proportionate participations, even when they feel a little queasy about the chance of selling these larger participations, just to enhance their status in the ad. Calling Lee Higginson and Co., for example, the manager may offer a thirty-third—adding, quickly, "That puts you in the bracket with Hornblower & Weeks and Dean Witter. You'll remember that you and they shared a bracket in the last Wapping Power issue." If a firm does an outstanding job in selling one issue—perhaps absorbing some bonds that another firm had found itself unable to move—it may conceivably get a better bracket in the next. The improvement of position represents such a major triumph for a firm, and such gall and wormwood for the other firms that used to share its bracket, that a manager takes his courage in his hands every time he promotes an associate.

The budget for the ad is set in the syndicate manager's advertising department, according to the size of the issue. Not long ago somebody in First Boston's advertising department decided to save a few pennies and made the ad a little smaller. Eight or so firms were thereby cut out of the ad completely, and they screamed for weeks. They are probably screaming still.

6

Johnniest-come-lately of the big underwriting firms is, of course, Merrill Lynch, Pierce, Fenner & Smith, Inc., which in 1958, according to the *Investment Dealers' Digest,* managed corporate underwritings of $554,787,000. Although the original Merrill Lynch was an underwriting house, it passed few men on to We the People's present underwriting department, which has been rebuilt almost from scratch in the last dozen years.

Merrill Lynch's greatest asset in its underwriting work is its 1,200 "account executives," its 400,000 customers and the immense retail sales possibility they represent. The firm is therefore, by the universal law of contradiction, proudest of its institutional clients, and the bulk sales to insurance companies and others made directly by its institutional department. By extension, it is also proud of its work in private placement.

Private placement is the direct sale of an entire issue by a corporation to an insurance company or some other wealthy institutional investor. The underwriter in these deals neither buys nor sells; he advises. Today half of all new corporate debt financing is privately placed; and perhaps half of that total is supervised by underwriting houses.

"We do a lot of such work," says Gilette Martin, "and we want to do more. But you have to fight for it. The insurance companies are always out soliciting loans on their own, and they snipe it out from under you." Once the insurance companies even went into competition with the underwriters and won a large issue at public bidding. In 1941 A.T. & T. solicited bids on an issue of debentures, $94,000,000 worth, and a group of three insurance companies—Metropolitan, Mutual and New York Life—won the bonds. All hell broke loose that afternoon and insurance companies have only rarely participated in competitive situations since. But they still try to persuade corporations that a loan from an insurance company is cheaper than selling bonds.

Private placement has one great advantage for a corporation: it eliminates the immense quantities of legal paper necessary under the Securities Act before a new security can be sold; it is also quicker. When an issue is privately placed with an insurance company it is not sold to the public at all. So the securities are exempt from the registration and prospectus provisions of the law—on the theory, quite correct, that insurance companies can take care of themselves.

In theory, it should also be possible for the company to eliminate underwriting costs by private placement, but many companies would rather have an underwriter in the deal, and pay an underwriter's fee. In some issues, an underwriter may be able to interest an insurance company that would remain unconvinced by the corporation's advocate—without the underwriter, the corporation stands hat in hand, begging for money. Finally, many corporations are dependent on underwriters for financial advice, and would hesitate to undertake a loan from anyone without an underwriter's okay, which means an underwriter's fee.

Actually, this insurance company market—which enters on all debt issues, not only private placement—is the reason underwriting spreads can be cut to half a point without cutting throats. Mechanically, a five-million-dollar sale to an insurance company costs about the same as a five-thousand-dollar sale to an individual (possibly less), and selling is the big expense of underwriting. But insurance companies do not usually buy stock, and here Merrill Lynch cuts the opposition deep indeed, because it can also underwrite stock issues successfully at a minimal spread. Merrill Lynch account executives work on a salary which must be paid whether or not they put part of their time in selling new stock. When a Merrill Lynch salesman sells something for the underwriting department it costs the firm the price of a telephone call. The same process costs other firms a 40-per-cent commission, because that is what a stock salesman gets.

Not long ago Merrill Lynch managed a syndicate that put in the high bid for a new issue of a stock traded on the New York Stock Exchange. The stock closed that day at 46⅞, which was its high for the week; Merrill Lynch told the other members of the syndicate that it was prepared to bid 46⅝ for the stock, with a public offering price of 47⅛. (Since this is a net price, it is fractionally lower than the Stock Exchange price, to which must be added about three-quarters of a point commission.)

"What could I do?" said the representative of one of the syndicate members. "They're taking 40 per cent of the issue, and they said that they would absorb whatever was left by any member who dropped out because he didn't like the price. Their salesmen, they said, had tested public reaction, and the public was willing to pay 47⅛, and half a point spread was enough. I didn't want to be a stinker and drop out. But I know damn well I can't make any money on the deal."

Perhaps for this reason, Merrill Lynch is more tolerant than other managers about people who drop out of its syndicates: "That's their business, and they're welcome next time, anyway."

7

When Section 5136 of the Banking Act of 1933 tossed the banks out of securities, it made an exception for bonds which are fully guaranteed obligations of the federal government, states and municipalities. Ordinary government bonds are not underwritten by anybody (in theory; actually, the Federal Reserve System used to be an all-powerful syndicate manager); but Public Housing Authority bonds and Land Bank bonds and the like need selling. So do the bonds of cities and states, which finance highways, waterworks, sewer systems, schools and such. Provided that the bonds are completely guaranteed by the governmental body which issues them, the banks can bid for them—and bid they do. In 1958 the First National City Bank of New York participated in syndicates that bid for $3,117,000 worth of these governmental securities and won $1,613,000. First National City does not keep records of the amount it actually managed, because syndicates for municipal bonds will usually have half a dozen co-managers; but Bankers Trust Company, which does keep such records, show a 1958 total of $882,000,000 sold by syndicates in which Bankers was one of the managers. Chase, the third giant of the triumvirate, hit about the same figures.

All governmental bonds, like most utility bonds, are sold at public bidding, but the spreads are better. "We do a grassroots distribution job," says Delmont Pfeffer, First National City's Vice-President in charge of underwriting, a handsome, grey-haired, pin-striped banker. His office is on the eighth floor of the First National City Bank building, a vast expanse of green carpeting with very few desks. In the next room, men are trading municipal and special-purpose federal bonds, coming in every once in a while to consult about a price. "Because we do grass-roots distribution, we need a bigger spread. We can't sell to life insurance companies or pension funds, because what we're selling is a tax-exempt bond paying a low rate of interest. Life insurance companies and pension funds are mostly free of tax liabilities, so the tax-exempt feature of the bonds doesn't help interest them. More than a third of all municipal bonds are sold to individuals in high tax brackets, who are willing to take the lower return in order to escape the tax. Moreover, your underwriter of corporate securities wants the big issues, where a small spread becomes multiplied to a reasonable amount of money by the number of bonds involved. We're bidding all the time for the little issues you never hear about, the one-million to ten-million issue put out by a town in Indiana. In order to bid for those, we need a better spread on all of them. Generally speaking, I suppose the spread on tax-exempts is about twice the spread on corporate bonds—if the corporate bond underwriter gets half a point, we'll get a point."*

The banks find it easier than the underwriters to judge

---

* 1959: Now that the corporate underwriter is up to ¾ of a point, the municipals underwriter is up to 1⅜-1½.

whether or not they wish to bid for a bond: if they feel that they want to keep some of it in their own investment port-folios, they bid. "It's a guarantee to our customers, and to ourselves," Pfeffer says. "We don't expect to sell everything we underwrite, and we won't sell anything we wouldn't want to own ourselves. Very often, when we lose an issue to a higher bid, we'll buy some of the bonds from the winning bidders. We get a dealer's discount, of course." First National City, espe-cially during the days of the excess profits tax, often had more than half a billion dollars' worth of municipal bonds in its own portfolio. Corporate underwriters, on the other hand, are sellers of all they buy, and cannot judge customers' atti-tudes by their own. As a matter of fact, the S.E.C. insists that corporate underwriters may not take advantage of their dealer discounts to buy bonds for themselves.

Corporate underwriters often have municipal departments, organizing syndicates to bid against the banks; and corporate underwriters and dealers form an actual majority of most of the syndicates headed by the banks. Out of the nation's 14,000 banks, only 100 or so are active in the municipal market as a regular matter, and participations in municipal underwritings are usually small because the bonds must be sold to individuals in small pieces. More than 2,300 banks and dealers once par-ticipated in a single municipal bond distribution. While this record looks safe for years to come, it is a rare municipal un-derwriting that takes the services of fewer than fifty firms.

First National City has twenty-five to thirty people working in its underwriting department. "That's very small," said Pfeffer. "Bankers' and Chase's are much bigger." This state-ment came as news to Bankers, which has twenty-four people including stenographers, in its underwriting department; but Chase has nearly twice as many. The banks investigate every issue quite carefully, because they expect to hang on to some of it themselves if they win it. Most of the executives of these departments have been in municipal bonds all their working lives, and have never had much interest in corporates. "You know how it is," Pfeffer says. "Everybody thinks his own field is the best."

8

"This book you're writing," said George Woods, Chairman of the Board of The First Boston Corporation, "is it a profit-able investment of your time?"

Maybe, maybe not.

"Well, how much money do you think you'll make from it?"

God knows.

"Are you entirely dependent on sales, or do you have a guarantee?"

There is an advance against royalties. So far as the publisher is concerned, that advance is dead; he's already paid it.

"What about the publisher? Does he expect to make money?"

Yes. He does.

"How many copies does he have to sell to make money?"

He will say seven thousand. He may even say ten thousand. Probably, he breaks even at five thousand.

"Well, would a five-thousand sale represent a profitable investment of your time?"

No.*

"Why are you doing the book, then?"

Prestige. Magazine assignments. Fame and glory.

"Oh."

It was remarked to Wallace Fulton, Executive Director of the National Association of Securities Dealers, that Mr. Woods takes a very keen interest in the minutest minutiae of money-making. "Humph," said Fulton. "Tell your publisher to watch out—he's probably going into the book business.

"Take a look," Fulton continued, "into back issues of *Variety,* at the people who back hit shows. Behind the big hits you'll usually find the firm of Woods and Martin, otherwise unidentified. That's George Woods and William McChesney Martin, Chairman of the Board of Governors of the Federal Reserve System. Wherever there's money, there you are likely to find Mr. Woods."

George Woods is a slightly awkward, black-haired man with a sidewise smile; he is nobody's Wall Street smoothie. The son of a Navy officer, who was commandant of the Boston Navy Yard when Woods was born, and took over the Brooklyn Yard six months later, Woods came down to the financial market as an office boy just out of Brooklyn Commercial High School. He was a vice-president of Harris Forbes (one of the largest of the pre-crash underwriters) before he was out of his twenties. During the war Woods served as a colonel on the U.S. Army General Staff; today, at fifty-nine, he is generally

---

* 1959: Fortunately, we have all done better than this.

regarded on Wall Street as the greatest of modern bankers.*

The enterprise he heads is huge, immensely wealthy and infinitely imaginative, it combines the advantages of Morgan Stanley and Merrill Lynch. Its sales department works out of a dozen offices and serves both institutions and individuals; its buying department is headed by seven vice-presidents, who can turn for assistance to a staff of eighteen security analysts, many of them former stars of First Boston's own training program. The buying department, like every other buying department, receives corporate visitors with business to do and evaluates securities put up for competitive bidding. More than any other buying department, however, it goes out and develops business that never existed before.

Every underwriter, of course, goes around to corporations and tries to edge in between the corporations and its present banker. "Our clients get unexpected visits from our competitors," says James Lyles, "usually from a boy, and the boy says, 'You're happy with First Boston, aren't you?' If the company says, 'Yes, it's happy with First Boston,' the boy goes away and that's that. If the company says, 'Wa-al, we've been having a little trouble, nothing serious, of course,' the boy goes away and his employer sends in the talent." First Boston does a little of that, too; but it concentrates its efforts on developing deals which are entirely new and—until they have been completed—entirely secret.

"If I'm out of town," Lyles says, "my girl is under instructions not to say where I am, unless it's Chicago, Washington or Boston. Likewise my wife. There's many a deal that's been lost because somebody was able to trace the man who was working on it."

Perry Hall got a huge issue for Morgan Stanley by suggesting to General Motors that it might need some working capital, but Hall is limited by his firm's usual insistence on prime names. First Boston is interested in all sorts of deals, wherever there is money to be made, regardless of the history of the company. All history, to First Boston, is ancient history if the future look good. Morgan Stanley probably would not have touched Seaboard Finance at the time when Lyles took it on; Lyles had a different reaction: "I must say I was glad to see him—boy, did he need a lot of financing!"

This progressive eagerness for business is held down as

---

* 1959: Woods suffered a serious heart attack four years ago, and has been somewhat less active since.

hard as possible in the firm's executive conferences, because every underwriter must be careful not to put his name on something that turns out to be a stinker and because no underwriter can afford to bid a higher price than the public will pay. Sometimes, however, eagerness will overcome caution and the bid submitted will soar above the economic limit; when this happens, First Boston has the capital to take the situation calmly. Late in 1953 First Boston bid several points higher than its nearest rival for a large public utility bond issue. Asked about the sale of the bonds, William Caldwell, Assistant Vice-President in the syndicate department, replied with a kind of gay sadness. "We own the company. Want to buy a utility?"

To cover such situations, First Boston has a policy of clearing out an issue, regardless of price, after thirty days. "We like to take our lickings," Caldwell says, "and forget about them." Underwriters go out of business when their capital is frozen into an unsuccessful issue. This is the risk of underwriting, for which the underwriters are paid; and the underwriters, though they grumbled, could afford to work for the almost invisible spreads of 1954 because there had been little such risk for fifteen years. Inflation and general prosperity have guaranteed the sale of new securities, and if the initial offering turned out by some freak to be unsuccessful the underwriter had only to wait a couple of months for prices to rise and give him a profit greater than the profit originally contemplated in the spread. Times are changing now, and the narrow spreads do not seem to cover the risk.

"Well," Woods says, "perhaps. But nobody in this firm spends a terrible lot of time complaining about the smallness of the spreads—we're making a reasonable return on our capital."

"Besides," Woods adds, "we're a publicly owned corporation. Most of these guys, it's just themselves and their wives, and they can complain all they like. When you have eight thousand stockholders, and a quote over the counter on the stock, somehow you get a little added sense of responsibility."

[1959: Woods' attitude toward the usual complaints about spreads was justified by events—that is, spreads did widen when risks really increased, after the first big break in the bond market in 1956. Before that, however, his claim for First Boston's sense of responsibility had been considerably weakened by the firm's involvement in the Dixon-Yates affair, which brought the name of First Boston before a wide public for the first time, and put Woods himself in front of newsreel cameras.

The story is worth telling, because it illustrates a point. Wall Street feels very strongly about the issue of public versus private production of electric power. The Eisenhower Administration came to office pledged to support private utilities against any further encroachment of government-operated dynamos. (Indeed, the President once in an off moment referred to the Tennessee Valley Authority as an example of "creeping socialism.") No modern government, however, can remain entirely aloof from the question of what power is needed where, and the Administration felt the need for technical advice on the financing of privately-operated power plants. First Boston was approached to help out, and loaned the Administration Adolph Wenzell, a senior executive who was at retirement age and becoming relatively inactive within the firm.

One of the first problems with which the new Administration's new power policy had to deal was the Atomic Energy Commission's increasing need for electricity in its Tennessee Valley installations. TVA was unable to supply the power from its existing facilities without cutting down on service elsewhere. Engineering considerations forbade the construction of a special steam plant to service the new installation, which was already hooked into the TVA grid. The new power policy forbade authorizing TVA to build a steam plant of its own to increase production. The solution eventually reached was to have TVA contract with a private utility to build a plant which would supply electricity to the TVA grid, thereby releasing TVA power to the atomic engineers. First Boston's executive-on-loan represented the Budget Bureau in the negotiations on the planning of this contract, which was eventually authorized by a split vote of the TVA board.

The successful bid for the contract came from the Mississippi Valley Generating Company, part of the South Utilities company of the Messrs. Dixon and Yates. (It has been alleged that the specifications were so drawn that only Middle South could win, but nothing that could really be called evidence has been placed behind the charge.) First Boston was the banking firm which handled bond issues for Middle South. Woods and his associates were conscious of the danger that their conduct might be criticized if they undertook an issue planned to meet a government contract with an officer of the firm had helped to draw. Nevertheless, they were reluctant to lose their established relation with Dixon and Yates, and they felt that anything they could do to help private utilities break into the Tennessee Valley area would qualify as a public service. They solved their problem by agreeing to plan and sell Middle South's bond issue *without charging for their services.*

If First Boston thought it a public service to help private plants break into the Tennessee Valley, the Democratic Party thought it a public scandal. The TVA contract with Dixon-Yates did not require Congressional approval, but it was the sort of thing that Congress can legitimately investigate and perhaps forbid. Senators Anderson, Hill and Kefauver were outraged by the idea behind the contract, and went searching for material which might discredit it. They quickly found out about First Boston's involvement on both sides of the deal. Meanwhile, S.E.C. hearings on the registration of the Middle South bonds produced various pleas, technical and political, that the Commission should bar the sale of the securities.

Presently, high officials of the Administration took a hand in the proceedings, with great damage to all concerned. Presidential assistant Sherman Adams, whose telephone calls to independent agencies were later to become notorious, called the S.E.C. and ordered a postponement of the vote on the registration until a less politically dangerous time. Meanwhile, Budget Bureau Director Randolph Hughes and Chairman of the Atomic Energy Commission Lewis Strauss testified before an investigating committee headed by Senator Kefauver, and flatly denied that any representative of First Boston had sat in on the conferences in which the plans for a private steam plant were discussed, though Hughes finally admitted that some such person had given technical advice. This denial was, at the very least, an extraordinary lapse of memory. Together with Adams' peremptory order to a supposedly independent commission, it threw a haze of real knavery over what was, in fact, a completely respectable if not responsible transaction.

First Boston was horrified to read in the newspapers about the testimony given by Hughes and Strauss. An informal firm meeting was held to decide whether or not a statement should be issued, jogging the Administration's memory. In the end, it was decided that Hughes and the Administration had to know what they were doing. This decision was incorrect, and George Woods wound up before the cameras at a Senatorial inquiry, forced to claim that First Boston's transaction with

Middle South was a perfectly routine affair, in the face of the firm's most unusual refusal to charge for its services; forced to admit that he did not have the vaguest notion why Hughes and Strauss had denied an obvious fact.

The Kefauver hearings did not succeed in blocking the Dixon-Yates contract (an amendment which would have had this effect was defeated on the floor of the House). And the S.E.C. permitted the registration of the Middle South bond issue. But the dam had broken, and mere legal authorizations could not patch it. A ruling by the Attorney-General held that the contract was illegal—so completely illegal, in fact, that TVA could not reimburse Middle South for expenditures already incurred in connection with it. The Messrs. Dixon and Yates emerged from their experience several millions of dollars out of pocket, with a lawsuit against the government as their only recourse.

First Boston was bruised, but not really damaged. And it must be said to their credit that—while their opinions of Kefauver were not merely unprintable, but inexpressible—they put most of the blame on the shoulders of Hughes and Strauss. It did not occur to them, however, to blame themselves.

And yet, First Boston's role was the saddest in the play. Like the New York Stock Exchange in launching the Monthly Investment Plan, it had violated a cardinal rule of American enterprise by mixing politics and business. Whenever a *business* operation is conducted for an essentially political motive, the end result will reflect unfavorably on everyone involved. An understanding of this rule is the necessary foundation to any commercial "sense of responsibility." It should be said that Sullivan and Cromwell, First Boston's lawyers, had known all about this rule, and had urged their client either to withdraw Wenzell from the Administration or keep out of the bond issue—long before there was any Congressional investigation.]

Chapter 10

A Variety of Trades

"The most important man on Wall Street today," said Joe Lann, very sternly, "is Karl Marx."

There was a moment's silence, then a quavered objection: John Maynard Keynes, perhaps; more likely Alfred Marshall; most probably Adam Smith . . .

"No, no. Karl Marx. C-a-r-l, M-a-r-k-s."

2

This Carl Marks is a small, round, balding, unpretentious, very serious man, who has made himself the largest foreign securities dealer in the nation. Das Kapital, in this case, is 15 million dollars; less than thirty years ago it was ten thousand dollars, and the increase is mostly out of profits.

The saga of Carl Marks is the most remarkable story of a place where fantastic stories are normal; and he tells it best himself, very earnestly, anxious that every word shall be clear, every technicality easy to understand. "Everybody," he said, "has his own idea of what to do. I went into this business because it offered me most of the things I was looking for. One of them was that I didn't have to deal with the public. A second was that I could use my own judgment and be rewarded for it."

Marks paused. He was sitting on the red leather couch in his tiny private office, and before him was, for some reason, a bridge table. The couch stood against a wall, one end in the corner; on the next wall was a window and a bookcase, and across the way, in the opposite corner, was his desk. The bridge table occupied the open space in the room so effectively that it had to be shifted every time Marks wanted to go to his desk for a piece of paper or for the telephone.

"All business," Marks said, explaining the fundamentals, "is in two categories—the expense end and the money end. At the expense end are bookkeepers, cashiers, accountants, lawyers, doctors, architects. They seldom get paid in accordance with their knowledge and experience; there's always a question about the charges. If you're sick you'd pay a doctor ten thousand dollars to cure you; but after the operation he sends a bill for four hundred and you don't like to pay it—all he did was an hour's work, maybe less. When business turns bad, people on the expense end are always competing with beginners. Trying for security, they're always putting themselves in the hole.

"On the money end it's different. If you're a good salesman or in business for yourself you keep what you make. The salesman is a money-producer, and the employer is afraid to fire him. I was looking for something on the money-producing end.

"First I worked at a news-stand and then in factories—railroads and ammunition, I consider myself an expert machinist. I studied accounting on my own, and got a Wall Street job as a bookkeeper. At lunchtime I worked on the cables, and finally I took over the cable work. This gave me a taste for arbitrage; I knew I had found a type of work with which I could be happy. I quit a sixty-dollar a week job as a bookkeeper to learn arbitrage, and for five years I made about five dollars a week.

"Then I took a job as a commission trader, and went from firm to firm. I was always taken advantage of. Once, I was about to go on vacation and somebody called me up and asked me if I wanted to speculate in German marks. I said, Yes, but not too heavily—I don't have any money. I got back from vacation and I was told I'd lost two hundred dollars. I didn't ask any questions—what could I do? I began paying them off at once, two dollars a week. The man who had called me was impressed, and offered me a job.

"I was working for him at a 40-per-cent commission, and in three months in 1923 I made $100,000 in commissions. They should have paid me $40,000, but they said, No, and they gave me $7,500 plus what was in my drawing account, maybe as much as $5,000 more. I quit and went to another firm, and the same thing happened.

"A. H. Danino, who was a Syrian, he had a money exchange at the foot of Whitehall Street and South Ferry. In 1925 we went into partnership and we were making a lot of money when I found he was doing something I didn't like. I took out my original money, and the people I knew and liked, and went into business as Carl Marks and Company."

At the top of the wall beside Marks' desk is a rack with much enlarged pictures of half a dozen men. Marks waved at the pictures. "We started at the end of '25," he said, "and there are very few people here today who haven't been here more than twenty years. My policy was to surround myself with the best people I could find and treat them as I wanted to be treated myself. In my opinion anybody who establishes such a policy is sure to be successful. I decided at the beginning the smart thing was to pay the workers as much as I possibly could—a reasonable salary, then up to 40 per cent of the profits as a bonus. I made it 40 per cent because that's the highest commission paid for bringing in business. Then I set up a policy of a 10-per-cent salary increase every year, at least 10 per cent. We have a promotion system, too. We've had practically no turnover in the office. The bonuses run from three to four hundred thousand dollars a year. There are about fifty people who work for Carl Marks and Company. It's an immense business but we keep it small."*

This is an office that turns over $200,000,000 worth of foreign securities every year; it doesn't look it. The reception room is a wallpapered box with three delivery slots feeding into a cage. On the other side, with a picture window facing into the cage, is the trading room, locked and soundproofed. Behind the picture window, on opposite sides of a long, high switchboard, sit eight apparently ordinary men in shirtsleeves. There is not an inch of clear space on the two tables at which they work. One end of the room is a blackboard, with prices chalked beside the symbols of faraway securities. A private wire to London ticks away, and ordinary phone calls come in from banks, brokers and financial institutions all over the world (Carl Marks & Co. does no business directly with the public). Within this room is America's greatest market in the securities of Argentina, Australia, Belgium, Bolivia, Brazil, Canada, Chile, China, Columbia, Costa Rica, Cuba, Czechoslovakia, Denmark, Ecuador, Finland, France, Great Britain, Greece, Haiti, Holland, Italy, Japan, Mexico, Norway, Peru, Poland, Portugal, Russia, Salvador, Sweden, Switzerland, Uruguay and Yugoslavia.

Where there are exchange markets abroad in these securities Marks' traders will arbitrage them, buying in one place and selling in another, instantaneously picking up a small but important profit on each deal. The traders also make a normal over-the-counter market in the bonds of foreign governments, stocks and bonds of foreign corporations. They take big positions where they expect the prices to go up, as they did

---

* 1959: Bonuses are now half a million, with sixty people working in the office.

with Japanese securities in late 1953. And, finally, Marks' office does special, amazing deals directly for the accounts of foreign governments.

"We have one man," Marks said, "who speaks at least a dozen languages; he travels round the world for us. Another man trades with central Europe. He has an assistant because the securities are quite active. Another man deals with continental securities. Another only in sterling securities. Another only in dollar securities, bonds which were issued over here by foreign governments and sold for dollars, with dollars to be paid in interest. Most of these are listed on the Stock Exchange, but we make the market. Another deals in Cuban securities, another in Canadian and Argentine.

"I claim that it takes you five years, sitting in the proper place, and with the proper advice, to get a background in this business; then another five years as an assistant, learning to trade."

In 1942 taxes began jumping and most companies started bonus plans for their employees. (As an employee said of an employer, "The old man found somebody he hated worse than the people who work for him—the government.") The federal tax authorities rather resented this reaction to the excess profits tax, and took steps. Carl Marks was paying his employees—traders, secretaries, everybody—the highest proportionate bonuses in the world, and the Internal Revenue Department hauled him up to explain. The fact that he had been paying such bonuses since the inception of his firm, back before there was a corporation income tax, let him off the hook. But to solidify his position he prepared a memorandum of his reasons for high bonuses; one section described his traders, who are "executives" of the firm:

(1) Executives must apply their full and undivided effort to their work to the exclusion of all outside interests. They may not participate or engage in any other undertaking whatsoever, directly or indirectly, regardless of whether same is in a similar or entirely different business sphere.

(2) . . . . these "Key Employees" remain at their desk uninterruptedly, even for lunch. It is not unusual to work long after regular hours and on Saturdays, Sundays and holidays. Study or research must be done after when possible.

(3) The Executive creates most of his own transactions. . . . Each man is irreplaceable, and when absent or on vacation, the greater portion of his dealings may be considered as lost. . . .

(4) Executives must have a natural talent and a highly special-

ized training. Each person requires from five to ten years of intensive, supervised training and active experience in this type of business before assuming complete responsibility. When he is able to create his own original business in which he becomes one of the foremost authorities in his field, he becomes a "Key Employee." The steps are gradual, as in a school, and continuous study, hard work and untiring effort are required to maintain this position. At his work he is subject to continuous mental strain caused by the necessity of making extremely important decisions at any given instant, by the pressure of time in which to accomplish his purpose and by the high nervous tension required to maintain an ever alert mind. His outside activities must be regulated so as to obtain sufficient rest and sleep and special attention must be given to his health, so that he will be able to attain, without effort, that high pitch of attention so necessary to the best performance of his duties. . . .

(6) The "Key Employee" must have character and personality. He must be able to meet and favorably impress representatives of banks and brokers, as well as officials of Foreign countries, graded from Financial Counsellor to Finance Minister or even Governor or President. He is expected to make constructive suggestions to Foreign Governments. . . .

(7) An Executive must have a broad accurate knowledge of Foreign and Domestic economic conditions, of International and Foreign Law, and of exchange restrictions and regulations and their relation to the firm's business. There are very few branches of art or science that do not tend to improve a trader's ability.

(8) An Executive must be an expert arbitrageur. . . . He must be able, without hesitation, to discern the possibilities of buying securities in one Foreign market and selling same in another. To do this the trader . . . must take into consideration market fluctuations in the respective Foreign countries, expenses involved in each market, such as commissions, taxes, stamps, shipping, cost of finance, length of time required for completion of transactions, and possible risks and penalties involved. . . .

(9) A "Key Executive" for our firm is a small Stock Exchange in himself. . . .

Marks studied this document, which goes back some years now. "It's still true," he said, and passed it over. "On the secretaries and the others, you can understand how important it is to me that nobody on the outside shall ever know what our plans are at any time."

This staff, and his own genius, have enabled Marks to cut out almost the whole of the foreign securities business for himself. When he opened his office, J. P. Morgan, Chase National Bank, Brown Brothers Harriman and Kidder Peabody were the giants of international finance; today they are just bankers, and Carl Marks & Co. does the risk work.

Morgan was responsible for the introduction of French securities to this country; by 1939 the great majority of American transactions in French internal bonds were done in the offices of Carl Marks & Co. German and Japanese bonds were brought back into the American market by bankers; today Carl Marks & Co. does 75 per cent of all trading in them.

Before the war Marks was the official agent of the German government, buying up for their account German securities held in this country. "In August, 1939," Marks recalls, "they told us to stop buying and to have everything delivered within two weeks. We told the State Department. It was one of the first signs the State Department had," Marks added earnestly, "that the Germans had set a time for the war."

Many of Marks' most profitable deals have been the result of his work for foreign governments. The bonds of foreign governments often sell at a considerable discount, and Marks works out ways in which the governments can buy them in cheaply and quietly. He does not worry about the credit ratings of foreign governments—"Not many people realize it," he says, "but there have been in all history only two repudiations of foreign debts—one in Russia and one in the United States. Confederate bonds. Even the Russian bonds aren't entirely dead; in 1933 Russia agreed to consider paying off its debts, which were only $75,000,000 then, and since then the debts have been reduced substantially by conquest and confiscation. Theoretically they aren't dead at all."* A few years ago Marks worked out a scheme by which the Italian government could redeem $40,000,000 of its $132,000,000 debt (then selling for only $160 per $1,000 bond), merely by paying the interest. Marks outlined the deal, which involved several bank loans and the use of the interest payments every year until 1967 to retire the loans. The Italian government took his outline over to a Swiss banking house, which offered to do the job for less money than Marks would charge. "That was fine with us," Marks said. "We saw the deal starting, because you can't buy that many bonds without making something of a stir in the market. So we bought a couple of million dollars of bonds, sold at a higher price and made more money than we would have made if we had done the deal ourselves.

"You see," Marks said patiently, "we knew the plan.

---

* 1959: Technical considerations in a recent proposed payment plan have made Russian bonds almost unsaleable. But, obviously, they still aren't dead.

Others can't do that to us because they don't know anything about our plans except what we tell them. Back in 1937, we had the sole order to repatriate Chilean bonds, on a fee basis. We say, 'We want to buy $4,000,000 face value of bonds at $250 each—and we'll buy 'em from anybody.' Anyone who tries to ride with us is speculating on our timing, our future intentions. It's not often profitable for him."

Marks has some trouble getting bank loans to finance his clearings and his special inventory positions. "They say, 'You folks make the market—how do we know what the real price is?'" There is the same problem with the trading prices, but Marks takes care of that in his typical manner. "This," he says, "is the type of organization that can accept responsibilities. We guarantee that any execution is as good as can be got—and we will adjust at any time if the customer could have got a better deal. A bank wants to sell $20,000 of Norwegian Kroner bonds; we say they're worth $115 a thousand. How does the banker know what they're worth? But we guarantee to protect him. Everybody is entitled to know all the transaction details on everything we buy or sell, if he wants them. I say, 'This is the best price you can get anywhere.' You can check me, and I'm right."

In 1958, Carl Marks and his little office of sixty people made a gross profit of almost $5,000,000; a net profit better than $2,000,000. (Four years ago these figures were $2,000,000 and $1,000,000; "The world is getting smaller and smaller," Marks wrote in a recent letter, "and people are becoming much more interested in 'foreign' shares than ever.") Much of it came from very small transactions, in markets all over the world; telephone calls, cables, letters, all the expensive minutiae of doing business at long distance. Somebody mentioned to Marks recently that this tiny piecing together of enormous deals must be a considerable nuisance.

He was surprised. "Nothing is a nuisance," he said, "where you can make money."

For the past few years, Marks has also been working energetically on a cherished side project which would bring him nothing whatever. It is a plan to broaden and ease world trade through an international group, a voluntary organization of nations, each of which would set up a National Exchange Bank. This bank, by bilateral agreements, would guarantee the accounts of foreign purchasers, enabling them to do business without the present worries over international credit ratings and currency exchanges. The plan would thus effectively reduce the costs of foreign trade, and could be made self-insuring. Marks has taken weeks of his immensely valuable time to promote the plan with U.S. and U.N. and World Bank officials, who have responded by patting him on the head and thanking him for his interest.

"Eventually, however," he said, "it has to come. The only people who profit by the present system are the international currency gamblers; everybody else loses. It's just commonsense that nobody but governments should have to worry about international exchange. So my plan, or something like it, is inevitable—in fact, the way the plan would punish defaulters is by making them return to the way they do business today. That would be so horrible they wouldn't risk it."

3

There is domestic arbitrage as well as foreign arbitrage. A stock will often be traded on several different exchanges, and whenever the prices at two exchanges get even slightly out of line there is money to be made buying on one exchange and selling on the other. More important, there are always mergers and reorganizations, new securities coming out to be exchanged for old ones; and inevitably both old and new exist together for a period. If two of the new are to be exchanged for one of the old, and the new does not cost *exactly* half as much on the market, there is money to be made by playing the different pieces of paper against each other. Finally, there is the arbitrage in A.T. & T. convertible debentures, which involves marketable rights to buy the debentures, the price of the debentures themselves and then a payment to convert the bonds to stock. These three prices added together—the price of the rights, the debentures and the conversions—will always be very slightly less than the market price of the stock. So there is a sure, quick 2 per cent or so to be made by selling the stock short and buying the rights. A month after the last set of rights was issued, the "short interest" in A.T. & T. was more than fifty thousand shares (which was eight million dollars' worth of A.T. & T.) on the New York Stock Exchange alone.*

The man who had sold those fifty thousand shares of A.T. & T., and runs almost every other large domestic arbitrage, is Gustave L. Levy of Goldman, Sachs & Co., a tall,

---

* 1959: It seems likely, in the light of the recent stock split, that we have seen our last issue of A.T. & T. convertible debentures.

black-haired Southerner in his early forties, the biggest money man on Wall Street. He can summon spirits from the vast deep, and money instantaneously from almost any commercial or investment banking house in the country. He is also that necessary insurer of risks, the man who will bail any reputable house out of almost any situation. If an underwriter is embarrassed by a shelf sagging under the leftovers of an unsuccessful underwriting, he calls Gus Levy and Gus Levy gives him a price. Levy's sense of the market is the most acute on Wall Street, and Levy's price is a wholly accurate, fair statement of his market insight. He was a legend before he was out of his twenties, and today, in his middle forties, he commands from his fellows the kind of respect that far more famous men might envy.

"I remember once," said an officer of the American Stock Exchange, "we had a broker come in here very disturbed. His teletype or telephone had got a message garbled, and he'd sold twelve hundred shares of a stock he didn't own and his customers didn't own. Goldman had bought it, but the broker didn't have the nerve to call up himself and try to make a settlement. He was working up the nerve, but he hadn't done it yet.

"Well, I felt sorry for the guy, who was in some trouble, and I called Gus Levy and I told him the story. Levy said, 'Did the guy give you a hard time?' I said, No, he was just unhappy, he hadn't tried to blame the Exchange for it. Levy said, 'Did he ask you to call me?' I said, No, it was my own idea. Levy said, 'Do you like the guy?' I said, Yes, he's a nice person.

" 'Okay,' Levy said. 'Cancel the deal. We'll get the stock some other time.' "

A moral was drawn: "If you give Gus Levy a straight story, and you're square with him all down the line, he'll go down the line for you. All he wants to know is that you're level with him."

Levy is a kind of folk hero, a John Henry of finance, and he lives in a place that only a folk hero could tolerate—the Goldman, Sachs trading room. This unornamental, narrow box looks like the wardroom of a destroyer, and sounds like the engine room of a battleship.* There is nothing to absorb the sounds made by the wire system to branch offices in Boston, Chicago, Detroit, Philadelphia and St. Louis, to

---

* 1959: Shortly after this book was published Levy had a heart attack. The Goldman trading room has moved to less barbaric surroundings.

correspondents in Atlanta, Buffalo, Dallas, Los Angeles, Montreal, Pittsburgh and San Francisco. Goldman makes over-the-counter markets in more than 150 common and preferred stocks, and about 75 bonds; and arbitrage is the profitable offshoot of the trading business.

Levy started as a runner in a New Orleans brokerage house at the age of eighteen, and five years later he was a trader for Goldman, Sachs. "*The* trader, as a matter of fact," he says. "There wasn't anybody else." That was in 1933, after the demise of the ill-starred Goldman, Sachs Trading Corporation, and business was pretty grim. In 1946 he was made a partner in the firm, and he holds the firm's seat on the New York Stock Exchange. "I never go down there, though, except to say hello to friends. Never have executed an order on the floor." He supervises the over-the-counter department, which takes the services of a dozen traders. "We carry very big inventories," he says. "Most of the time, too big." But arbitrage is his first love.

"Most arbitrage situations," he says, "arise out of mergers, convertible issues, stock rights, simplifications of capital structure. We wait to see the proxy statement before we move—we've been wrong on occasion, especially in mergers. We want to be sure that the deal won't take too long to go through, and that the security we buy isn't overvalued, regardless of the possible arbitrage.

"The work itself, of course, is mostly financed by bank loans. The profit is very quick but very small, and if you can convince a bank to put up 80 per cent of the money, your profits increase five-fold. Since it's quick, the interest you pay is no hindrance."

Arbitrage, of course, is the most exotic plant in the financial greenhouse; it is no task for amateurs. "You need a lot of capital," says Levy modestly, "good credit and know-how."

4

Goldman, Sachs is a rich firm, and Levy can call on many, many banks to help finance his work; but sometimes a job gets so big that outside help is needed. That happened with the A.T. & T. 1953 issue of convertible debentures, and Levy turned to Wertheim & Co., which was glad to take a piece of its 22-million-dollar capital and give Levy the use of it in a joint account.

Wertheim is always ready for special deals; it is the special situations firm *par excellence*. Its most spectacular and famous deal was in the common stock of Nedick's, Inc., the New York chain of hot-dog and orange-drink stands which went bust in the early thirties. The late Maurice Wertheim, one of the founders of the firm (and of the Theatre Guild and half a dozen other cultural enterprises), bought the company, very casually, at a total cost of $60,000, including lawyers' fees. That was in 1934; between 1934 and 1951 Wertheim took out of Nedick's more than $2,000,000 in dividends, and in 1951 sold it to National Phoenix Industries for nearly $4,000,-000. The total profit was some $5,900,000, or nearly 10,000 per cent.

This is regarded at Wertheim as a successful deal, but there have been others even more successful, especially in Cuban sugar properties. Cuban sugar properties have gone down seriously in value since 1949, which Wertheim is sorry about —but not hurt. Wertheim sold out in 1948.

Wertheim in 1958 took underwriting participations high in five figures, did substantial business in brokerage and made a number of markets over the counter. Its primary work, however, is in the investment of its own capital. It takes risks that nobody else on Wall Street would dream of taking, and it makes the kind of profits that everybody dreams of making. Some of its work is with previously unknown companies, now expanding and looking for lots of risk money not available in ordinary underwriting channels. Another part lies in mass purchasing of listed and unlisted securities which, in the opinion of the firm, are radically undervalued.

A writer once called these securities "cats and dogs," the Street phrase for low-priced securities with no present earning power behind them, and Wertheim screamed for the police. " 'Cats and dogs,' " said Henry Hottinger, a partner in the firm, "well, the way it is with cats and dogs, you buy them and then you put them away in the attic and you hope that when you die your relatives won't find them." Actually, Wertheim's animals are usually good companies fallen in the doldrums. Where possible, Wertheim likes to buy a majority interest in the company, so that its voice will be heeded if its voice must be raised.* Often the companies Wertheim buys are in need of financial reorganization, and Wertheim likes to be able to advise on how the reorganization shall be

* 1959: This is not true. Wertheim wants its voice to be heard, but it does not wish to undertake the responsibilities involved in actual ownership. Indeed, if it doesn't like and trust the existing management, it will not buy.

carried through. It will not ordinarily interfere, however, in the business management of the company.

The other side of the operation, supplying new money to expanding corporations, is even more difficult, and more valuable to the economy at large. Here the central judgment that must be made is a judgment on the value of the management. There are many owners of middling-small businesses who can handle their middling-small volume so brilliantly that their companies seem assured a huge future. When the money for expansion is supplied, however, they fall on their faces: they are small-business executives, not large-scale co-ordinators. Wertheim's people have developed a second sight into the psychology of enterprise, which men can and which men cannot manage a big, expanding business; and this is perhaps the most amazing example of special skills on Wall Street.

Wertheim's people are always out looking for deals, and deals are always flooding into the office, which occupies a quiet half a floor of the enormous Equitable Building at 120 Broadway. Among the other tenants are the odd-lot dealers Carlisle & Jacquelin, the Bankers' Club and, wedged against the elevators in a corner of the ground floor, the smallest, noisiest and most crowded lunch-counter in the district. The building itself occupies the entire block bounded by Broadway, Nassau, Pine and Cedar streets, and soars some fifty stories into the sky. It is one of the few real estate corporations listed on the New York Stock Exchange, so that nobody owns all of it. Wertheim used to own a controlling interest, however; bought it cheap, sold it dear.

5

Not all the special occupations on Wall Street involve big money; some of them are very small indeed. B. S. Lichtenstein & Co., for example, is Ben Lichtenstein and one girl, on the thirteenth floor of 99 Wall Street. Another man might be lonely out there, near the East River, where all his neighbors are commodity brokers; but Lichtenstein is obviously a man incapable of gloom or depression. "Life dazzles me," he says.

He runs an insurance business somewhat similar to Gus Levy's insurance business; but while Levy buys from underwriters perfectly good securities that have been overpriced, Lichtenstein buys junk. Unless a corporation has surrendered its charter (which means that the stock represents nothing, and cannot even be transferred), Lichtenstein will probably be willing to bail a broker's customer out of it. He does no business with the public directly, and most of the business he does with brokers will involve stock that neither the broker nor Lichtenstein nor anybody else ever heard of before a customer called up and said he wanted to sell it.

"The idea," Lichtenstein says, "is that out of every thousand stocks that I buy, one or two or three or four or ten will suddenly come to life and get profitable. I have better odds than most people, because I have ways of checking whether the corporation is still sufficiently in business to give the stock a chance. Even when I can't check, though, I'll sometimes take the gamble, because that way I do a service for a broker and some day he'll do a service for me. I won't tell you how I check up on stocks, because if I did you'd set up in competition with me. This is a profitable business. If it were a sufficiently profitable business I'd be retired. I'm a very lazy man."

Lichtenstein is all energy. He has seriously weak eyes, so weak that special secondary lenses must be taped on to his already thick glasses to enable him to focus, and the telephone on his desk has a special large disc around the dial to enable him to read the numbers. Nevertheless, he is an omnivorous reader, interested in everything. He advertises his business as dealing in "obsolete securities," and in his little two-inch ads he gives full rein to whatever may be interesting him at the moment. For example, he goes to the theatre:

"KIND SIR"
We're kind, sir, to obsoletes

In 1953 he made a long trip to Europe and had a wonderful time. "I could talk for weeks about my business," he said, "it fascinates me. But I'd rather talk about Europe. Don't miss Greece, whatever you do." Since he pays a yearly bill for his ad in the *Commercial and Financial Chronicle,* and gets a great kick out of writing advertising copy, he celebrated his business even while he wasn't around to do it:

We've left the cats and dogs here
to visit the alleyways of Europe
BIG BEN
OF LONDON
And Ben L. have one thing
in common—"obsolete"

"I went into the securities business on May first, 1926," he says, "and I was interested in this end of it on May second, 1926. And when I finally went out on my own, in 1937, I was busted—I couldn't afford to get in good companies. I had to get into junk.

"Actually, 'obsolete' is a misnomer. There is in my mind a terrific difference between no market value and no value. A corporation worth ten million dollars can have no market value because one family owns all the stock, and there's no market. I deal in stocks of corporations which have got so deeply into trouble that the market for their stock has disappeared. That doesn't mean the stock has no value.

"For example, a broker called me a while back about a streetcar company in Canada. His customer had twenty shares, for which he'd paid some money many years ago, and now the customer wanted to sell out and take a tax loss. There were only twenty shares involved. I checked up on the company, couldn't find out much about it. It was still in business, all right, running lots of streetcars, it had a lot of money and it owed a lot more money. No market for it anywhere. Well, I took the chance; I offered a nickel a share and bought the twenty shares for a dollar. Nobody else would have bought them at all.*

"About eighteen months later, I got a letter. A minority stockholder in the company wanted to buy up the ownership, and he offered $6.93 a share. That was a big profit—$138.60 for stock that had cost me a dollar. But it doesn't happen often, and there are fifty to five hundred that I buy which will never return a penny." The worst of them, however, can sometimes be sold in another market; on several occasions Lichtenstein has supplied worthless certificates to traders who want wallpaper for a rumpus room.

The telephone rang and Lichtenstein picked it up. The voice on the other end said, "Hello, Mr. Lichtenstein, this is Chapman at Merrill Lynch. How are you?"

"Terrible, thank you," said Lichtenstein cheerfully. "And you?"

"Oh—uh—fine. I have some Blank Double Zero stock here

---

* 1959: It might be well to stress more strongly the tax loss aspect of these transactions, which otherwise look silly—all that fuss to collect one dollar for a bundle of waste paper. But the internal revenue agent tends to be sticky about capital-loss debits on income-tax forms unless the paper has actually been sold. And the established loss may represent a very large tax saving. If Lichtenstein does not buy the stock, he may be able to supply proof that the corporation has disappeared, and the stock is eternally worthless—and such proof satisfies the tax collector as well as a sale. This is what Lichtentein means when he says he "runs a free statistical service."

that a customer wants me to sell for him——"

"I'm sorry, that's worthless," Lichtenstein said, equally cheerfully.

"Oh, I thought——"

"No, it had some value until the fall of 1952, but then the company went completely out of business and surrendered its charter. Completely worthless—sorry!"

"Thanks for the information—and good-bye."

"Good-bye."

Lichtenstein regarded his glorious view of the East River, and the bridges marching across, one after the other. "R. M. Smythe was in my business," he said, "a very peculiar man. He advertised himself as 'No-Telephone' Smythe, and he wouldn't have a phone in his office. He left his papers to the Marvin Scudder Library of Worthless Securities, up at Columbia. It's an interesting place to visit."

He looked out the other corner, to the magnificence of the Wall Street skyline, all of it to the west of him, etched clearly about and above him. "People are decent," he said. "I run a free statistical service here; I get information that brokers are too lazy to get for themselves; besides, it wouldn't pay them to get it. Then I give them that information to give to their customers, and if the stock has any possibility of value I buy it. So when they can do me a favor, they're glad to do it."

6

Further away from corporate finance, but far closer to the zigs and zags of the market, is the options business—Puts and Calls. Options for securities are like options for the services of movie stars, or options to buy buildings. A real estate broker, trying to put together a large parcel of land on which to build a skyscraper, may go around to the owner of a bar-and-grill and say, "Joe, I think I may want to buy your building at a real good price—a hundred thousand dollars. I haven't got the thing put together yet, and I need all the buildings on the block: the deal falls through if I can't get them all. I'll give you five hundred bucks right now, though, if you'll give me an option to buy the building at a hundred thousand." Joe figures it out carefully and sees that he has nothing to lose—he's willing to sell for a hundred thousand, and he get five hundred whether or not the broker buys. He gives the broker an option, and takes his five C's.

An option to buy a stock is known as a Call; an option to

sell is known as a Put. The basic principle is that the price of the stock is thereby fixed to the man who buys the option. If U.S. Steel is selling at $89, a Call on one hundred shares of U.S. Steel for the next thirty days might cost $137.50. (This is the traditional price for a thirty-day option; it apparently originated in Holland, where tulip bulbs were traded wildly and options were the prime means of speculating on them.) For this $137.50 the man who buys the Call gets the right to buy one hundred shares of U.S. Steel at $89, at any time during the next thirty days. If the price goes up to $95, he exercises his call, buys one hundred shares for $8,900, goes to the Stock Exchange, sells one hundred shares for $9,500, and winds up ahead by $600, less commissions and the $137.50 he paid for the option. If the price goes down, he simply lets the option expire. Whatever happens, his risk is no more than $137.50.

Puts work in exactly the opposite manner. A man who buys a Put on U.S. Steel at $89 has the right to *sell* one hundred shares of U.S. Steel at that price at any time during the next thirty days. If the price goes up he is not interested; but if it goes down, say to $83, he will go to the Exchange and buy one hundred shares for $8,300, then exercise his option to sell one hundred shares for $8,900, winding up ahead by $600, less commissions and the money he paid for his option. His risk, too, is only $137.50.

Options are usually available in periods of 30, 60, 90 and 120 days, six months and nine months. The longer the option, the more it costs. An option on a high-priced stock costs more than an option on a low-priced stock (a five point fluctuation is small for a $100 stock, large for a $25 stock). Moreover, the price of the option will also be influenced by prevailing market opinion: if the general belief around is that U.S. Steel will shortly be selling for $93, a Call on U.S. Steel at $89 will probaby cost $400 instead of $137.50 (this figure is a little low, anyway). Alternatively, the customer could probably buy a Call at $93 instead of $89, and pay 137.50. For the customer to make money on this latter option, the price will have to go from $89 to $94½ (4 points plus 1⅜ plus profit); while he can make money at $93⅛ by paying more for his option and taking it at the current price. The reason for the difference is that cash in the hand is worth twice protection in the bush; the man who sells the former option will make only $137.50 if it is not exercised, while the man who sells the latter must make $400 and is therefore willing to give the customer a better break.

Options are most obviously a cheap way to gamble in stocks, and often a very effective way, too. In a widely fluctuating market a lengthy option can produce immense profits even though the stock winds up where it started: by giving its purchaser an anchor it lets him play in safety. Suppose, for example, he buys a six-month Call on U.S. Steel at $89, and the price goes up to $95. He need not exercise his option at all. He sells short at $95, knowing that he can buy at $89 if he wishes. Then suppose the trend reverses, and U.S. Steel backs down to $83. He simply buys U.S. Steel at $83, making $1,200 on his short sale. He still has his Call, unused. And while the market was heading downward he was enjoying that dream of glory—the riskless gamble. If the market should now go up again, he can play the game again, over and over for six months on one Call, as long as the market gyrates around his contracted price. (The same process, in reverse, works on the Put: the price first goes down, the customer buys stock and holds it, selling out when the price goes over the level of the Put. Since he can always sell at $89, he runs no risk in holding on to the stock he has purchased.)

Beyond the gambling aspect, options can be used to hedge, and as such they are more effective than the stop-loss order on an Exchange.* The example of the stop-loss order is the man who buys at $89 because he thinks U.S. Steel is going up; and if his calculations are right he believes the stock should not fall below $85 in any market swing. If it does fall to $85, he is willing to admit that his calculations were wrong, so he asks his broker to enter a stop-loss order, which will sell him out at $85. The stop-loss order has two problems: it sells the customer out of his stock, even though he may be right and the longer trend is up; and it may prove ineffective, since a rush of selling orders may push the price well below $85 before it can be executed by the specialist. By purchasing a Put, the customer insures himself a selling price of $89 and limits his possible loss to the cost of the Put. He does not have to worry about the short-term fluctuation and he has no reason to panic out if the stock drops sharply. In short, he need make only the judgment that the price is going

* 1959: The Put is also, of course, more expensive than a stop-loss order, which costs nothing until it becomes effective, and then only standard commission.

up; he does not have to bother about the even trickier judgment of how low it may go before it does start heading up. If the price goes up, the cost of the Put is deducted from the profits.

These are the reasons for buying options; the reasons for selling them are simpler. A man who owns one hundred shares of U.S. Steel can sell them for only $8,900 if the market is $89; if he sells a Call for $137.50, and the Call is exercised, he sells his stock, in effect, for $9,037.50. He has sacrificed some of his profit potential on the stock, but he has been paid for the sacrifice. The sensible seller of options regards them as ways to reduce the cost of the stock he owns; if he paid $85 for his U.S. Steel, and sells a Call for $137.50, he can figure that his stock cost him only $83⅝ a share—$85 less $1.375. If the Call is exercised he has a profit; if the price of the stock goes down, and the Call is not exercised, he has reduced the effective cost to him of the stock he owns.

The options business is a little business; but not very little. In an average year, the volume of shares on which options are bought and sold will run about 1 per cent of the volume of trading on the New York Stock Exchange—six million shares, say, or sixty thousand option contracts. All these options are bought and sold by fewer than thirty firms, all in New York and all members of the Put & Call Brokers Association. Although they occasionally sell the options themselves, their more usual method is to find purchasers for people who want to sell options, or supplies for people who want to buy options. They make their own livings by taking a price mark-up on each deal. If the average mark-up is fifty dollars (it is probably a little higher), the Put and Call brokers among them may make a gross profit of two and a half million dollars a year, an average of nearly a hundred thousand dollars a firm. There is no such thing as a Put and Call broker's office which employs more than three people or occupies more than two rooms in the back of a building; so business is pretty good, considering.

The Put and Call broker lives by his list of customers, his ability to find buyers and sellers of options. The competition among these brokers is severe, but it is not really a price competition because two options on the same stock often represent completely different pieces of goods. A thirty-day Call at today's market is very hard to compare to a six-month Call at a price a few points higher. Nevertheless, three firms regularly place one-column, four-inch ads in the *New York Times* and the New York *Herald Tribune,* offering options for sale. The response is small; but every response is a new name to call tomorrow, and tomorrow, and tomorrow; and once a customer gets used to options he may buy a lot of options in a year.

The usual spokesman for the options business is Herbert Filer of Filer, Schmidt & Co., a tall, white-haired man erect as Cleopatra's needle, who loves his business and will spend hours patiently explaining it. Like most people on Wall Street, he spends two-thirds of his working day on the telephone, but his soliciting is probably a little more active, a little more in the salesman tradition. And he has more than the usual trouble bringing in new customers, because however carefully they are explained, options are complicated.

For example, there are Spreads and Straddles in addition to Puts and Calls—Spreads which give the customer the right to buy *or* sell at a fixed price during the life of the option, Straddles which give him the right to buy *and* sell during the life of the contract. And . . .

Chapter 11

The Money Managers

"I REMEMBER when I was a boy," says Harry I. Prankard, managing partner of Lord, Abbett & Co., one of the largest managers of mutual funds, "my father brought me down from Troy for a visit to New York. It was in 1915 or so, and I remember reading in the newspapers about the trial of what must have been the last big bucket-shop operator in New York.

"In case you're to young to know it, a bucket shop is just like an ordinary brokerage office—except that the operator doesn't belong to any exchange, and doesn't execute any orders for his customers. If a customer comes in and 'buys' a hundred shares, the bucket-shop operator just makes a mark in a book, saying that he owes so-and-so a hundred shares. In effect, he goes short of the stock. In reality, he bets against his customer.

"Well, this particular bucket-shop operator was confused and disappointed that he had been hauled into court. He was an honest man, he said; he'd never gypped any customer. Anybody who was ahead and wanted to sell could get his money. The operator wasn't hurting a soul.

"What was more interesting to my young mind was the operator's records—very scrupulously kept. His records showed that he made money on *87 per cent* of all his transactions—in other words, that the public was right only thirteen times out of a hundred. And I don't think the proportions have changed much over the years."

2

Roger Babson, dean and general oracle of investment analysts, not long ago announced that in his half-century of experience 90 per cent of all investors have lost money on their investments. Considering the fact that there has been a secular trend upward in the stock market, at the rate of 3 per cent a year, Babson's figure was astonishing. But of all the Wall Street professionals to whom the figure was mentioned, only Merrill Lynch thought it was wrong.

Such statistics as are available indicate that the public in general starts buying a stock as it nears the crest of its rise, holds on to it stubbornly as it drops down the other side of the wave, and then sells resignedly well before the top of the upswing.* Enthusiasm for a security percolates down from the professionals to the customers' men (who are not professionals in the sense of having a profession) to the public only after the price has risen substantially; disappointment, or the sentiment that the thing is now overpriced, percolates down only after the price has reflected the new attitudes. The individual investor, at the mercy of his emotions, his incomplete anaytical equipment and general ignorance of economics, will rarely make an accurate decision as to whether a stock is overpriced or undervalued at the present market.

This situation has been generally recognized for some years, and various people have opened various doors to help the public out of it. There are several thousand investment advisers or investment counsels registered with the Securities and Exchange Commission and selling advice to the public. Firms such as Lehman Brothers run extensive investment advisory services, Wertheim & Co. gives its customers an opportunity to participate in its deals, Gus Levy will allow some of Goldman, Sachs' clients a piece of his work in arbitrage. The Mellon family hires Charles Davis to invest the Mellon money; the trust departments of banks invest dead men's money for the benefit of their widows; and Kuhn, Loeb guarantees that it will increase the income from the investments if the widows will kindly transfer their money from the banks to the trustee division of Kuhn, Loeb.

These services, however, are not available to the ordinary man. Lehman Brothers, for example, limits its investment advisory program to those with $400,000 or more to invest; Wertheim (which charges no fee) has no interest in small accounts; Gus Levy extends his courtesies only to Goldman's best customers. The fee for investment advisers is generally one-half of one per cent of the money invested; which means that the fund to be invested must hit $100,000 before the annual fee reaches $500. Trust departments of banks are notoriously cautious and unimaginative (the laws which govern their operations make them hideously liable for the client's losses unless the money is very conservatively in-

---

* 1959: Unless he needs the cash or quits on the market (both of which are likely to happen near the bottom of a downswing), the investor usually does *not* sell at a price much below his original cost. This is why stocks run into "resistance areas" as they near their previous highs—people who have held the stock through the dip decide to sell while they are even or almost even, and the supply of the stock rises sharply.

vested, so they have a great stake in caution); and even large customers find it almost impossible to get personal attention from trust departments. And the Mellon family is one of the very few that could afford to hire the likes of Charles Davis to manage its money.

Still, people need help with their investments and are willing to pay, within reason, for any help they receive. To catch this audience, business newspapers and magazines generally contain at least a column or two devoted to tips from alleged experts on the stock market. The Thursday edition of the *Commercial and Financial Chronicle,* for example, is devoted almost entirely to the important speeches made that week by businessmen, economists and government officials; but room is found on the second page for a regular feature, "The Security I Like Best," by two analysts. *Financial World,* a magazine with forty-thousand circulation (and a subscription price of twenty dollars a year) gives most of its space to analyses of specific stocks and columns on the general state of the market by an editorial staff of thirty-five. The magazine also protects its subscribers by refusing to accept ads from people it doesn't respect (which includes everybody else who advises about investing, and individual dealers and underwriters whose reputation is not of the highest); and about a thousand of the subscribers also take *Financial World's* investment management service, which costs $225 a year and up, depending on the amount of money managed. *Barron's* and *The Magazine of Wall Street* and *Forbes, Moody's* and *Standard and Poor's* all offer analyses of specific securities. Major L. L. B. Angas, a shy, nervous gentleman with a British accent, who writes pamphlets predicting the general trend of the market, infuriates Wall Street with his attitudes ("the market is mostly a matter of psychology and emotion, and all that you find in balance sheets is what you read into them; we're all guessers to one extent or another, and when we guess wrong they say we're crooks"), his advertisements ("OUR CUSTOMERS HAVE YACHTS!") and the titles of his literary productions (one of them, in early 1954, was called "PREPARE ONCE MORE TO SCURRY"). Major Angas himself thinks most highly of one rival service, Quinn's *Factographs* ("the man is literally decades ahead of all the rest of us—oh, here I go, making enemies again"), and bemoans, perhaps with a certain self-interest, that Quinn has often had bad luck with his actual forecasts. . . .

One of the biggest and most highly respected of all the investment services is Arnold Bernhard's *Value Line,* which makes four reports a year on every one of some six hundred stocks, predicting future market prices on the basis of a complicated multiple-correlation statistical analysis. A graph is drawn, with twelve little up-and-down lines in every year to show the monthly range of prices for the stock; then the statisticians juggle with five factors influencing stock prices until they have found a formula which explains every important price movement in the last twenty years. Bernhard's staff then makes an educated guess about the company's earnings and dividends for the coming year, and the statisticians, applying their formula, draw a line on the graph to indicate where the price should go. Examining the present price and this new line on the graph (called "the rating"), *Value Line* gives each stock one of five labels—"Especially Recommended," "Buy/Hold," "May Be Held," "May Be Held/Switch," or "Switch." In addition to these weekly reports on regularly monitored stocks, *Value Line* offers its 23,500 subscribers (who pay $120 a year per subscription) a weekly Supplement, a monthly recommendation of a Special Situation, a "model account" and a fortnightly commentary on the general state of the economy. There is also an "Over-the-Counter Special Situations Service" with 1,500 subscribers.

Value Line has got safely away from Wall Street itself, far enough away not to be influenced by the tides of emotion that sweep through the canyons. It occupies all of a narrow, five-story building just off Madison Avenue two blocks from Grand Central Station in midtown New York. Bernhard himself has had minimal experience with the brokerage business; he started as a reporter for *Time* magazine, writing about the theatre; moved on to *Moody's Investors Service* and went out on his own as an investment adviser in 1931. (His interests still extend well beyond finance: he is president of the Auden-Barzun-Trilling Mid-Century Book Society.) He started *Value Line* in 1938. "I used to write it, develop the ratings and print it on an offset machine—all by myself," Bernhard said recently. "In a way, I hated to see it grow, I loved the printing end so much." Bernhard is a tall, slightly stooped man with a fringe of black hair over the ears, a toothbrush moustache and a stern expression frequently relaxed by broad, questioning grins. An economist of wide training, ten statisticians, a mathematician and thirty security analysts work on each week's report, which is put in final shape every Tuesday morning at a special staff meeting in Bernhard's office.

Most of the security analysts are young men Bernhard has taken out of the colleges or business schools (every one must have an arts rather than a science degree), and he has trained many of them himself. Each one is assigned an industry or two to watch, and before he makes his Tuesday report another young analyst "proctors" his findings and predictions. The resulting estimates of each company's future earnings and dividends are then sent down to the statisticians and graph-drawers, who project the "rating." Before this material goes to the printer, however, Bernhard gives his young men a Socratic lesson in security analysis.

Every rating that will appear in that week's report is brought up to Bernhard's fifth-floor office, and every prediction must be defended. All the analysts are expected to comment and produce thoughts on what *Value Line* should say about the stock. The attitude is that of the economist rather than that of the market guesser; and *Value Line* will sometimes give greater consideration than the market to the fundamental economic picture. Bernhard saw the market declining in 1954, because the economy was declining; he underestimated the extent to which public relations could influence investors. But consideration of underlying economic factors gives the service a long-run conservatism as regards its customers' assets, which is what its customers need.

This does not mean that *Value Line* is unconcerned about short-term price fluctuations; if it advises a customer to switch, it wants to see the stock go down rather than up in the three months that pass between the regular reports on any one item. Examining the graph at a Tuesday meeting, Bernhard sees a "May Be Held/Switch" recommendation on a relatively low-priced stock that has gone up a point and a half since *Value Line's* last report on it.

"What did we have on that one last time?" he says to the analyst.

" 'May Be Held/Switch.' "

"And it went up, didn't it?"

"Yes."

"Not so good. What did we tell him to switch to, if he switched?"

"Loew's, at eleven."

"That's up four, isn't it?"

"Yes."

"Well, he did all right then," Bernhard says. "Let's look at the next one."

The analysts in the meeting are expected to pay attention at all times, and the atmosphere has some resemblance to a classroom. An analyst caught yawning, for example, may be sent out of the room:

"I'm sorry, sir, but the baby had me up all night."

"That's all right," Bernhard says, very firmly. "I don't doubt you've got a good reason to be tired. Just go back to your desk and catch up on your sleep. I'll call you when we need your report."

What gives *Value Line* its outstanding position among the investment surveys is not the graph and the multiple-correlation analysis, but the very quick, readable and useful report presented in little lumps of fact and language underneath the graph. To some extent, Bernhard recognizes that the factual information may be more important to the customer than the *Value Line* prediction; a note on every page tells the customer how to project his own rating if he feels that earnings and dividends in the months to come will be higher (or lower) than those forecast by the service. In his portfolio management department and his three mutual funds (total assets: $110,000,000), Bernhard sticks by his ratings.

3

Serving many more investors than all of the services, and handling much more money than all the investment counsels put together, are the investment companies, also known as investment trusts and mutual funds. At the end of 1958, these companies had some fourteen billion dollars in net assets, representing the savings of more than two million people. Here is the fastest-growing part of the financial market, and the worst sufferer of growing pains.

Ordinary corporations sell stock to raise money to put up factories and produce goods; investment companies sell stock to raise money to invest in other stocks. The man who buys an investment company stock buys a piece of an investment portfolio with shares in many corporations in many industries, and the services of a professional money manager. In theory at least, his investment is protected by this "diversification" and by the skills of the management.

Investment companies come in several varieties, of which the most important are the open-end mutual fund and the closed-end investment trust. The mutual funds are called open-end because their stock issue is never fixed: they will always (except in time of utter collapse) buy back their own stock on demand from their stockholders, paying the net asset value of the stock; and they will always sell new stock to customers at the net asset value plus a fixed sales commission. Closed-end trusts are exactly like ordinary corporations: their stock issue is more or less set, and the stock is traded over the counter or on an exchange. As a general rule, shares in a closed-end trust will be traded for less than the net asset value behind them, so that the purchaser buys more investment for his money; but this advantage partly disappears when he sells his shares, because he receives less than their net asset value in payment for them.

A special section of the internal revenue code exempts these companies from the corporation income tax, provided that they pay out to their stockholders every year all their capital gains and at least 95 per cent, after expenses, of their dividend and interest receipts. Aside from this break on taxes, however, the stockholder in a fund pays all the costs of indirect investment. The company's bookkeeping, letter writing, dividend paying and annual report-making expenses come out of its earnings, as does a management fee, usually paid to people who are officers of the company, ranging from one-third of one per cent to one per cent a year on the money invested. By the time all the costs of the investment company have been paid, somewhere between 12 and 35 per cent of the dividends earned by the investment have vanished. In times of rising stock prices, however, investment companies have been able to make up this cost through profits on their long-term trading operations.

There are investment companies for every purse and every purpose. Christiana Securities, the du Pont monster, is basically an investment company; and its shares in 1959 topped sixteen thousand dollars each. On the other side are speculative mutual funds with prices of fifty cents to two dollars a share. Some funds undertake to manage all of a customer's money, keeping a certain proportion in government or high-grade corporate bonds; others are common-stock funds which are designed to handle only that proportion of the customer's money which can be risked on stock ownership.

Some funds are devoted to special situations, such as Atlas

Corp., a closed-end trust traded on the New York Stock Exchange, which made its early millions by purchasing other closed-end trusts selling, as usual, for less than their net asset value, and then liquidating its captives. The law now bans such cannibalism by forbidding investment companies to buy more than 10 per cent of any corporation's total stock issue, and Atlas has gone looking, sometimes in very strange places, for other gimmicks. In 1953, for example, it picked up 500,000 shares of Webb & Knapp common stock, which is liquid paper. Atlas of course, is not in this project to make dividend income—Webb & Knapp's watery common stock is not likely to pay a dividend in the foreseeable future. But Bill Zeckendorf of Webb & Knapp is one of the most astute publicity getters in America, and enough publicity might yield Atlas considerable capital gains.

Lehman Corporation, too, concentrates on long-term capital gains, which are taxable to the stockholder at only one-half his income tax rate to a maximum of 25 per cent. But unlike Atlas, which is practically uninterested in dividends, Lehman keeps a balance. More than 60 per cent of its money is usually invested in high-grade and reasonably conservative securities, and only a limited amount is used in special situations. Two of the most remarkable of these were Dome Explorations and Monterery Oil, on both of which the profits, when the stock is finally sold, are likely to better twenty-fold.

This is far and away the most respected of the closed-end companies, and since 1949 it has usually sold at a mark-up from its asset value, one of very few closed-end trusts that has ever done so. Lehman Corporation was started on (ouch!) September 4, 1929, with a capitalization of $100,-000,000, underwritten and sold to the public by Lehman Brothers: present and past partners in Lehman Brothers, their families and trust accounts have held about 10 per cent of the stock from the beginning. The management arrangement is unusual, in that Lehman Brothers gets a management fee of $225,000 a year, which is only one-fifteenth of one per cent of the fund's net asset value; but the corporation also pays salaries to a staff of fifteen senior analysts and a number of statisticians, who help the Lehman Brothers investment advisory service pick good stocks. Total expenses, including all salaries and other corporate costs, plus brokerage fees (90 per cent of which went to Lehman Brothers as brokers), ran to slightly more than $1,100,000 in fiscal

1954—0.7 per cent of the company's assets, 21 per cent of its dividend and interest receipts, 10 per cent of the total dividends, interest and capital gains.

[1959: Last year Lehman launched a giant of a mutual fund, the One William Street Corporation, which started with $250,000,000 of investable money, raised through conventional underwriting plus a soupçon of special publicity. A separate management and investment advisory staff was established to handle the fund, which is organizationally a thing apart from Lehman Bros. & Lehman Corp.]

Perhaps the most fascinating of all investment companies is State Street, founded in 1924 by Richard C. Paine, Richard Saltonstall and a pug-faced, brilliant Boston Cabot named Paul. State Street started as an open-end company, and Cabot and his friends founded it mostly as a way to pool their own money. When the fund reached seventy million dollars, Cabot closed one of the open ends. Seventy million was as much money as he wished to manage, he said; from now on, State Street will redeem its outstanding stock as asset value, but will issue no new stock. The result of this announcement was to set up an over-the-counter market in the stock, with a floor under the bid at a price slightly above the net asset value of the stock—since State Street would redeem at the asset value, a redeemer would have to bid more than the asset value to buy the stock. Public and dealer confidence in Cabot has been such that since 1944, when he closed the books for the last time, he has never had to redeem any stock; it sells constantly at a high premium (sometimes 20 per cent) over the asset value. Among the remarkable special situations in which State Street has participated was the Western Leaseholds proposition; when Morgan Stanley brought it out, State Street's holdings received a market value of many times what they had cost. Cabots, though in many ways an older and more distinguished family, are friendly with Morgans.

The public's confidence in Cabot is shared by Harvard University, which has entrusted its investment fund to his management. This fund has a special purpose: the income from it must make up the yearly deficit that afflicts every educational institution of quality. Cabot, as Treasurer of the University, sets a rate of return on the fund at the beginning of the year, so that everyone can make plans, and then tries to earn more. If he does earn more, he puts the difference into a surplus that will be used if and when income from the fund decreases—and may be used to pay the University its expected income when and if Cabot decides that the market is about to crash and the University's funds had better get out of the investment picture. Cabot would never put Harvard's money into special situations, of course; but he has made some startling profits with it. He employs a research staff of thirty and divides up his brokerage business among nearly one hundred firms, in proportion to the value of the information they give him—and he has a large ear to the ground. In fiscal 1954, the market value of Harvard's investments increased by $57,000,000; by December 1958 the value of the fund was approaching $400,000,000.

Open-end mutual funds got their start in Boston, and many of the biggest—Massachusetts Investors Trust, Keystone Custodian Funds, Boston Fund, Eaton & Howard—are still there. The fourth largest of them all, however, with net assets of nearly $560,000,000, is on Wall Street—Affiliated Fund, managed and sold by Lord, Abbett & Co., which also manages and sells American Business Shares. Affiliated has 152,000 stockholders who own more than 73,000,000 shares of stock—the price is low to tempt the small investor. Its president is Harry I. Prankard, 2nd, who is also president of American Business Shares, and managing partner of Lord, Abbett & Co.

Prankard is a large, stooping awkward man in his early fifties, an accountant who was invited into Lord, Abbett & Co. after the founder died in 1946. Before that he had worked for several accounting firms, maintaining a special interest in mutual funds. While an accountant, he was chairman of the New York State CPA's Investment Trust Committee; like the ASE's Edward McCormick (a personal friend), he has worked both sides of the street. In 1950, when the S.E.C. took after mutual fund literature, he headed the committee from the business that worked out the final Statement of Policy governing investment company sales material.

Affiliated Fund represents money management in its pure state, with the general objective of providing both present and future income to its shareholders. Unlike some other funds, it does not limit its investments to stocks or preferred or bonds (though it is primarily a common stock fund), to "growth" securities or conservative securities, to securities in any industry or nation. If it thinks the market is about to go sour, it can pull out into governments; if it thinks the market is way undervalued, it can borrow money (up to a quarter of its assets) to put into securities. In short, Affiliated hopes to act as a large, young, intelligent and imaginative investor would act on his own account.

Affiliated's lesson to its shareholders, drummed into their skulls by each annual report, is that every stock is a good buy at one price and a bad hold at another: the bluest chip can get too highly priced, and the snarlingest dog can go too far below its value. The fund cannot tie up its money in special situations, as Lehman and Atlas can, because it is obliged to buy its stock back from the holders on demand and therefore must be able to sell its investments fairly quickly, if necessary. Affiliated will limit its holdings in any one stock to the amount of the stuff traded in an average month, up to a maximum of 5 per cent of the corporation's total stock issue. The amount of research necessary to find a good investment is the same whether the investment is in a large company or a small company; and Affiliated, with some $550,000,000 to invest (plus a checking account of $10,000,000 to buy back its own stock and pay running expenses), must make large investments. So the fund concentrates its work and its purchases in the stocks of four hundred large corporations. "Basically," says F. B. Wadelton, Jr., Vice-President in charge of investing the wad, "we make money by knowing when to sell one blue chip and buy another."

About sixty-five people work for Lord, Abbett & Co., which sells and manages Affiliated and American Business Shares; fifteen of them, not counting the four partners, do research work on securities. "We're great people for forms," Wadelton says, "and we file everything, for a while, anyway." News stories, opinions from investment services, statistics, mail, reports by Affiliated's people on their interviews with management—all go into the files, which are periodically reviewed. Wadelton himself managed a very rich man's money before he went with Lord, Abbett; before that he had worked for the National City Bank and for the U.S. Navy, flying torpedo bombers. He is a tall, thin man with curly, sandy hair and a pointed nose; he plays squash with such skill that although he went to Yale the Harvard Club recently drafted him, temporarily, on to its squash team. He promptly wrenched a muscle in his foot.

The offices of Lord, Abbett & Co. show the Boston influence on the business; they are maple, New England, early

American style. The senior securities analysts have glassed-in cubicles by windows looking west on Wall Street, the juniors sit in a bull pen, and Wadelton sits in a more or less private corner. Across a wall from his desk is another valuable member of the firm—Henry Kuipers, a natty and rather nervous gentleman who sits all day at a ticker and a switch-board, and buys and sells stocks for Lord, Abbett's two funds. His market expertise is another asset purchased by the buyer of a share in Affiliated or American Business Shares.

"When we buy," he said recently, stopping the ticker for a moment, "we buy a lot, and you might think that would push up the price. But we pride ourselves on paying less for our last hundred shares than we paid for our first hundred shares. For example, right now I'm picking up a listed stock. I bought two hundred shares on the floor, at $20\frac{1}{8}$. Then I got a call from an over-the-counter dealer, offering me a thousand shares off the floor at $20\frac{1}{8}$. I said, No, I'll bid 20; and I bought the thousand at 20. Well, that's a net price, over the counter, so it cost me about three-eighths of a point less, counting brokerage, than I was paying on the Exchange. Of course, I ran the risk of losing the stock."

Wadelton was standing by, amused. "Brokers are always asking us," he said, " 'What do you guys care about an eighth of a point—you're buying the stock because you think it's going to triple, aren't you?' Still, we're interested in the eighth." (There is a reason for this care over trifles: if Affiliated sold $30,000,000 worth of new shares and and switched $50,000,000 of its present investment during the course of a year, and the average price paid for stock was $40, an eighth of a point saving would represent $400,000. The fund's entire management fee is only $800,000.)

"Sometimes," Kuipers added cheerfully, "the specialist will get the idea that I'm buying and he can hold me up. But I'm an awfully patient man. I can wait until there's somebody who wants to sell, big, and who'll cut his price to mine. Excuse me." He flicked a switch, and the ticker ticked on again.

Affiliated changes the nature of its portfolio considerably from year to year, to meet changing conditions and to sell stocks that were good buys at low prices but have become bad hold at high prices. In 1950 nearly 30 per cent of the Fund's assets was in oil stocks; by the end of 1953 the per-centage in oil was 4.5. So Affiliated was not damaged by the decline in the price of oil stocks in 1953; Affiliated had seen it coming. The money that went out of oil went mostly into electric light and power stocks; and, as the 1953 annual report proudly stated, "Of the thirty-five electric light and power companies in which we now own stocks, twenty-six increased their dividends after we bought them. . . . Since the end of our 1950 fiscal year the market value of the electric light and power stocks we then owned (all but one of which we still own) increased 42 per cent." Everybody who invests makes mistakes, of course, and Affiliated like everybody else has taken its baths. But unlike the average investor (who, as Prankard puts it, "thinks he's done well if he breaks even in a bull market"), Affiliated will take its losses from the unforeseeable rather than the logical.*

One factor in its business saddens Affiliated—its inability to put its stockholders' money into what might be real growth situations. "Not long ago," said Wadelton, "we thought it might be a good idea to go into electronics stocks. But aside from the big companies—the General Electrics and such, which have other price considerations—there just wasn't anything worth our while. The companies are too small to give us a chance at more than a fifty-thousand-dollar investment, and too unpredictable to make the investment sensible. Everybody talks now about motors as the growth industry of the 1910's—but most of the motor companies of that period are now dead, and the investors simply lost their money. It's all very easy to say that you should have put your money into Monsanto in 1928—but how could you know it in 1928? We'll stick with what we can see—sound companies with a more moderate, but far more visible, chance to grow. Still, it *is* a shame. . . ."

4

Affiliated's problems are considerably less severe than those of the mutual fund business as a whole. "Mutual funds," said a broker recently, "are the lowest form of life in finance"; and after making an exception for Affiliated and perhaps a dozen others, he could easily have proved his point. The problem is the costs: the investor in mutual funds pays somewhere between 6 and 10 per cent more than the

---

* 1959: This, of course, is the definition of a market professional; there is no implication intended that Affiliated alone among the funds is professional, or that individuals do not play their own accounts at least as shrewdly as any fund.

net asset value of his stock, then pays expenses of 10 to 30 per cent of the dividends earned by that asset value. And the management service he gets for it is often something next door to worthless.

Just about anybody can start a mutual fund simply by opening an office, filing a few papers with the S.E.C. and putting an ad in the newspapers. It is cheap, easy and profitable. Mutual funds are sold to the public by dealers, who send out direct-mail advertising closely followed by doorbell-ringing salesmen. Most of the established mutual funds charge the customer 8 per cent over net asset value, which is calculated twice a day; the dealer's commission is 6½ per cent. New funds will charge as much as 10 per cent, and give the dealer an 8-per-cent commission, which means a strong self-interest in selling the new fund.* Prankard discounts this possible conflict of interest—"The dealer," he says, "has to live in the same town with his customer, and wants to do more business with him; he can't afford to sell the man a lemon." In point of fact, however, the dealer often does not expect to sell any more to this customer— tomorrow his salesmen will be on another road. The established funds can keep themselves leaders in selling because they have another gimmick to offer: they give out tens of millions of dollars' worth of brokerage commissions a year, and can allocate their brokerage to dealers in proportion to the dealers' sales of their own stock. A special campaign by a dealer, to "saturate" an area, merits an even higher proportionate share of the brokerage. Chairman Demmler of the S.E.C.† has cast a dubious eye on this policy, which certainly has little to recommend it; but with all its faults it is better than charging the customer a heavier sales load.

Some of the mutual funds are managed and operated by brokers; others have brokers sitting in prominent positions on their boards of directors. Here there is an immediate and sometimes even a noticeable conflict of interest: the broker wants brokerage business, and firms controlled by brokers will often turn over their portfolios more rapidly, paying

---

* 1959: Several long-established funds charge no sales load at all, most notably Scudder, Stevens & Clark and Loomis, Sayles. The first of these mingles its shareholders' money with that of the Carnegie Corporation, which it manages, and thus provides a more conservative than usual portfolio. No fund which refuses to pay commissions to brokers is available through a broker's office—obviously. You have to ring the doorbell yourself.

† 1959: Mr. Demmler has since had two successors in the job; he is now practicing law in Pittsburgh.

extra brokerage commissions out of their stockholders' pockets. Worst of all, there is almost no way for a customer to find out how rapidly a mutual fund is being churned, because the financial statements of mutual funds do not report the amount of brokerage commissions paid.* Here again, Prankard discounts the danger: "Funds that play that game show a bad record, and can't sell stock." But mutual funds are not at present sold on their records; they are sold on a certain glamor, an aura of romance which they sturdily cultivate.

Every year sees a few new ones with remarkable names: Canadian Fund, when Canadian stocks were big news; Atomic Energy Fund; Television Fund. Now, there is ordinarily no advantage in restricting investments to one industry, which merely cuts down the number of good investments available to the fund. But a salesman who shows up with a picture of an atomic submarine sliding on its test run, and a prospectus for Atomic Energy Fund, has a good deal better pitch than a salesman who talks the important matters of facts and figures.

Mutual fund salesmen are recruited from all over, and what they sell often has little relationship to finance. United Funds, for example, is managed by a Kansas City dealer and sold by travelling salesmen on a nation-wide basis. The feature of the sales pitch is the name "du Pont," which is never far off the salesman's tongue. With some reason: United's board of directors is loaded with du Ponts. Selling United, the salesman does not talk about the fund's performance record—which is not much to talk about, anyway—but about the du Ponts big and little. And what housewife wouldn't admire having her money managed by du Ponts?

"Of course," said a dealer rather cautiously, "there is a corrective." So there is—a high but not very thick book called *Investment Companies*, revised every year and published by Arthur Wiesenberger & Co., members of several exchanges and dealers in mutual funds. It is known in the business as

---

* 1959: The prospectus does, however. One of the most interesting advertisements of 1958 was a special section of the *New York Times* taken by the Dreyfus Fund, a branch of a brokerage house. The section was a legal prospectus for the issue, presented in a relatively new, illustrated manner. Among the many interesting items of information in the prospectus was the fact that the fund had paid in commissions to the sponsoring brokerage house during the previous year more than half the income received from dividends on investments. It must be mentioned, though, that Dreyfus is offered as a highly speculative proposition—a trading operation as much as an investment operation—and therefore *should* show a high ratio of commission expenses to dividend income.

"the Bible." Written in simple, clear language and stuffed with figures that are immediately comprehensible to anybody, it compares the performance of almost all the mutual funds against the Dow Jones average. The final ratings are given in terms of "volatility" rather than ability, under the assumption that a fund which gains faster than the averages in a rising market will lose faster in a falling market. There is some justification for this assumption (aside from the fact that the boys would lynch Wiesenberger if he used any other), because balanced funds, which keep a high proportion of their assets in bonds, must inevitably trail the stock averages going up and down; and certain funds are by their own statement speculative in purpose, which would make them more "volatile." In another section of the book, however, the purposes of the funds are plainly set out in large, children's-book type, and when the prospective purchaser finds a non-speculative fund to which Wiesenberger gives a high "volatility" rating he is home. Management which keeps ahead of the averages on the up side will probably do better than the averages on the down side, too; and for 8 to 10 per cent of his total investment, plus 12 to 30 per cent every year off the money earned by that investment, the customer deserves management that can beat the averages.* "Anybody who doesn't read up before he buys a fund," said the dealer more cautiously, "is a fool, and a fool and his money are soon parted. The one thing the public has to get through its fool head is that you can't buy stocks without thinking—and you have to think as hard about an investment company stock as about any other kind of stock. The beauty of mutual funds is, once you've thought it out correctly you own a stock you'll never have to change. If you buy U.S. Steel and it goes up ten points, you're probably best off selling U.S. Steel and finding another stock. If Eaton & Howard is a good stock today, however, it's likely to be a good stock forever."

Even Prankard, who will vigorously defend the investment companies as a whole, would like to see some better regulation of the business, and is grateful for the regulation that exists. "I have no quarrel with the S.E.C.," he said recently.

---

* 1959: In the sharp recession of 1957-58, according to an analysis by Alfred Morgan, common-stock funds which had beaten the averages on the way up dropped slightly more than the averages on the way down. But it was true that funds which stood highest in relation to the averages at the top of the boom still stood highest, with reference to a distant base point, at the bottom of the bust. Their upward "volatility" was greater proportionately than their downward "volatility."

"It costs me a lot of money, but I actually couldn't do business without it. There's an awful lot of chisellers in this world."

5

With a few exceptions, the investment companies have the same purpose as individual investors—dividend income and possible capital appreciation. About fourteen billion dollars of investment money has gone into them, which is a good deal of scratch, and makes them important in the financial market. But even more important, these days, are the pension funds and their managers in the banks.

They have nearly twenty-two billion dollars to invest; and the amount is rising rapidly, because labor unions are successfully pressing for new pensions, and because the already existing pensions are still building their funds. "In theory," says an officer of the Bankers Trust Company pension department, "a fund ought to show quite a build-up in size for twenty-five or thirty years. Then the fund is all set up, and the earnings on the fund pay the pensions; the fund stops building. In fact, the fund never does stabilize, because the company grows, wages change, and pensions to be paid keep going up."

A pension fund has a specific purpose—a guarantee that there will be enough money in the future to pay pensions to retiring workers. The money *must* be there; no gambling allowed. But the income to be earned on the money is important, too: "We figure that if we can earn one-half of one per cent more on the money, it reduces the cost of the pension plan by 12 per cent." Bankers Trust has its own pension fund dating back to 1913, one of the oldest in existence, and manages the pension fund of American Telephone and Telegraph and its subsidiaries, the largest in existence, totalling well over a billion dollars. Corporations, unlike individuals, usually know something about investing, and pension fund managers will consult with the corporations whose pension funds they manage before making any major changes in the portfolio; nine-tenths of the time, however, the manager himself has the authority and the responsibility of investing the money. The decision that interests the corporations is usually not which stock or bond to buy (that's what the manager is paid for) but what proportion to keep in stocks, what proportion to keep in bonds.

Pension funds are primary purchasers of new bond issues,

and the managers will be wooed assiduously by underwriters. They have no interest in tax-exempt municipals, because the funds are themselves tax exempt; and they will only rarely risk low-grade bond issues because their first job is to keep out of trouble with the corporations that have given them the money to manage. "The trusts are irrevocable," says Bankers Trust, "in that the company can never get its money back. They aren't irrevocable as regards the trustee."

Most of the big banks in New York have trust departments panting to get a piece of the pension fund business; they advertise regularly in the New York newspapers. Bankers Trust puts an occasional ad in the national business magazines, but no more; "We have," says another officer, carefully, "the only fully integrated pension fund department." Of the 22 billion dollars' worth of pension funds managed by banks, Bankers Trust is supposed to have more than a fifth. Eleven officers and 30-odd lesser folk work in investment research, studying and recommending investments; unlike many other money managers, Bankers Trust sends its people around the country all the time and places more reliance on their observations than on published statistics. An investment committee composed of senior officers of the bank makes the actual decision to buy or sell and the bank's bond department will do the buying or selling, choosing the time by its feel of the market. Like the investment companies, the pension funds can often sit back on their haunches and wait until somebody wants to sell at their price; but they are limited in their patience by the fact that they have money coming in all the time and the money must be put promptly to work. If they don't like the look of the existing corporate bond market, of course, they can put it into governments; pension funds are among the best customers of the government bond dealers.

In addition to the forty investment researchers, the Bankers Trust pension fund department has 134 clerical people and a corps of company officials, and dozens of I.B.M. machines sit in its spacious halls, making out the checks that go to pensioned employees. This job, like the paying out of corporate dividends—which is also handled, as a rule, by a bank —used to take many millions of man-hours a year; and the man-hours were devoted to work that approached the state of perfect dullness. Now the faithful I.B.M. machines calculate the money and punch holes in cards and print checks—and Bankers Trust has brought the Addressograph Company and I.B.M. together to see if between them they can't design a machine that will also address the envelopes. Bankers Trust would buy a lot of these machines if somebody made one. . . .

6

Other pension fund money, and billions of dollars of premium payments, is invested by the life insurance companies; and the money management policies of the insurance companies are probably the most important factor in the bond market. Here is the opposite end of the private placement picture; here are the wholesale customers who buy in such large lots that underwriters can afford to bring out new bonds at a price mark-up of less than 1 per cent. Here, too, is the loudest gripe in finance.

"We're long-term lenders," says Metropolitan Life. "When we buy a thirty-year bond, we expect to hold it for thirty years." But the corporations won't let the life insurance companies hold their bonds for thirty years, not if the interest rate goes down in the meantime. Most corporate bonds of the highest grade are "callable"—the corporation can buy back its bond, at a slight premium, any time it sees fit. If the general interest rate goes down, and the corporation can raise new money at a lower coupon, the corporation will see fit. It will sell new bonds at the new, low interest rate, and use the proceeds to buy back the old bonds; and the life insurance companies, which cannot afford to let their money stand idle, are stuck with less interest on their investments. "We sign a contract for thirty years, and we live by it for thirty years. If the interest rate goes up, and we could get more interest on our money, we have no way out of the contract. If the interest rate goes down, however, the borrower of the money can force us to take a lower return. The result is that life insurance costs the public more than it should—there are no stockholders in most life insurance companies; it's the policyholders who own the business and get the benefit of the investments. Back in 1930, we had a rate of return on our bond investments better than 5 per cent a year; by 1947 it had gone down to 2.88 per cent." [1959: Metropolitan Life's average return on all its investments averaged 3.8% in 1958.]

Insurance companies, like banks and pension funds, are regulated in their investments; but they can buy preferred stocks fairly freely. They stay in bonds, however, because bonds pay almost as much return as good preferred stocks, at a far lower risk; and because preferred stocks can offend the eye on the yearly balance sheet. This balance sheet "window dressing" is strangely important to the big financial institutions; banks, for example, will sell government bonds every December in order to show a strong cash position in their annual report. By law, insurance companies can carry high-grade bonds on their books at their amortized value, even though the market price for the bonds is lower; while preferred stocks must be carried at market valuation. The purchase of a preferred stock, therefore, risks an apparent loss smack in the middle of the window display in the balance sheet; so the insurance companies hate to buy preferreds unless they can easily justify the paper loss by a real increase in their return on the money.*

The big insurance companies, of course, are not limited to securities in their search for places to put their money. Since they are owned by their policyholders, they represent the public far more than the most widely held corporation, and they like to invest their money in places that serve the public weal. (Fire, casualty and such insurance companies are different: they are owned by stockholders, and try to make a profit by writing insurance.) Shortly after the war, when interest rates were minuscule and the housing shortage was acute, companies such as Metropolitan, Equitable, Prudential and others invested their policyholders' premiums in middle-class housing projects as well as corporate bonds. Prudential, as a New Jersey organization, bought lots of Jersey Turnpike bonds; then sold them six points over par.

Imagination helps. Safety is the first consideration, always, since the companies are selling insurance; but sometimes there is money to be made in safety. Since the war, Metropolitan Life alone has put half a billion dollars into natural gas pipe line companies; the companies were new and had no earnings record to show, but they needed huge quantities of money to create their business. Since they were new, they had to expect to pay for their money. Metropolitan hired geologists to study the gas pools from which the lines would draw; Metropolitan's lawyers studied the contracts that the lines had made with the utility companies to which they would feed; Metro-

* 1959: During the last few years, insurance companies have been buying small, scattered lots of common stocks for their portfolios. One large company—Prudential—has announced plans to issue a "variable annuity" which would be based on common stock investments and would pay policyholders a compensating bonus if the level of prices rose between their initial purchase and their receipt of the annuity. Such an insurance policy, obviously, would compete directly with common stocks for investor's funds, and the New York Stock Exchange has led the fight before state insurance commissions to make "variable annuities" illegal.

politan's financial experts drew up bonds with ironclad sinking fund provisions, so much to be paid off per year, the rate to accelerate if it seemed to the geologists that the pools of gas were giving out faster than expected. Then, while prime commercial names were selling bonds at a 2¾-per-cent coupon, Metropolitan graciously let the natural gas pipe line people have their $500,000,000 at 4-per-cent interest.

"We're long-term lenders," says Metropolitan with considerable poise. In theory, the insurance companies should plan their investments according to an actuarial table: so many policyholders to die in 1981, so many in 1982. Actually, they can buy whatever looks good without worrying about maturity dates, and they never have to be nervous about selling their investments to pay their policyholders. Even in the worst years of the depression, Metropolitan took in more money in premiums than it paid out in death benefits and cashings-in. All the investment companies put together have fourteen billion dollars in assets; all the trusteed pension funds put together have almost twenty-two billion dollars in assets. Metropolitan Life alone has more than sixteen billion dollars in assets.

Chapter 12

The Law

"I REMEMBER," says Baldwin Bane, a white-haired Southern gentleman who was the first administrator of the Securities Act and until recently a special adviser to the Securities and Exchange Commission, "a man who came down here to Washington and raised hell with us. He was trying to sell stock in a gold mine, and he'd entered a registration statement for the stock, full of engineers' surveys and comparisons, showing a lot of gold just sitting in the hillside, waiting to be plucked.

"Well, I was pretty suspicious of the whole thing right from the beginning, because I'd learned over the years that a man with a real, honest-to-God gold mine doesn't have to come East to raise money to dig his mine. The people right in his own neighborhood will be glad to buy his stock. So we turned his engineers' surveys over to our own engineers, and pretty soon they reported back, 'Nope. Just isn't true.'

"We held up his registration, wouldn't let him sell the stock, and he came down here to argue with us. We set up a conference with our engineers and everybody else, and we were all sitting around, and he was yelling about how we were keeping the public from making fortunes in his gilt-edged mines, when my secretary came in and dropped a telegram on my desk.

"The telegram had been sent to this promoter, 'care of Baldwin Bane.' Well, it was dropped on my desk, so I didn't look at the name. I just opened it. Well, it was signed by this promoter's partner, and it came from out at the site of the mine. It read: 'CANCEL REGISTRATION. HAVE FOUND GOLD.' "

2

The financial market is a wonderful machine, intricate and delicate as a jewelled watch, strong as a bulldozer, honest as the day is long. It may run for years on its own oil; and then, suddenly, it flies apart. A long time has passed since its last explosion and the people who live in the machine wish that everybody would now forget the number 1929. But the disasters of the period 1927-37 were not accidents; the machine is not foolproof.

Basically, the financial catastrophes of the late twenties and early thirties were caused by three factors: excessive credit, a very low ethical standard on stock exchanges and an even lower ethical standard among securities salesmen. From the vantage point of today's financial market, the ordinary practice of twenty-five years ago seems scandalous—even criminal. Such practice would, in fact, be criminal today, which is one of the reasons (by no means the only one) why the Street works differently these days.

First came the margins, and very low they were. In the 1920's it was possible for a man to buy $10,000 "worth" of stock on a payment of only $1,000. His broker lent him the rest, and in return got the commission on a $10,000 purchase, plus a zooming interest rate on the loan. The "margin" put up by the customer was 10 per cent.

Thereafter, the rule was that this margin, called "the customer's equity in the account," could never go below one-tenth of the market-value of his purchase. Since it was the customer, not the broker, who was gambling in the market, any increase in the market price of the stock was added on to the customer's equity, and any increase was deducted. This created interesting possibilities.

Suppose that the customer bought with his $1,000 margin 1,000 shares of a $10 stock, and the price went up to $15. His purchase was now worth $15,000, of which only $9,000 was broker's loan; so $6,000 was "customer's equity." On $6,000 of equity, he would own $60,000 in stock, so he went out and bought another $45,000 "worth" of stock. The market advance was only 50 per cent—but the customer's holdings went from $10,000 to $60,000. And all he ever had in the market, cash money, was $1,000.

The technical word for this phenomenon was "pyramiding," accurate enough if the pyramid is regarded as inverted. For the slightest shift of weight, and the whole structure would quickly collapse.

Consider, for example, this particular customer. After his second purchase, he owned 4,000 shares of a stock selling at $15; and he owed his broker $54,000. If the price now dropped 10 per cent, or $1.50 a share, his holdings would be "worth" only $54,000—in short, the "customer's equity" would vanish. So would the customer, because his broker was taking no chances with that loan; the broker would (after giving him the chance to put up $5,400 additional dollars, or 5.4 times what he had put up in the first place) promptly sell him out. This was known as a "margin call," and it provided for many people a sad but rapid exit from the stock market.

The tragedy involved in all this was somewhat less than it may seem, because all the customer ever had invested, cash money, was $1,000. As Walter Levering of Carlisle & Jacquelin puts it, "Lots of people tell me they lost a hundred thousand dollars in the market in '29. I always ask them, 'How much did you have in the market—cash?' And the answer always is, 'Oh, five thousand.' So I tell them, 'You didn't lose a hundred thousand, you lost five thousand.' You can't lose more than you put in."

Nevertheless, there was a kind of magnificence to the whole system. No other racetrack in the world ever gave all the customers a chance to play with borrowed money; no other banking system ever allowed its lending facilities to be so thoroughly geared to the demands of gambling. And no other market before or since has been run according to this amazing margin gimmick, by which demand increased automatically as prices went up, and supply was forced into the market whenever prices started down.

Then there were the antediluvian ethics of the stock exchange. The code countenanced—even encouraged—the grossest sort of distortion of market values. Prices were pushed up and down every day by organized gangs called "pools," and a large part of the nation hung over ticker tapes, guessing at what "they" were doing.

The pool would start with the purchase, or hire, of a few financial columnists. Then its members would get in touch with the larger stockholders in the company whose stock they were about to rig, and buy options. The options were doubly useful; they guaranteed that stock would be available to the pool at a fixed price and in large quantities; and they assured the pool that no large blocks of stock could be offered to damp down the price, as the pool pushed it up. With these pledges of publicity, stock and safety, the pool would get to work, buying stock.

When a small bundle had been quietly gathered, the pool would start buying noisily, moving the price. Then the first "news story" might come out—an exaggerated sales figure for the preceding month, perhaps, or some tale of growing demand for the company's product. With this "reason" for increasing prices, the operators would give the stock a solid push, buying perhaps 10,000 or 20,000 shares in the process. A great deal could be done by means of "wash sales," in which members of the pool sold the same shares back and forth amongst themselves, on the floor of the Exchange, creating both volume and price rises. This move would lift the stock well above its previous price, and the pool would now pick up its options on the large blocks, buying quietly, off the floor of the exchange, another 50,000 or 60,000 shares. Then a breathless market columnist would report the possibility of an increased dividend based on the previously reported increased sales, and the pool, aided by the now-bemused public, would shove the price up another dozen points—twenty points or so above its starting place—and pick up sufficient stock to round out its holdings to 100,000 shares.

Now, if everything had been carefully prepared, the company would declare an increased dividend (it was always safest and best to have a few directors of the company in on the pool). Then the public would run to the market to buy stock in this expanding business—and the pool would sell, slowly so as not to damp enthusiasm, its 100,000-share bundle.

Properly conceived and executed, such a pool might—and often did—sell its entire 100,000 shares at prices twenty points above the prices at which the stock had been bought. The entire operation might take a month or six weeks, and the profit would be spectacularly good on the actual cash investment, because 90 per cent of the money necessary for the job would be put up by the banks.

Once the pool had distributed its stock it was usual for "a reaction" to set in: the price of the stock would drop steeply, often to a point below the price at which the deal had started. The pool would often re-form to help this reaction along, selling the stock short on the way down, and doubling its profits.*

---

* 1959: A whiff of this era blew back into the market in 1958, when it was announced that speculator Louis Wolfson, who had become famous a few years previous by mounting a massive attack on the management of Montgomery Ward, was selling his large holdings in American Motors. Wolfson's purchases of American Motors—which had amounted to nearly fifteen per cent of the total stock issue—had undoubtedly helped the company tide itself over the days when it was losing money, before Rambler became a major make of automobile. The purchases had been loudly trumpeted at the time. If Wolfson was selling, and so large a block hung over the market, American Motors had become, obviously, a chancy thing. In fact, however, Wolfson had *already* sold, quietly, some time before, his entire holdings in American Motors—and was now substantially short in the stock, with a concomitant financial stake in declining prices. The S.E.C. brought out this information the day after the original announcement, in a controlled but bitter statement. Apparently the circumstances surrounding the news that "Wolfson

It was not all this easy to do, because pool operations required a high order of skill, company managements could not always be persuaded to co-operate and two pools with different notions might collide in a stock to the ruin of both. Sometimes not all the large stockholders could be reached, and one of them would take an inopportune moment to sell his holdings and flood the pool. Still, it worked most of the time, a constant noisy siphon drawing money out of the pockets of the public, through the stock exchanges, into the pockets of market manipulators.

On September 1, 1929, stocks listed on the New York Stock Exchange had a total market price of eighty-nine billion dollars. By January 1, 1932, their market price had shrunk to seventeen billion dollars.

Finally, there were the ethical standards of securities salesmen. There were no ethical standards for securities salesmen. During the 1920's there was no particular reason for a stock salesman to tell the truth about a security if the truth might hurt his sales: just a few state laws, hard to enforce and unpopular. New stocks and bonds were easy to sell (stock to the speculative citizen; bonds, supposedly safer, to the solid citizen). Very little cash had to be put up, since new stock, too, could be bought on margin. And some corporations, if they had no real use for the money they were raising by the sale of securities, could always put the money in the market and do a little gambling themselves. . . .

Worst of all, perhaps, the underwriters—always the most substantial members of the Wall Street community—got taken in by all the propaganda. Much later, in the thirties, Morgan and Kuhn, Loeb were able to boast that few of the securities they had underwritten turned out to be actually worthless; few other firms could say the same. Caught up in the gaiety of the party—and quite conscious that less reputable firms would immediately underwrite and sell anything they turned down—the major underwriters sold at par issue after issue that was never in reality anything more than scrap paper.

Between 1920 and 1933 underwriters took in fifty billion dollars in payment for new securities. In 1933 half of these

---

is selling" were too ambiguous to permit prosecution, and the matter was forgotten.

It is interesting to note that very similar "pool" operations are still commonplace—and apparently legal—on the London Stock Exchange, where "take-over bids" create price rises which allow the bidders to sell their existing holdings at high, untaxed profits.

securities had completely disappeared, and the other half was selling at a tiny fraction of its original cost.

3

It seemed too high a price to pay for the freedom of the financial market.

4

The laws which were written to prevent any recurrence of this collapse are among the most skilful and appropriate on the statute books; they have scarcely been amended since they were passed. The first of them was the set of amendments to the banking acts which ordered the banks out of the securities business. The second was the Securities Act of 1933, which set up strong civil and criminal liabilities for distorting the facts, or failure to give all the facts, concerning any new issue of stocks or bonds. The third was the Securities and Exchange Act of 1934, which set up the Securities and Exchange Commission, required stock exchanges to register with the Commission, gave the Commission power to change any rule on any exchange in the public interest and specifically banned under criminal penalties the manipulation of security prices anywhere by anyone. The 1934 Act also gave the Federal Reserve System power to set margin requirements on all exchanges, and forbade dealers to run margin accounts in over-the-counter transactions and in sales of new securities. In 1959 the minimum margin on stock exchanges was fixed at 90 per cent; it has never, since the Act, been less than 40 per cent.

Except for margin regulation, which is in the hands of the Federal Reserve Board, all these laws are administered by the five commissioners of the S.E.C., helped by a staff of some 880 skilled analysts, accountants, engineers, lawyers, market technicians, clerks and secretaries. Two-thirds of the staff is in Washington, half the remainder in New York and the rest scattered through eleven regional offices all over the country. Among the men who have served as Chairman of the Commission are such well-known citizens as Justice William O. Douglas, former Ambassador Joseph P. Kennedy and Dean James M. Landis. In 1959 the Chairman was Edward N. Gadsby.

Headquarters is near Union Station in Washington in two of the many "temporary" World War I buildings which have the look of beaverboard but apparently were built to last. Both buildings are narrow, three-story walk-ups with long corridors and fairly rudimentary comforts; both, thanks to the work of the budgetary broadsword, are only partially occupied. The S.E.C.'s total appopriation runs under seven million, of which two and a quarter million comes back to the Treasury through the fees which the Commission charges to register new securities and license stock exchanges. The S.E.C. offices are pure Washington caste system: commissioners have large private offices with a carpet on the floor, *and* their secretaries have large private offices with a standing wardrobe in the corner; directors of divisions have private offices with carpets, but their secretaries sit in bull pens; more important technicians have substantial private offices with ante-rooms and linoleum on the floors; less important technicians have little private offices, answer their own telephones and must summon secretaries from a pool. There are two libraries: one in the North building for employees of the Commission, the other in the South building for the public. The South library contains complete files on every security issued since 1933, and on every action initiated by the Commission since its foundation in 1934. It is one of the most valuable and interesting paper storehouses in Washington.

In fiscal 1958 the Division of Corporate Finance accepted 810 filings of registration on public issues representing some $16,489,735,521 worth of new securities, of which more than eighty per cent was intended for cash sale. The money figure has more than doubled over the last five years. It is a very good bet that few of these issues were sold on the basis of misleading advertisements or literature—not because the S.E.C. staff catches everything, but because the law itself is wide and deep and stiff, and very discouraging.

The principle of the Securities Acts is the principle of full disclosure. The thought behind the principle is that the government cannot hope to save a sucker from himself, but can give him the tools necessary for self-protection. If a man starts a corporation to mine uranium on the moon, and wants to sell $1,000,000 worth of stock to keep himself in steaks while he tries to figure out some way of getting to the moon, the S.E.C. will not stop him; it will merely insist that these facts be given to investors. Before any security issue of more than $300,000 can be offered to the public, the issuing corporation and the underwriter must file a registration statement giving all the relevant facts about the corporation and the issue, and including documents to support the facts.* And the only argument permitted in selling securities is the "prospectus," which must contain all the material information given in the registration statement.

It is illegal to sell any new security unless a registration statement for that security is "in effect." In the absence of any objection from the S.E.C., a registration statement becomes effective twenty days after it is filed with the Commission. In theory, these twenty days are to be used for extensive circulation of a "red-herring" prospectus—an ordinary prospectus for the issue, which contains, printed in red on each page, a special legend:

INFORMATION CONTAINED HEREIN IS FOR INFORMATIVE PURPOSES ONLY, AND IS SUBJECT TO CORRECTION AND CHANGE WITHOUT NOTICE. UNDER NO CIRCUMSTANCES IS IT TO BE CONSIDERED A PROSPECTUS, OR AS AN OFFER TO SELL, OR THE SOLICITATION OF AN OFFER TO BUY THE SECURITIES REFERRED TO HEREIN.

Meanwhile, the Corporate Finance Division of the S.E.C. is casting a weather eye over the registration statement, looking for lies, errors and omissions. If it finds any trouble, it has the power to push off the date at which the registration statement is supposed to become effective, thus stopping any sale of the stock. (On special application the date can also be pushed forward, "accelerating" effectiveness.) Generally, the Commission will get in touch with the issuer by means of a rather formal letter, telling him what in the opinion of the Commission is lacking in his statement; and the issuer can then amend the statement (and his prospectus) to make everything in order. Depending on the seriousness of the error, the Commission can accept the amendment as part of the original registration statement (which will then become effective on schedule) or announce that the amendment starts everything over again, which means that another twenty days must

---

* 1959: If the security is to be sold to fewer than 25 customers, who will not resell it, the issue may qualify as a private placement, exempt from prospectus regulations. The rule is tricky to enforce (how long a time must elapse, for example, before the purchaser of a private placement can resell?), and is occasionally evaded. One of the most explosive cases of abuse of the private placement rule came to light after the collapse of *Collier's Magazine* and *The Woman's Home Companion*, properties of the Crowell-Collier corporation—which, it developed, had kept itself in the magazine business via questionable bond issues and loans on which usurious rates had to be paid. The mechanism by which the facts came out was an S.E.C. enquiry into the registration of the bonds.

elapse. Postponement is the Commission's most usual method, but in extreme cases it may issue a "stop order."

What solidifies the Commission's position is that it takes no responsibility for the accuracy or completeness of these statements; it merely says, "There's nothing wrong on the surface." If there is anything wrong under the surface (or any bit of carrion floating up top which escaped the notice of the Commission) both the issuing corporation and the underwriter are still liable to all the civil and criminal penalties of the Acts. On the front page of every prospectus there must appear, in boldface type, the statement that:

THESE SECURITIES HAVE NOT BEEN APPROVED OR DISAP-PROVED BY THE SECURITIES AND EXCHANGE COMMISSION, NOR HAS THE COMMISSION PASSED UPON THE ACCURACY OR ADE-QUACY OF THIS PROSPECTUS. ANY REPRESENTATION TO THE CONTRARY IS A CRIMINAL OFFENSE.

If the prospectus contained any "untrue statement of a material fact" or "omitted to state a material fact required to be stated therein or necessary to make the statements therein not misleading" (legal language is a marvellous device), the purchaser of the securities can, as an ordinary matter, sue and get his money back from the issuing corporation, any of its directors, any accountant or engineer who put his name on the false statements or any of the underwriters. And after these people have paid off the defrauded purchasers, they can still go to jail for five years.

This is big medicine, and its ingredients have been very carefully concocted. For example, it is required that the prospectus be printed in type "at least as legible as 10-point leaded type" (this book is set in 12-point Granjon solid)—except for financial summaries, which can be printed in 8-point type. Moreover, the Commission insists that every prospectus contain all the important arguments *against* buying this security, and that these arguments be presented up toward the front of the pamphlet.

Edward McCormick's book on *Understanding the Securities Act* contains a hilarious chapter on some of the changes that the S.E.C. has insisted be made in one prospectus or another. Consolidated Oil Company, for example, was forced to point out specifically that it was "in no way connected with Consolidated Oil Corporation," a more substantial organization. A controlling stockholder of the Longines-Wittnauer Watch Company was forced to point out that he was also an

officer of the Waltham Watch Company, and had been instru-
mental in getting the United States Government to work out
import quotas on Swiss watches, the only kind sold by
Longines-Wittnauer. The Alleghany Corporation, Robert
Young's little giant of a closed-end investment company, was
obliged to point out in a prospectus for the sale of stock then
held by insiders that because of the company's heavy debts
"an increase of $77,663,340, or approximately 100 per cent,
in the net indicated value of Alleghany's assets . . . would be
necessary before the net indicated value of such assets appli-
cable to the Common Stock would be zero."

Perhaps the most spectacular case of full, or three-dimensional, disclosure came, however, in the prospectus for
$1,000,000 of convertible debentures issued in March, 1952,
by Cinerama, Inc. The debentures, which were to be sold in
any denomination that the public might be convinced to pay
for them, were convertible into stock at the rate of one share
per three dollars of debenture. Page one of the prospectus
disclosed that of the money to be raised more than 16 per
cent would go to pay the underwriter. And on page three of
the prospectus there appeared a heading: SOME SPECIAL
ELEMENTS OF RISK; and under that heading appeared some
remarkable facts:

(1) The process was at that time untried, and might flop;

(2) The equipment for showing Cinerama is expensive; at
that time the company had only one camera, and was running
into considerable difficulties producing another one;

(3) "The first picture is not a high-budget picture by
Hollywood standards . . . its chief appeal may rest on the
novelty of the Process";

(4) "Three-dimensional and space perspective effects can
be created by methods and devices other than those of the
Cinerama process"—in other words, if the thing went over
big, there would be competition;

(5) The Company was broke, and would probably need
more money even after it sold this issue of debentures;

(6) The whole business was dependent on patents owned
by another company, Vitarama Corporation, and Cinerama
would have to pay royalties in the amount of $10,000 to
$50,000 a year to use its own equipment;

(7) "If the Corporation should fail . . . the entire investment in the Corporation might be lost, as was the case of a
former corporation (Cinerama Corporation)"—in short, the
whole thing had been tried before and gone bust;

(8) "At this time there are 1,749,300 shares for which the public paid $439,000. The purchasers of the debentures are, therefore, being offered securities which will be convertible into approximately one-fifth of the number of shares now outstanding, for an investment almost two and one half times the total investment in the Corporation to date.... Net worth on October 31, 1951, was 23¢ a share." (Further on in the statement it was revealed that the promoters had bought the first 170,000 shares for $7,877, or less than a nickel a share; the next 354,000 shares for 10 cents a share. That Reeves Soundcraft, a company controlled by one of the officers of the corporation, had purchased 1,050,000 shares for less than 15 cents a share. That the public had been permitted in January, 1951, to buy 100,000 shares at $2 a share. And that Cinerama Productions, Inc. (then known as Thomas-Todd, Inc., after its two central promoters, Lowell Thomas and Mike Todd) still had options to buy 200,000 shares of Cinerama, Inc. at 60 cents, 15,000 shares at $1, and 50,000 each at $2, $3 and $6. Don't go away yet, because the most remarkable part is still to come:

(9) All that Cinerama, Inc. could ever collect was:
25 per cent of the profits until it had received $500,000
20 per cent of the profits for another $200,000
15 per cent of the profits for another $300,000 and
10 per cent of the profits thereafter.

The rest of the profits from theatrical exhibitions of Cinerama would go to Cinerama Productions, Inc. And out of its share, Cinerama, Inc. had to pay Vitarama, Inc., which owns the patents, 5 per cent of its total receipts, with a minimum payment rising from $8,500 a year to $50,000 a year in 1955.

Briefly, then, there were three companies: (1) Vitarama, Inc., which owned the patents; (2) Cinerama Productions, Inc., which was to make the movies and which owned a majority interest, acquired at insignificant cost, in (3) Cinerama, Inc., which was to pay all the expenses of buying and installing the fancy equipment, pay the royalties to the patent owners and collect at best 25 per cent of the profits from exhibition. Cinerama, Inc. was the corporation in which the public was being invited to invest; it was definitely low man on the totem pole.

Now, all these facts were dutifully set out in the prospectus, and if a man chose not to read the prospectus that was his own fault. Nothing could be sold to him until he had been given a prospectus and told to read it. Nevertheless, the bonds were all sold, and if the customer moved fast enough he made some money on them. The "low-budget" movie opened in New York shortly thereafter and created an aura of romance about the stock, which rose to $8¼ a share at one time (bankrupting a sound Boston house which had sold it short at $6 because it so obviously couldn't be worth more than $2). If the buyer of the convertible debentures had converted quickly, and sold the stock quickly, he wound up substantially ahead on the deal. Still, on the evidence of the prospectus he had no business buying it.

There is much other evidence that the public does not read prospectuses, and buys on hunches or on largely uncontrolled oral arguments, much as it always did. Moreover, registration statements are quite expensive to prepare, and prospectuses are expensive to print. "I've heard," said George Jones of Wertheim, "that General Motors had to lay out half a million dollars on that big debenture issue, just to get all the documents in order. Now, isn't that a remarkable waste of money?"

The answers to this contention come in bits and snatches. In the first place, as an assistant to former Chairman Demmler pointed out, half a million dollars was less than one-half of one per cent of the $300,000,000 GM was raising by selling the debentures—"One-half of one per cent doesn't seem like too much to spend to protect the public." Beyond that, the registration statement and the prospectus, in the words of Commissioner Jackson A. Goodwin, "force the company that's issuing the stock to think the thing through from the point of view of the investor"—a most valuable discipline. And, finally, Baldwin Bane likes to quote his father to the effect that "You can lead a horse to water but you can't make him drink—*but,* if you keep leading him there, he's going to learn one of these days what that water's for." The S.E.C. receives thousands of letters about prospectuses from investors who have read them carefully enough to want further elucidation. "There are lots of people," says Bane, "who can't read financial statements— but they know other people, in their bank, for example, who can. They go and get the figures explained to them. The law's been on the books more than twenty years now, and investors have become prospectus-conscious.

Nevertheless, in 1954 the Commission instituted a new, single-page short form—the identifying statement—which would not replace the prospectus but would give the investing public a chance to see the essential facts of the situation in simple presentation, and the issuing corporation and the underwriters a chance to arouse interest in the security before the prospectus was delivered.

5

Wall Street does two jobs: it creates new securities and it provides a market for all securities. The Corporate Finance Division supervises the one; the Trading and Exchange Division regulates the other.

"We watch six to eight thousand securities, all the time," said Anthon H. Lund, a large, powerful, blond man who started as Baldwin Bane's clerk back before there was an S.E.C., and worked his way up to be Director of the Trading and Exchange Division. In 1954 he went on loan to the Foreign Claims Settlement Commission, and was replaced, perhaps permanently, by a man from within the business.* "There's a ticker down the hall, and a trained observer at the ticker; the observer happens to be a girl, but she knows her stuff. If she sees an unusual volume movement or price movement, she calls it to our attention. Then there are other girls, patiently writing on to file cards, every week, the prices of the six to eight thousand securities and the volume of trading in them. Besides that, we have nine experts, each specially trained as a security analyst in one industry or another. If there is any reason why a stock should suddenly start moving around, they'll probably know it."

The Division of T & E will investigate any sudden spurt in volume for a stock, and any unexplained shifting around of its price. They have subpoena power, and they can force brokers to reveal who bought or sold the stock, when and (if the broker knows) why. The usual investigation will start with the specialist, who knows what brokers have been interested, and what members of the Exchange have been trading for their own account. If the preliminary check indicates manipulation of the market (which is specifically made a criminal offense in the Securities and Exchange Act of 1934), the investigation will continue until every customer has explained satisfactorily why he bought or sold the stock. (Meanwhile, if the situation seems serious, the S.E.C. can issue an order prohibiting all trading in the stock.) "We aren't

* 1959: Lund is now an officer of Goldman, Sachs.

interested in whether the reasons are good ones or bad ones," Lund said, "except that we don't like to see anybody massaging the market."

Lund is a very cynical man, with the belief that many of the statements made by sellers of stock are pure hooey. He has a low view of market forecasters and money managers, and an even lower view of professional traders. When the Stock Exchange cries about volume, Lund is not moved: "Three-quarters of that volume in 1929," he said, "came from professional, inside traders, churning and manipulating the market. Sure, the boys made money; but it was all against the public interest."

Lund's cynicism and expertise make him a much admired man on Wall Street, because the Street in private conversation is pretty cynical about itself. ("You know what the mutual fund managers do," says an officer of the New York Stock Exchange. "They put pins through the stock list book." And, "Over there at the Stock Exchange," says an over-the-counter dealer, "all they do is run a booth, selling tokens. They expect to make a lot of money out of that booth." And nobody has ever criticized Baldwin Bane's famous statement to a group of amused investment bankers: "You gentlemen have no profession. A barber is different—he's a professional man, he needs a degree and a license. . . .") Besides, Lund knows whereof he speaks; and he is that necessary element in a community, the man who is a sonuvabitch to everybody.

Lund's view of the market forecasters is based on statistical studies made by his Division. On the day after Labor Day, 1946, the market broke ten points—ten dollars a share, which in total meant several billion dollars.* There were no economic signs pointing to it, no generally held belief that the market was over-priced, no apparent reasons. The Division of Trading and Exchange therefore took this day as its sample, hoping to find out how and why the market moves, wondering whether there was any manipulation involved. A staff that included dozens of people looked into every transaction on the floor of the New York Stock Exchange on the day of September 3, 1946, investigating both the buying and the selling end. The idea was to get an absolutely complete record

---

* 1959: Recently, ten-point drops and gains have become relatively commonplace, because the market, despite the advance in volume figures, is still relatively thin—and because prices are so much higher. A ten-point drop from 600 points is a far less spectacular development than a ten-point drop from 200 points.

of one important day's business on the New York Stock Exchange.

They got the record. It took one solid year of work.

And the results proved a number of small technical points, plus the truth of everybody's guess that the market is wholly unpredictable. (This did not make the work worthless, by any means; the fact that the investigation proved little was important in itself.) Out of some 350 investment advisory services whose predictions the Division studied in connection with this report, exactly three had predicted a serious market collapse. The rest believed that the market was going up or at the least holding steady; and the market promptly dropped ten points.

"Back in the thirties," Lund recalled, "a group of investors subsidized two very important economists, and they did a study of the factors that effect stock market prices. They went back as far as 1870, and they studied the economic picture and the market in relation to each other. At the beginning, they thought there might be 112 separate factors which could make the market move in one direction or another. They worked several years, and decided that there were exactly twelve. Finally they produced a book, full of charts and graphs and figures, showing how each of these twelve factors influenced the movement of stock prices. They sold three hundred copies of the book, which was a big sale considering that they didn't have much time and the price was *five thousand* dollars a copy.

"I've got a copy here. I didn't pay any five thousand dollars for it—they sent it to me as a gift.

"Well, the book came out in August, 1939, and in September, 1939, you may recall, there was a war. That knocked all the calculations into a cocked hat. But they weren't baffled, no, sir. One thing they had learned for sure was that commodity prices always go up in wartime. So they formed a company to speculate in commodities, and President Roosevelt promptly put a ceiling on commodity prices.

"You can't outguess the market, you can't predict the market. But most people will always think that you can, just as most people will always buy in at the top and sell out at the bottom.

"That's not our concern. Our job is to keep people from massaging the market."

6

Just as the Division of Corporate Finance relies partly on

the strength of the laws behind it, the Division of Trading and Exchange relies partly on the organizations of the market —the exchanges and the National Association of Securities Dealers, which has a government-created monopoly of the over-the-counter market. The N.A.S.D. came into being as the direct result of the Maloney Act, passed in 1938 as an amendment to the Securities and Exchange Act of 1934. Like the exchanges, it is a private association of member firms; and like the exchanges it derives its power from its rule that discounts on prices or commission rates can be given by a member firm only to another member firm. All the big underwriting houses and even the smallest over-the-counter dealers are N.A.S.D. members.

The N.A.S.D., like the exchanges, shows the advantages of working for private employers rather than the government: while the offices of the S.E.C. are bare of all but the minimum comforts of work, the Washington headquarters of the N.A.S.D. is decorous in the modern manner. It occupies the basement of a new office building in the luxury-hotel section of the city, and what with air conditioning and such the absence of windows becomes merely an incentive to chic. Outside, in the waiting-room, are all the magazines of the investment business: *Investment Dealers Digest, Finance, American Banker* and others. The N.A.S.D. is designed to help the over-the-counter dealers as well as regulate them, and earns part of its dues by supplying a clearing-house for ideas and lobbying on behalf of legislation desired by its members.

Basically, however, the N.A.S.D. is a regulatory body, and is registered as such with the S.E.C. For ease of administration, it is divided into thirteen districts; and the ruling Board of the Chicago market, three from California and one apiece from every other district. Disciplinary action against a member usually originates with a complaint from the district committee of the Association (complaints from the public have played only a minor part), and may be appealed by easy stages to the Board of Governors of the N.A.S.D. and thence to the S.E.C. and the courts. In cases where it feels the N.A.S.D. cannot or will not act, the S.E.C can revoke a dealer's membership on its own initiative, just as it can expel members from an exchange. When a dealer joins the N.A.S.D. he agrees to open his books on demand to any of the Association's thirty examiners; and refusal to open the books is grounds for discipline. Otis & Co., for example, was suspended from the N.A.S.D. after it welshed on the Kaiser-Fraser underwriting, not because of the welsh (that was a matter for the courts, which eventually decided that K-F was as guilty as Otis, and a plague on both their houses), but because Otis had refused to give an N.A.S.D. district committee information about the case. The information was later revealed in court, Otis & Co. went out of the securities business and the N.A.S.D. dropped proceedings.

Many of the measures which have cleaned out and upgraded the over-the-counter market were initiated by the N.A.S.D. itself, and every once in a while the N.A.S.D. has been slapped down for overzealousness. To keep the cheapjacks out of the business, for example, the N.A.S.D. once set up minimum capital requirements of $5,000 for member firms which did business with the public, $2,500 for member firms which did an entirely professional business. This maneuver could have cost the N.A.S.D. a quarter of its membership; but the Association felt the step was necessary to protect the other three-quarters. The S.E.C., pointing out that the Maloney Act had (rather unintentionally) given the Association something resembling a monopoly of the over-the-counter business, refused to allow such standards, though it sympathized with their aim—and had, in fact, given a green light for such rules during "informal discussions." Later, after a statistical survey of some sixty thousand transactions, the N.A.S.D. decided that 5 per cent was a reasonable mark-up on any transaction in which a dealer bought from one man and sold to another at the same time—giving him no risk, and no expenses except the two telephone calls and the clearing operation. The result of the decision was an "interpretation" to the effect that on such transactions a mark-up of more than 5 per cent would be investigated as a possible violation of the Rules of Fair Practice. Here, too, the S.E.C. in one case proved timid and restored to membership a dealer kicked out for overcharging.

There are roughly 3,000 firms which are members of the N.A.S.D., and actions have been brought against as many as 120 members in a single year.* In its disciplinary functions, the N.A.S.D. tends to be considerably rougher than any of the exchanges. An exchange, after all, is a club; its members

* 1959: In 1955-56, the N.A.S.D. acted so vigorously against distribution of questionable uranium stocks in the Denver-Salt Lake City region that about twenty per cent of its Mountain States membership was forced out of business.

live together all day long, and their regard for each other is built on personal rather than professional grounds. Over-the-counter dealers work in separate offices in separate cities scattered through the country; they may transact a lot of business and scarcely know each other. A man's charm is no help to him when he is caught off base in his business; so the N.A.S.D. can move more quickly and sternly against its own malefactors, and has far less tendency to turn its troubles over to the S.E.C., which the exchanges do regularly in hard cases, because they are afraid to offend a member. The N.A.S.D. represents genuine self-discipline in the securities business, and as such it is a unique phenomenon.

An organization such as the N.A.S.D., which acts as both spokesman and cop for an industry, must inevitably have one man who takes all the punches. The man here is Wallace H. Fulton, a lean, leather-skinned San Franciscan who was hired by the organizers of the Association and has been its Executive Director since its foundation in 1938. He combines a profound intolerance for those members of the industry who chisel around in the smaller aspects of their work, and a profound agreement with the industry's own attitudes toward the larger aspects. Few combinations are so likely to make a man unpopular with elements of his membership.

Early in 1949 the *Commercial and Financial Chronicle*, which speaks with the most intensely anti-governmental voice on Wall Street, circulated a questionnaire to over-the-counter dealers, asking their opinion of the N.A.S.D. One thousand and one registered representatives replied, giving the following results:

75.4 per cent were against the 5-per-cent policy;

74.1 per cent were against the N.A.S.D. policy of checking on prices at periodic intervals;

76.4 per cent were against the N.A.S.D. policy of examining everybody's books every once in a while;

85.4 per cent were against the N.A.S.D. method of handling disciplinary actions;

69 per cent were against the fundamental rule which forbids members to split commissions or discounts with non-members;

64.2 per cent were against the Maloney Act itself.

In view of this apparent overwhelming resentment, it is somewhat surprising that Fulton year after year gets support from the democratically elected Board of Governors which employs him. The reason seems to be that few of these anonymous grousers would have the guts to stand up in a public meeting and shoot their popguns at the N.A.S.D. The Association has done its job too well for that.

Fulton, whose background was in financial publishing, was drafted for the top regulating job in the over-the-counter market because an outsider was needed to clear up a mess. For the same reason, the N.A.S.D. pushed into the regulation of mutual fund sales literature. In one month after the N.A.S.D. set up rules about investment company sales material, Fulton's office examined two thousand separate pieces of literature. It was through N.A.S.D. that the mutual funds and the dealers who sell them got together in a committee (Harry Prankard was chairman) and worked with the S.E.C. to set up standards for sales pitching. It was Fulton, too, who insisted that all salesmen (and all traders for over-the-counter firms) be registered with the N.A.S.D. Registration, unfortunately, comes almost automatically unless the would-be registrant is a convicted felon. "There ought to be admittance standards," Fulton growls, "in all phases of the securities business.

"For example," he said recently, "fifty applications came in one day from one large dealer in mutual funds. He was registering new salesmen. Well, they were former policemen and firemen, streetcar conductors and shoestore clerks. A few days later I was in this dealer's home territory, making a speech, and I saw him in the audience; so I went into the need for standards, and mentioned the fifty applications— without giving his name, of course.

"After the speech was over he came up to me and he said, 'You were talking about me, weren't you?'

"I said, 'I sure was.'

" 'You know,' he said earnestly, 'we really want to do something about that situation.'

" 'I'm glad to hear it,' I said.

" 'In fact,' he said, 'we've started a school, and everybody who sells funds for us must pass a course first at the school. We'd like you to help us set up the program.'

"That was very encouraging," Fulton says, nodding. "So I asked him what the program was now. 'Oh,' he said, 'it's a three-day course. On the first day, we teach them all about investment banking. . . .' "

7

Regulation is the soil in which lawyers grow, and the increasing rôle of government in corporate and financial affairs has produced an orchard of law firms on Wall Street. There are literally hundreds of them, scattered through all the buildings in the area, and nearly a dozen of them are enormous, employing eighty or more attorneys-at-law.

The names themselves are impressive. Two of the big firms keep a simple, small-town, two-name structure: White & Case and Sullivan & Cromwell. Others flourish luxuriantly: Dewey, Ballantine, Bushby, Palmer & Wood; Davis, Polk, Wardwell, Sunderland & Kiendl; Cahill, Gordon, Reindel & Ohl. From these firms have come many of the leading figures of the national scene: Wendell Willkie (of Willkie, Owen, Farr, Gallagher & Walton)*; John W. Davis, Democratic nominee for President in 1924; John Foster Dulles; Arthur Dean, our special negotiator in Korea; Justice Harlan, who went almost directly to the Supreme Court from a partnership in what was then Root, Ballantine; "Wild Bill" Donovan, wartime chief of the O.S.S. and Ambassador to Thailand under the Eisenhower Administration; Henry Stimson (of Winthrop, Stimson, Putnam & Roberts); Winthrop Aldrich, who was a lawyer before he was a banker; and many, many others. The Dewey in Dewey, Ballantine went the other way: from public life to a Wall Street law firm.

These Wall Street firms (with a few exceptions) do every kind of legal work except patent law, admiralty law and criminal law. They are enormous enterprises, with pay-rolls running into millions of dollars every year; and the "retainer fees" paid by their large corporate clients can run as high as $400,000. No investment banking house has so many employees as the dozen largest of these law firms; and according to investment bankers no investment banking house makes such profits, either. (There are two sides to this feud: "Take a hundred-million-dollar private placement," said a lawyer recently, "the investment banker gets at least a hundred and fifty thousand, and a lawyer's lucky if he gets thirty thousand. But the lawyer does a lot more work. In fact, I can't for the life of me see what the investment banker does at all." The participants in this argument can safely be left to their own devices, which are plentiful.)

These firms spread over several floors of the large Wall Street office buildings, and sometimes spill over into adjoining buildings. One of them (Dewey, Ballantine, etc.) has a

---

* 1959: Actually, Willkie like Dewey became a partner in a Wall Street law firm only *after* he had been Republican nominee for President.

weekly intra-office newspaper, called *The Bull;* another (Cahill, Gordon, etc.) serves afternoon tea to all partners and associates in the library at four o'clock. The young lawyers who start with these firms take home an initial pay check of one hundred and thirty dollars a week, and one-thousand-dollar, year-end bonuses are by no means uncommon. In return, they work like dogs, often until eleven o'clock or midnight, and they make constant trips out of town to comfort corporate clients.* The late hours produce a side problem in the office (in addition to a major problem in the home); a man leaving his desk at midnight has no incentive at all to return to the library the law books he has been using. The next day somebody (perhaps even a partner in the firm—the biggest firms have thirty-five partners) wants that book; and he has to crawl around all the offices to find it. One fine day Dewey, Ballantine (then Root, Ballantine) became disturbed about this situation and established a system: "Look," said the managing partner, "we know you're tired when you quit for the night. We don't ask anything unreasonable. Just one favor: as you put your stuff in order to go, look at the books on your desk. Those you don't need any more, knock off the desk on to the floor. One wave of the arm will do it. Then, early the next morning, before anybody comes in, two of the office boys will go around with a canvas cart, pick up all the books on the floor, and return them to the library. Is it too much to ask?" It wasn't; and today the early-morning visitor to Dewey, etc., will see the floors of the various offices neatly stacked with books no longer needed.

One branch of every firm is devoted to the legal problems of banks; "It seems," Leighton Coleman, a partner in Davis, Polk said recently with some satisfaction, "that whatever a bank does it needs a lawyer. The banks are regulated by two sets of laws—state and Federal Reserve if they're state-chartered; national and Federal Reserve if they're nationally chartered. In New York they're also subject to the general corporation or stock corporation law. Every time they lend money we draw the loan agreement, and we tell them whether or not the collateral is good under the law. When the banks act as trustees they need legal advice. Then the under-

---

* 1959: In his book on *The Cravath Firm*, Robert Swaine tells a charming story about a complaint to his partner Hoyt Moore that the "associates" were being worked too hard. "Nonsense," Moore replied. "There wasn't a light on in the office when I left at two this morning."

writing departments—there was a question, can banks under-write revenue bonds? The answer is No, but it's tricky—when is a revenue bond not a revenue bond? When it's backed by the full faith and credit of the state or municipality that issues it. What's full faith and credit? Oh, the banks need lawyers all the time."

In 1954 the biggest department in most of the law firms was the tax department—"You can't have anything, these days," says Colonel Joseph M. Hartfield, senior partner of White & Case, "that doesn't involve taxes." The wills and estates department, too, is always busy. Registration state-ments, trust indentures and private placement agreements will be prepared mostly by the corporations department (the men who write these lengthy, dull documents call it "boiler-plate work," but the fees on it can run from six to forty thousand dollars). Finally, there is the litigation department, which does the actual trial work in the courts and before the various administrative bodies. "I'm in charge of litigation," says Colonel Hartfield, "but my part's mighty little."

Litigation, of course, is the center of any law practice, even though a firm does little of it: no matter how persuasive a lawyer may be in private conference, his record depends on his ability to persuade judges. One of the Wall Street firms (not White & Case) even runs speech classes for its young lawyers to train them in proper vocalizing of their arguments: "Who's got the ding-dong?" they sing, red-faced but pear-shaped, "Who's got the bell?" Hartfield himself is generally regarded as one of the most effective trial lawyers in the country; and he is also one of the last, great colorful figures on the Street. In an age when so mild an idiosyncrasy as the boutonniere has all but disappeared, Colonel Hartfield wears nothing but black and white. His huge, square office, looking out between the enormous ornamental columns at the top of the Bankers Trust building, is furnished in the flexible old black leather that has gone out everywhere else. He is a small man physically, and when subjected to an interview he walks rapidly around his room, glancing now out the window, now at his visitor, now at some item in his bookcases.

"I'm not really senior partner," he says, "that distinction belongs to Mr. Case, but he's eighty-two now and pretty much retired." Hartfield is in his seventies. "And it's a mistake to think of us as primarily the attorneys for U.S. Steel—we never had much connection with them until they borrowed our Mr. Olds for a few months, and kept him for years to be chairman of the board. My own specialty, starting in 1912 and continuing for more than twenty years, was in the reorganization of bankrupt railroads and corporations."

Colonel Hartfield, a Kentuckian, is that rare blossom on Wall Street, a confirmed and active Democrat; and this was before the 1954 elections. "There'll be some more of that work, pretty soon," he said, "don't you worry."

Chapter 13

This Side of the Street

THOMAS HUXLEY tells a story about a woman who stood and stared for fifteen minutes at the hippopotamus in the London Zoo, and finally turned to the attendant. "Keeper," she said, "what *sex* is that hippopotamus?"

"Madam," said the keeper solemnly, "that is a question, the answer to which could be of interest only to another hippopotamus."

Most of what excites Wall Street is like that, too: of interest only to another hippopotamus. Broker versus dealer, competitive versus negotiated underwriting, Eastern versus Western banks—these matters are unsalted caviar to the general, and with excellent reason. What counts, in any public reckoning, is how well Wall Street works, how well it serves the national interest.

And today Wall Street works more efficiently than ever before, and more responsibly. Over the last twenty years the financial market has changed from a rough-house guessing game to a profession. Its leaders, by and large, are no longer the rich and the lucky, but the imaginative, the experienced and the scrupulous. There are standards now, standards of excellence and ethics, where once there was honor among thieves. The problems that arise within the Street are solved quickly and intelligently; ability is recognized; incompetence and corner-cutting are punished.

This is within the Street, inside a professional world that knows a man by his actions rather than his background. To the outside, however, the Street even today too often presents its old face of class pride, the pride that props up the Street's ugliest habit: its insistence that the ordinary man is incapable of handling his own money.

History as well as prejudice lies behind this general distrust of the public intelligence: Wall Street has seen generation after generation of otherwise capable middle-class people throw away their savings in the market through avarice, ignorance or laziness. But finance is a public business, dependent for its very existence on public participation and understanding. The premise of public incompetence leads finally to attitudes of either timidity or arrogance, both equally damaging.

Timidity is in the argument that the public should be discouraged from any participation in finance. "Money," said an underwriter recently, "is always money. You have to work to earn it, and you need skills. Not many people can handle two professions at once, and the man who earns his money as a doctor doesn't have the time or the training to earn money as an investor. He can't buy advice—bad advice is so cheap he gets it for nothing, and all the good advice is reserved for people like me and my brother-in-law. Even the good advice isn't worth very much: as the old saw says, 'Inside information and a long pocket-book have ruined many a man.' So the ordinary man who comes down to Wall Street to invest is actually gambling with the family savings, because he has no way of knowing what he's doing, he's just counting on his luck. Don't tell me about mutual funds. I know about mutual funds.

"Personally," he went on, warming to the thought, "I'd rather we had a wholly professional market, so we didn't have to worry about what Walter Winchell would say next Sunday on television. We have a job to do down here, and it's not an easy job at best, and the government makes it harder every year. Sure, a lot of people live on public interest, and a lot more live off the public's mistakes. But except for the fact that some of my friends would lose their jobs, I'd see no reason to grieve over the bankruptcy of three-quarters of the member firms of the New York Stock Exchange. The public would be better off, because it would hold on to its money; and American business would be better off, because we could do our job more efficiently without this haze of alternating panic and enthusiasm. You can't stop people from playing the market, and you shouldn't try to stop them; but for the love of God let's not encourage them."

This is not a new attitude: it has been for fifty years the accepted philosophy of the Street's most responsible, most conservative men. Appalled by the daily mistakes of their own highly-trained subordinates, they see no hope for the untrained public. They would say, moreover, that they are not denying to the public the rewards of capitalism: "Everybody earns money on his savings, and through the financial market, too. Your doctor friend can put his money in the savings bank, or in life insurance, and the bank or the insurance company will invest it for him. Sure, they're very conservative and take big fees out of the earnings. But they guarantee the safety of his money, and pay him a small income on his savings, and that's a far better result than he's likely to achieve if he goes into the market by himself."

But the end result of this intelligent, timid attitude is that people who work outside the financial market earn 3 or 4 per cent a year on their money, people who work the Street earn 6, 8, even 10 per cent. Staying out of the market is not the prudent solution: in today's economy, a man loses money by not investing his savings almost as surely as if he had invested them in a bad stock.

Timidity would bar the gates; arrogance, less responsible, tries to hustle the public thoughtlessly inside: "If you don't know what stocks you'd like to buy, your broker will be glad to advise you." Starting with the attitude that they know best what should be done with the public's money, semi-professional publicists print and distribute every year millions of pages of misunderstood over-simplification. Finance, they say, is not complicated at all; we can tell you how it works in four short paragraphs, written by our advertising agency. Now, all you have to do is drop the enclosed postcard to your stockbroker, and he will invest your money for you. . . . [1959: Thus the Stock Exchange and the big brokerage houses like to boast that the "little man," the M.I.P. customer and his ilk, buys big-name corporations, not speculative ventures. But this is meaningless—the little man has always bought the most publicized securities. Nobody who has watched the market can have any doubt that there are times when the "blue chips" are the most overpriced and dangerous securities listed on the New York Stock Exchange. It is the blue chips, after all, which make up the Dow-Jones Index —and the Dow-Jones fluctuates much more rapidly than the Standard & Poor Index which includes eight times as many stocks.]

Investing is like marrying: each man has his own plans and resources, and must make his own choice. An investor needs help in understanding long-run prospects, and the factors that influence them; brokers live on the day-to-day fluctuations of the market, and have no foundation from which to judge long-term trends. The broker knows when to switch; the customer must know what to buy.

Some of the knowledge that an investor needs comes from the better brokerage house research departments; some is cast his way by the professional public relations people of Wall

Street: Tom Waage of the Federal Reserve Bank, Lou Engel of Merrill Lynch, Jim Conway of the National Association of Securities Dealers, Ed McDougal of Bankers Trust, John Sheehan of the American Stock Exchange, Fred Reiniger and Dick Callanan of the New York Stock Exchange. These men work mostly within the financial community, supplying information to people who need it. When they go out among the public they talk seriously about serious subjects—securities as a way to make money with money banking as a service industry.*

Wall Street needs more like them, and more and better research departments. The Street cannot survive as an active or useful market if intelligent, middle-class people continue to hand over all their savings to banks and trust departments, life insurance companies and mutual funds. In the final reckoning the Street lives by selling imagination, a commodity that cannot ordinarily be sold to the dead-white brains of institutional investors. Insurance companies must buy high-grade bonds, they have no choice in the matter; and Wall Street can scarcely expect to be well paid or much loved for marketing Aaa debt securities to Aaa institutions. Corporations can do such work themselves, and will.

What will save finance as a profession is individual customers who can ask the right questions and measure risks, but warm to the flame of imagination. To win such customers Wall Street need merely mind its own business, quite literally. When the Street speaks of home and mother and the American Way of Life there arises a smell of stale candy; when the Street speaks of money, it speaks with authority.

The 1950's are a new period in time: puritanism and class guilt have both gone out of fashion. Young men are no longer reluctant to come down to Wall Street and work with stocks and bonds; people in general are no longer ashamed of making money with money. Money has, at long last, become respectable.

So has Wall Street, and by its own efforts. Respectable—but rarely dull.

1959: Nevertheless, there is some reason to ask pointed questions about the future of the financial market. The past

---

* 1959: It is pleasant to report that these men have done extremely well in the intervening years. Engel, Waage and Reiniger are all vice-presidents of their institutions, with responsibilities far wider than public relations; McDougal, after achieving his vice-presidency, left to become proprietor of an automobile agency; Conway has his own public relations firm, with the N.A.S.D. only one of his clients.

five years have seen a continuous erosion in the relative position of the financial trades as against the other occupations in the economy. Finance no longer holds center stage in the great drama of capitalism. The loudly advertised campaigns to extend the benefits of corporate ownership to the Man in the Street has concealed the accelerating collapse of investment capital as a factor influencing the course of the economy.

Money may have become *too* respectable, too unwilling to assert its importance in a highly developed market economy. The managerial revolution heralded by James Burnham and celebrated by Peter Drucker has not only diminished the rôle of the owner in the operation of industrial enterprise; it has made the financing of industrial expansion largely independent of market considerations. Earnings retained by corporations—to be spent by their managements almost without outside control—made it possible for automobile companies, appliance manufacturers, steel makers, aluminum fabricators to expand their current capacity well beyond the community's ability to absorb the increased production. This excess of capital investment in the first seven years of the decade was the root cause of the sharp recession of 1957-58, and continues to threaten the prosperity of the early 1960's.

Temporary over-expansion of capital plant is certainly nothing new in economic history; the novelty lies in the fact that the managers who built the redundant facilities were able to do so entirely on their own initiative. They did not have to compete in the financial market for their share of the available investment funds, or to justify their expenditures to anyone other than their own Boards of Directors.

It can be argued effectively that the financial market used to exert far too great an influence on the course of the economy. The winds of fashion blow more strongly in the canyons of Wall Street than on the plains of industry. As a means of allocating investment resources, the free financial market has been, historically, both inefficient and wrongheaded. The man who can convince the financial market that he will make profits on new money is not necessarily the man who has the most rewarding project on his drawing-board.

Nevertheless, the financial market is an independent force, and the corporate manager is committed. It is difficult to find room in capitalist theory for the company which "diversifies" by purchasing firms in other industries, simply to rid itself of an embarrassingly large lump of retained earnings. If the "operation of the free market" is the best way to determine whether enterprises prosper or decay, then the free market must also be the best allocator of capital resources.

We have grown so used to the words "free market" as a shibboleth that we tend to forget the greatest single virtue of the capitalist market-place: its unitary nature. Especially where the transfers involved are mere pieces of paper, a free market presents over an entire political entity the same supplies, demands and prices. This impersonal unity compensates for the obvious inefficiencies introduced into any market by imperfect information, psychological quirks and herd movements. Logically considered, in fact, the words "decentralized free market" are a contradiction in terms. Only the most severe physical or legal restrictions can prevent the growth of arbitrage, operating between separated markets to create a single market.

On the working level, therefore, despite all the propaganda from both sides, a free market can live with fairly stringent central government controls—simply because they are unitary. The controls which have operated in the United States have undoubtedly increased rather than damaged market efficiency, because they have acted to improve the quality of information available to the market. What cannot be tolerated in a capitalist system is the widespread growth of individual power centers, private or governmental, which assert their independence of the market. Such centers have been growing, egged on, usually, by business economists and management-glorification societies. One of the most depressing developments in modern American thought is the rationalized hatred of the free market which now passes for sophisticated economics at the business schools and within the large corporations.

At its present state of economic development, the United States can certainly afford a high level of random inefficiency in its capital markets, but there is good reason to ask whether it can really afford the kind of *directed* inefficiency represented by investment decisions arrived at without reference to the market. Peter Drucker's supposedly empirical justification of the big companies' independence—the theory that investment plans would be stable, simply because they would not require support from the always uncertain market—collapsed finally in 1957-58, when the big companies put an even heavier foot on the brake than did their smaller, more "dependent" contemporaries. The sort of "planned capitalism" which so delights today's apologists for the whims of management actually carries with it most of the practical weaknesses and few of the moral strengths of socialism.

Wall Street is a cheerful and stimulating place partly because it utters so little of this self-serving, cartel-worshipping, corporate claptrap. Though it is no longer the center of capitalism, as it was in the days when Bryan and Lenin fixed a century's radical ideology, it is still the center of the capitalist spirit—the spirit of secular adventure, of individual shrewdness, of controlled greed, and of risk. Especially the spirit of risk.

In the long view, this is the problem Wall Street must face: can *risk* be made respectable? Both the customers and the clients of finance, the public and the corporations, have always lusted after a riskless market. When finance was overwhelmingly powerful, Wall Street could laugh at their foolish desires. But the terms of trade have shifted violently against the money market, and Wall Street can no longer control the attitudes of its patrons. Somehow, finance must convince the corporations and the public, against all their instincts, that a riskless market is by definition a useless market, that markets exist not merely to reward the right decision, but also to punish the wrong one. The task will not be easy; it will not even be possible unless Wall Street maintains its newly achieved integrity and efficiency, and its respect for the gambling spirit.

Index

Index